An Important Message to Our Readers

GET THE MOST OUT OF YOUR RETIREMENT AND MEDICAL BENEFITS

KEEPING UP TO DATE

To keep its books up to date, Nolo.com issues new printings and new editions periodically. New printings reflect minor legal changes and technical corrections. New editions contain major legal changes, major text additions or major reorganizations. To find out if a later printing or edition of any Nolo book is available, call Nolo.com at 510-549-1976 or check our website: www.nolo.com.

To stay current, follow the "Update" service at our website: www.nolo.com. In another effort to help you use Nolo's latest materials, we offer a 35% discount off the purchase of the new edition of your Nolo book when you turn in the cover of an earlier edition. (See the "Special Upgrade Offer" in the back of the book.)

This book was last revised in: February 2000.

SEVENTH EDITION	
SECOND PRINTING	FEBRUARY 2000
EDITOR	BARBARA KATE REPA
BOOK & COVER DESIGN	JACKIE MANCUSO
PRODUCTION	SARAH TOLL
INDEX	SAYRE VAN YOUNG
PROOFREADER	ROBERT WELLS
PRINTING	CONSOLIDATED PRINTERS, INC.

Matthews, Joseph L.
Social Security, medicare, and pensions : get the most out of your retirment and medical benefits. — 7th ed. / by Joseph L. Matthews with Dorothy Matthews Berman.
p. cm.
Includes index.
ISBN 0-87337-487-8
1. Social Security—Law and legislation—United States—Popular works. 2. Medicare—Popular works. 3. Pensions—Law and legislation—United States—Popular works. I. Berman, Dorothy Matthews. II. Title
KF3650.M37 1998
344.73'023—dc21 98-22231
CIP

For information on bulk purchases or corporate premium sales, please contact the Special Sales department. For academic sales or textbook adoptions, ask for Academic Sales, 800-955-4775, Nolo.com, Inc., 950 Parker Street, Berkeley, CA 94710.

Acknowledgments

Many thanks to Barbara Kate Repa for her considerable and thoughtful input to the content and structure of this book, and for her thorough editorial work on various drafts of the manuscript.

Special thanks go to the National Council of Senior Citizens in Washington, D.C., for many helpful suggestions on the original edition of the book, and to Bruce Campbell, Karen Fuller and Sue Schwab of the Health Care Financing Administration office in San Francisco for their assistance in sorting out the many state variations in Medicaid.

Special thanks also to the Health Insurance Counseling and Advocacy Program and Legal Assistance for Seniors office in Oakland, California, as much for their example in tirelessly serving the interests of low-income seniors as for their suggestions for improving this book.

Contents

4 Social Security Dependents Benefits

5 Social Security Survivors Benefits

6 Supplemental Security Income

7 Applying for Benefits

8 Appealing Social Security Decisions

9 Federal Civil Service Retirement Benefits

10 Veterans Benefits

11 Private Pensions and 401(k) Plans

12 Medicare

13 Medicare Procedures: Enrollment, Claims and Appeals

14 Medigap Insurance

15 Medicare Managed Care Plans

16 Medicaid and State Supplements to Medicare

Appendix

Index

About This Book

Are you 55 or over? Do you help support someone who is?

If so, you may be facing a series of problems for which you are unprepared: getting the most retirement and pension income and obtaining the broadest medical coverage you can afford. People in their retirement years often have access to a wide variety of programs to help with financial support and medical care. But many people are unaware of the extent of programs that exist for them, or are unable to wade through the rules and regulations that apply to those programs, and so do not receive all the benefits for which they are eligible.

For people who are or soon will be on fixed incomes, the unnecessary loss of benefits and protection can cause critical problems. This book is intended to help you get all the benefits to which you are entitled: Social Security, private pensions, Supplemental Security Income, veterans' benefits, civil service benefits.

Most people over 55 are particularly concerned with getting the broadest possible medical coverage they can afford—knowing well that a serious medical problem can cost a fortune. Almost everyone is aware that Medicare is available, but few people understand how it works and what it does and does not cover. This book carefully, completely and in plain language explains Medicare rules and regulations and explains how the holes in Medicare can be filled by medigap private insurance, managed care health plans and Medicaid.

Using This Book

Each chapter in this book explains a different benefit program or set of laws designed to protect the rights of older Americans. It explains how each particular program works, and also how it may relate to the other programs discussed in the book. Not all of these benefits will apply to you. However, even if you don't think you are eligible for a particular benefit, take a look at the general requirements discussed in that chapter. You may be surprised to find that a program, or some part of it, applies to you in ways you had not previously realized. Pay special attention to explanations of how your income, or your participation in one benefit program, might affect your rights in another program.

You Have Earned These Benefits

A key word in this book is "entitled." Almost all of the benefits discussed here are paid to you because you worked for them and earned them through contributions you made during your working life. If you are an older American facing retirement and a fixed income, you need all the financial support these programs are supposed to provide. And you are entitled to it.

Depending on your age and stage of life, there are a number of major issues you should consider as you first scan through the book.

If You Are Age 55 or Over and Not Yet Retired

- Check the rules regarding the age at which you are eligible for Social Security retirement benefits. (See Chapter 2, Section B.)
- Learn how much your Social Security retirement benefits will be reduced if you retire early or increased if you retire later. (See Chapter 2, Sections B and C.)
- Find out how much income can be earned without having it affect Social Security benefits. (See Chapter 2, Section D.)
- Look into civil service retirement benefit rules, if you have ever worked for the federal, state or local government or any public agency or institution—school system, library, public health facility. (See Chapter 9, Sections A and B.)
- Check the rules of your private pension plan—if you worked for any private company that had a pension plan, or if you belonged to any union—including whether your pension will be affected by your Social Security benefits. (See Chapter 11, Sections A, B and C.)

If You Are Within Six Months of Your 65th Birthday

- Obtain a current estimate of your retirement benefits from Social Security, civil service and private pension plans. (See Chapter 1, Sections A and G; Chapter 9, Section E; Chapter 11, Sections E and F.)
- Determine whether you should delay claiming your Social Security retirement benefits if you are going to continue to work after you turn 65. (See Chapter 2, Section D.)

- Go over the rules regarding Medicare eligibility and coverage. (See Chapter 12, Sections B, C and D.)
- Investigate the availability of medigap health plans to supplement Medicare, or HMOs or managed care plans. (See Chapters 14 and 15.)
- If you have low income and few assets, find out the eligibility rules in your state for assistance with medical bills from Medicaid. (See Chapter 16.)

If You Are 65 or Over and Retired

- Review the rules of Social Security or civil service retirement programs concerning the effect of current earned income on the amount of your benefits. (See Chapter 2, Section D1; Chapter 9, Section B.)
- If you have low income and few assets, see whether you might be eligible for financial assistance from Supplemental Security Income (SSI). (See Chapter 6, Section A.)
- If you require medical treatment, understand the Medicare rules to ensure that you will get maximum coverage. (See Chapter 12.)
- If you have low income and few assets, check to see whether you are eligible for Medicaid or other state programs that can help pay your medical bills. (See Chapter 16, Section B.)
- If you were in the military, find out whether there are Veterans Administration financial or medical benefits to which you are entitled. (See Chapter 10.)

If You Can Work Very Little or Not at All Because of a Physical Condition

- Consider the rules regarding Social Security disability. (See Chapter 3, Sections A and B.)
- If you have low income and few assets, check the rules regarding Supplemental Security Income (SSI). (See Chapter 6, Section A.)
- If you were in the armed forces and your physical condition is in any way related to your time in the service, investigate the rules regarding veterans' disability benefits and medical care. (See Chapter 10, Sections B and E.)

If You Are a Surviving Spouse or Former Spouse of a Worker Who Is Retirement Age

- Review Social Security and civil service rules on survivors' and dependents' benefits. (See Chapters 4 and 5.)
- Obtain an estimate of your own retirement benefits, and compare them to estimates of survivors' or dependents' benefits. (See Chapter 1, Sections F and G.)
- Check the rules of the pension plan of any company or government entity for which your spouse worked for more than three years. (See Chapters 9 and 11.)
- If you or your spouse was in the military, see if there are any veterans' benefits to which you might be entitled. (See Chapter 10.)

If You Are Age 60 or Over and Are Considering Getting Married

- Find out what effect marriage would have on your right and your intended spouse's right to collect Social Security retirement, survivors' and dependents' or disability benefits, and on the amount of those benefits. (See Chapter 2, Section C; Chapter 4, Sections A and E; Chapter 5, Section A.)
- Determine what effect marriage would have on your and your intended's eligibility for Supplemental Security Income (SSI) and Medicaid. (See Chapter 6, Section A; Chapter 16, Section B.)

Unofficial Marriages and Benefit Programs

As you go over the rules of the specific programs, you will notice that eligibility for and amounts of many benefits to which you may be entitled often depend on your marital status. While Social Security and other programs provide a number of benefits to the spouse of a worker, they do not provide for people who live together without being married.

On the other hand, eligibility for some benefits and the amounts to which you may be entitled depend on the combined amount of income and assets of a claimant and his or her spouse. If you are not married, your partner's income and assets are not generally counted in determining your financial position, and so you are more likely to be eligible for benefits.

Many people live together in the belief they have a common law marriage—a legally recognized marriage—even though they never went through a formal ceremony, took out a marriage license or filed a marriage certificate.

In fact, common law marriages are only recognized in: Alabama, Colorado, District of Columbia, Georgia, Idaho, Iowa, Kansas, Montana, Ohio, Oklahoma, Pennsylvania, Rhode Island, South Carolina, Texas and Utah. If you do not live in one of these states, you do not have a common law marriage, no matter how long you have lived with another person, shared the same name, life and family.

If you do live in one of these states, you will only be considered to have a common law marriage if you and a person of the opposite sex intend to be considered as married. You can show this in a number of ways—including living together as husband and wife for several years, using the same last name, referring to yourselves as married, having children together and giving them the family name you share, owning property together.

Anything that shows that you consider yourselves married can be considered as evidence that you have a common law marriage. You can even write out an agreement that says you regard yourselves as being in a common law marriage. However, there is no one thing you can count on to absolutely prove the existence of your common law marriage. And nothing guarantees that Social Security or other programs will consider you married when making a decision about your benefits.

Finally, no matter how much evidence you have that you have a common law marriage, if either you or the person with whom you live is still lawfully married to someone else, there can be no common law marriage.

Social Security: The Basics

Social Security is the general term that describes a number of related programs—retirement, disability, dependents and survivors benefits. These programs operate together to provide workers and their families with some monthly income when their normal flow of income shrinks because of the retirement, disability or death of the person who earned that income.

The Social Security system was initially intended to provide financial security for older Americans. It was meant to help compensate for limited job opportunities available to older people in our society. And it was intended to help bridge the financial gaps created by the disappearance of the multi-generational family household—a break-up caused in large measure by the need for American workers to move around the country to find decent employment.

Unfortunately, this goal of providing financial security is today increasingly remote. The combination of rapidly rising living costs, stagnation of benefit amounts and penalties for older people who continue to work have made the amount of support offered by Social Security less adequate with each passing year. This shrinking of the Social Security safety net makes it that much more important that you get the maximum benefits to which you are entitled.

This chapter explains how Social Security programs operate in general. It is helpful to know how the whole system works before determining whether you qualify for a particular benefit program and how much your benefits will be. Once you understand the basic premises of Social Security, you will be better equipped to get the fullest benefits possible from all Social Security programs for which you might qualify. (See Chapters 2, 3 and 5.)

A. History of Social Security

Public images of our society generally render invisible many millions of economically hard-pressed older Americans. The older person with little income and assets is left out of the standard media pictures of two-car, two-kid suburbanites and of wealthy retired couples in gated luxury communities. Modern Western capitalism produces expendable workers. And the most vulnerable, such as people over 65, are the most easily expended.

In the most advanced of modern industrial nations, the United States, the position of expendable workers is the worst. The richest 1% of U.S. households controls 40% of the nation's wealth, and the poorest 20% of the population earns just 5.7% of total after-tax income. These figures for the distribution of wealth are twice as large as those of Great Britain, a society commonly thought to have a wide divide separating rich and poor.

During periods of extreme economic retrenching, the number of people cast off by the economy spills over the normal barriers of invisibility. And with so many people during these crises sharing their complaints about economic injustice, it is sometimes difficult to keep them all under control. One such period of extreme economic dislocation was the Depression of the

1930s. Many millions of people were displaced—not only from job, home and family, but from any hope for a place in the economy.

1. The Beginning of Social Security

Faced with this crisis and with the possibility of massive social upheaval, Franklin Roosevelt and Congress decided to act. Whether motivated more by an abiding concern for the common man or woman or by fear of social revolution, Roosevelt pushed through a number of programs of national financial assistance—one of which was a system of retirement benefits called Social Security, enacted into law in 1935.

When benefits began, Social Security retirement cushioned slightly the crushing effects of the Depression. But the new retirement program established no real or lasting security. Retirement benefits were set at levels that were never enough to guarantee a standard of living above the poverty line. In 1939, Social Security benefits were extended to a retired worker's spouse and minor children; in 1956, to severely disabled workers. These extensions helped cover more people in need, but neither new program deviated from the basic premise of Social Security: provide just enough to keep starvation from the door, but not enough to guarantee a decent standard of living.

2. Current Threats to the System

The United States is presently in the throes of yet another economic upheaval, one that rivals the Depression. In the gluttonous 1980s, large capital interests, with the assistance of government, stuffed their pockets with profits and paid off their upper management with overblown salaries. There was much talk then of these sums trickling down to the remaining 98% of the population.

But the 1990s have revealed that the only thing trickling down is the perspiration of financial worry: for the millions of workers who have been "downsized" out of their jobs; for the millions of children sinking into poverty; and for the millions of older people who find it increasingly difficult to get by on their meager pensions, their low-paying part-time jobs and their Social Security benefits.

Despite its limited benefits, many people depend on Social Security. In 1999, over 30 million people received Social Security retirement benefits, which averaged about $750 per month. Over six million widows and widowers received survivors benefits. Those averaged about $700 per month. And over three million spouses of retired or disabled workers received dependents benefits that averaged about $380 per month. These Social Security benefit amounts, standing alone, are far from sufficient to support a decent standard of living. And if you are in the half of the retired, dependent or survivor population who receive less than the average, your situation is likely to be even more dire.

If these figures were not grim enough for people facing their retirement years, the federal government—following the dictates of monied interests who do not depend on retirement benefits—is currently looking to cut Social Security and Medicare benefits. (See Chapter 12.) And Congress has already begun to raise the regular age for retirement benefits from the long-standing 65 years. (See Chapter 2, Section B.) Other cuts in Social Security programs—further penalizing older people who continue to work, making disability benefits harder to obtain—are also being contemplated.

3. What You Can Do

In response to this deteriorating situation, anyone facing retirement should take two important steps.

First, understand the rules regarding Social Security benefits. (See Chapters 1 through 5.) That will enable you to plan wisely for your retirement years, including answering the basic questions of when to claim your benefits and how much you can work after claiming them.

And second, become aware and active concerning proposed moves by Congress regarding the Social Security and Medicare programs. Local senior centers and national seniors organizations such as the National Council on Senior Citizens in Washington, D.C., are good sources of current information.

If you are even beginning to think about your retirement, it is not too early to begin trying to safeguard it.

B. Social Security Defined

Social Security is a series of connected programs, each with its own set of rules and payment schedules. All of the programs have one thing in common: benefits are paid—to a retired or disabled worker, or to the worker's dependent or surviving family—based on the worker's average wages, salary or self-employment income in work covered by Social Security.

The amount of benefits to which you are entitled under any Social Security program is not related to need, but is based on the income you have earned through years of working. In most jobs, both you and your employer have paid Social Security taxes on the amounts you earned. Since 1951, Social Security taxes have also been paid on reported self-employment income. Social Security keeps a record of these earnings over your working lifetime, and pays benefits based upon the average amount earned. However, the only income considered is that on which Social Security tax was paid. Income such as interest, dividends, sale of a business or investments and unreported income is not counted in calculating Social Security benefits.

Four basic categories of Social Security benefits are paid based upon this record of your earnings: retirement, disability, dependents and survivors benefits.

1. Retirement Benefits

You may choose to begin receiving retirement benefits as early as age 62. But the amount of your benefits permanently increases for each year you wait, until age 70. The amount of your retirement benefits will be between 20% of your average income (if your income is high) and 50% (if your income is low). For a 65-year-old single person first claiming retirement benefits in 2000, the average monthly benefit is about $800; $1,350 for a couple. The highest earners claiming their benefits in 2000 would receive about $1,430 per month; $2,000 for a couple. These benefits increase yearly with the cost of living. (See Chapter 2.)

2. Disability Benefits

If you are under 65 but have met the work requirements and are considered disabled under the program's medical guidelines, you can receive benefits roughly equal to what your retirement benefits would be. (See Chapter 3.)

3. Dependents Benefits

If you are the spouse of a retired or disabled worker who qualifies for retirement or disability benefits, you and your minor or disabled children may be entitled to benefits based on the worker's earning record. This is true whether or not you actually depend on your spouse for your support. Married recipients must determine whether they will receive a greater sum from one Social Security benefit and one dependent benefit or from two Social Security retirement benefits, if both partners are entitled to one. They may be awarded retirement or dependent benefits, but not both. (See Chapter 4.)

4. Survivors Benefits

If you are the surviving spouse of a worker who qualified for retirement or disability benefits, you and your minor or disabled children may be entitled to benefits based on your deceased spouse's earnings record. (See Chapter 5.)

Getting Benefits From More Than One Program

You may qualify for more than one type of Social Security benefit. For example, you might be eligible for both retirement and disability, or you might be entitled to benefits based on your own retirement as well as on that of your retired spouse. You can collect whichever one of these benefits is higher, but not both.

C. Eligibility for Benefits

The specific requirements vary for qualifying to receive retirement, disability, dependents and survivors benefits. The requirements also vary depending on the age of the person filing the claim and, if you are claiming as a dependent or survivor, on the age of the worker. However, there is a general requirement that everyone must meet to receive one of these Social Security benefits. The worker on whose earnings record the benefit is to be paid must have worked in "covered employment" for a sufficient number of years by the time he or she claims retirement benefits, becomes disabled, or dies.

1. Earning Work Credits

All work on which Social Security taxes are reported is considered covered employment. About 95% of all American workers—about 135 million people—work in covered employment. For each year you work in covered employment you receive up to four Social Security work credits, depending on the amount of money you have earned. And if you have accumulated enough work credits over your lifetime, you, your spouse and your minor or disabled children can qualify for Social Security benefits.

The amounts of work credits you need to qualify for specific programs is discussed in Chapter 2 (retirement benefits), Chapter 3 (disability benefits), Chapter 4 (dependents benefits) and Chapter 5 (survivors benefits).

The Social Security Administration keeps track of your work record through the Social Security taxes paid by your employer and by you through FICA taxes. The self-employed—people who take a draw from a self-owned or partnership business, or who receive pay from others without taxes being withheld—earn Social Security credits by reporting income and paying tax for the net profit from that income on IRS Schedule SE. Income that is not reported will not be recorded on your earnings record. Although many people fail to report income to avoid paying taxes, a long-term consequence is that the unreported income will not count toward qualifying for Social Security retirement or other benefits, and will reduce the amount of benefits for those who do qualify.

The Importance of Names and Numbers

The Social Security system does everything—records your earnings, credits your taxes, determines and pays your benefits—according to your Social Security number. On every form you fill out or correspondence you have with the Social Security Administration, you must include your Social Security number. You should also use your name exactly as it appears on your Social Security card. This will make it easier for Social Security to track the correct records.

If you have used more than one name on work documents, indicate all names you have used on correspondence with the Social Security Administration. As long as you have used the same Social Security number, your records should reflect all of your earnings.

If you have changed your name and want to ensure that all your future earnings will be properly credited to your Social Security record, you can protect yourself by filling out a form at your local Social Security office. The Application for Social Security Card form allows you to register your new name and match it with your existing Social Security number. You will be sent a new Social Security card with your new name, but same number.

To complete this form, you must bring to your local Social Security office the originals or certified copies of documents which reflect both your old and new names. If your name has changed because you married or remarried, bring your marriage certificate. If your name change is due to divorce, bring the final order of divorce which includes reference to the return of your former name. If you have any questions concerning the type of documents you may bring to show your old and new names, call Social Security at 800-772-1213.

2. Coverage for Specific Workers

There are special Social Security rules for coverage of some workers in certain sorts of employment.

a. Self-employed before 1951

Self-employment earnings have only been covered by Social Security since 1951. Self-employment earnings before then had no Social Security tax obligations and so were not applied to a worker's earnings record. If you had self-employment earnings before 1951, they will not help you qualify for any type of Social Security benefits. Certain types of military service may also make you eligible. (See Section C2e.) And if you do qualify for benefits, the amounts you earned in self-employment before 1951 will not be counted in figuring how much those benefits will be.

b. Federal government workers

If you were hired as an employee of the federal government on January 1, 1984, or after, all your work for the government since then has been covered by Social Security just as if you worked for a private employer. If you worked for the federal government before 1984, your work both before and after January 1, 1984, has been covered by the separate federal Civil Service Retirement System. (See Chapter 9.)

c. State and local government workers

Most state and local government workers are not covered by Social Security. State government employees are usually covered by their own pension or retirement systems, and local government employees have their own public agency retirement system, or PARS.

However, some state and local government employees are covered by Social Security instead of—or in addition to—a state or PARS pension system. This is because some state and local governments chose Social Security coverage for their workers instead of depending entirely on a system of their own. If so, they and their workers pay at least some Social Security taxes. And workers under these plans are entitled to Social Security benefits if they meet the other regular requirements.

State and local government workers who are not covered by their pension or retirement plans—mostly part-time, temporary or probationary workers, or workers who were too old to qualify for the retirement plans when they began employment—are covered by Social Security for their government work.

If you are a government employee and aren't sure whether you are covered by Social Security, check with the personnel office at your workplace. And remember, even if your employment at a state or local agency does not entitle you to Social Security benefits, any other work you have done during your lifetime may qualify you, if you paid Social Security taxes.

d. Workers for nonprofit organizations

Since 1984, all employment for charitable, educational, religious or other nonprofit organizations is covered by Social Security. Before that time, however, nonprofit organizations were permitted to remain outside the Social Security system, and many chose to do so. Because people who worked for such organizations were left out of any retirement plan, the Social Security system now permits some of them to qualify for benefits with about half of the normal number of years of work credit.

If you reached age 55 before January 1, 1984, and you worked for such a nonprofit organization, you and your family can qualify for Social Security benefits with a reduced number of work credits. The exact amount you need for each benefit is discussed in the chapter which covers that specific benefit—retirement (see Chapter 2), disability (see Chapter 3), dependents (see Chapter 4) and survivors (see Chapter 5).

Employees of Churches or Religious Organizations

Certain church organizations and religious groups do not contribute to the Social Security system for the people who work for them. Apparently these churches believe that the spiritual security they offer will compensate their workers for the lack of Social Security. And bowing to a rather exaggerated notion of the free exercise of religion, the federal government lets them get away with it.

As a result of this free ride for churches and religious groups, the people who work for them must pay not only their own share of Social Security taxes but also the share normally paid by an employer. That amounts to a 15.3% Social Security tax on an individual's wages, in addition to income taxes.

Employees of these non-paying churches or religious organizations must file a self-employment tax form (Form 1040, Schedule SE) and pay this full Social Security tax with their federal tax return. By paying the tax, the employee's work is credited to his or her Social Security earnings record.

e. Members of the military

Whether your service in the military was considered by Social Security to be covered employment depends on when you served and whether you were on active or inactive duty. From 1957 on, all service personnel on active duty have paid Social Security taxes and so all active service from that date is covered employment. Since 1988, periods of active service, such as reserve training, while on inactive duty have also been covered. (See Section D.)

If you served in the armed forces between 1940 and 1956, you may also have accumulated some Social Security work credits if you met certain additional conditions. (See Section D.)

f. Household workers

Household work—cleaning, cooking, gardening, child care, minor home repair work—has been covered by Social Security only since 1951; work before that date is not credited on a worker's earnings record.

A major problem for household workers is that most employers do not report their employees' earnings to the Internal Revenue Service and do not pay Social Security taxes on those earnings. Of course, a lot of domestic workers do not want their earnings reported. They are paid so little that they prefer to receive the full amount, often in cash, without any taxes withheld. One result of this non-reporting, however, is that the earnings do not get credited to the worker's Social Security record. So when the worker or worker's family later seeks Social Security benefits, they may have trouble qualifying, and if qualified will have lower benefit amounts.

If you want your earnings from household work reported to Social Security, you have several options. If you work for a number of different employers and make less than $1,000 per year from any one of them, you can report that income yourself as self-employment income and pay 15.3% self-employment tax on it in addition to the regular income tax. Paying self-employment tax, on federal income tax Form 1040, Schedule SE, credits the earnings to your Social Security earnings record.

If you work for any one employer who pays you a total of $1,000 or more over the course of a year, you can ask that employer to withhold Social Security taxes from your pay, report your income to Social Security and pay the employer's share of the Social Security tax on that income, as the law requires. (See explanation below.) If the employer refuses, you are faced with a difficult choice. You can report the refusal to your local Social Security office. This will permit you to begin the process of gaining Social Security credit for your earnings. It will also mean that you will have 6.75% of your pay deducted for your portion of Social Security taxes. And, of course, it is likely to strain relations with your employer.

If you did household work between 1951 and 1993, employers were required by law to report your income and pay Social Security taxes on it if you earned more than $50 per quarter-year. Very few employers did so, however. If you want to get Social Security earnings credit for any of those years, you may be able to do so by providing the Social Security Administration with some proof of your income. Before you report this income, request a copy of your earnings record from Social Security, which will tell you what work has already been credited to your record. (See Section E.) Then, if you have any kind of written proof of unreported income—copies of pay stubs, checks, bank deposits, income tax returns—you may show it to your local Social Security office and have that income credited to your earnings record. Be aware, however, that if Social Security credits you with these previously unreported amounts of income, you may have to pay your share—6.75%—of the previously unpaid Social Security tax.

Employer's Duty to Report Earnings of Household Workers

If you hire a household worker—cleaner, cook, gardener, child sitter, home care aide—who is not employed by and paid through an agency, and you pay that worker a total of $1,000 or more during the year, you are required by law to report those payments and pay Social Security taxes on them. This rule exempts any worker who was under age 18 during any part of the year.

You can report these taxes on your own federal income tax return Form 1040, and pay your Social Security tax obligation as employer along with your income taxes. To file and pay these taxes, you need the name of your employee as it appears on his or her Social Security card, the employee's Social Security number and the amount of wages paid.

g. Farm workers

Since 1954, farm and ranch work has been included in the Social Security system. If you do crop or animal farm work, your employer must report your earnings, pay Social Security taxes on them and withhold your share of Social Security taxes if you earn $150 or more from that employer in one year, or if the employer pays $2,500 or more to all farm laborers, regardless of how much you earn individually. Any amounts you are paid in housing or food do not have to be reported by the employer.

As with household workers, farm workers have long faced the problem that many employers do not pay their share of the Social Security tax. An employee gets Social Security credit for earnings only if the earnings are reported to the Social Security Administration and Social Security tax is paid. If your employer fails to pay its share of tax, and fails to withhold your share of Social Security taxes from your paycheck, the burden of Social Security taxes falls unfairly on you. Either no Social Security taxes are paid at all, in which case you do not get earnings credits that will eventually lead to retirement or other benefits; or, you pay Social Security taxes as a self-employed person, which is twice the tax rate you should be paying.

To make sure your farm work is counted toward your Social Security record, check your pay stub to see if Social Security taxes—labeled FICA—are being withheld and ask the person who handles payroll for paperwork indicating that Social Security taxes are being paid on your earnings. If your employer is not paying Social Security taxes on your earnings, or you get the run-around and you are unsure what the employer is doing, ask your local Social Security office to find out for you. If you are worried about your employer finding out that you are checking on this, ask the Social Security worker to make a confidential inquiry. Social Security can request all the employer's wage records without letting the employer know which employee in particular has brought the matter to its attention.

D. Earning Work Credits

To receive any kind of Social Security benefit—retirement, disability, dependents or survivors—the person on whose work record the benefit is to be calculated must have accumulated enough work credits. The number of work credits you need to reach the qualifying mark—what Social Security calls insured status—varies depending on the particular benefit you are claiming and the age at which you claim it.

You can earn up to four work credits each year, but no more than four regardless of how much you earn. Before 1978, work credits were measured in quarter-year periods: January through March, April through June, July through September and October through December. You had to earn a specific minimum amount of income to gain a work credit for that quarter.

- Between 1936 and 1978, you received one credit for each quarter in which you were paid $50 or more in wages in covered employment.

- Between 1951 and 1978, you received one credit for each quarter in which you earned and reported $100 or more from self-employment.
- Beginning in 1978, the rules were changed to make it easier to earn credits. From 1978 on, you receive a credit for each fixed amount of earnings from covered employment regardless of the quarter in which you earn it, up to four credits per year. That means that if you earned all your money during one part of the year and nothing during other parts of the year, you could still accumulate the full four credits. The amount needed to earn one credit increases yearly. In 1978, when the new system was started, it was $250; in 2000, it had increased to $780.

Example: In 1950, Ulis was paid $580 between January and March, nothing between April and July when he could not work because of a back injury, $340 in August and $600 in cash from self-employment in October and November. For the year 1950, Ulis earned two credits: one credit for the first quarter in which he was paid more than the $50 minimum; nothing in the second quarter, so he got no credit; one credit in the third quarter because he earned well over the $50 minimum even though he worked only one month; and nothing for the last quarter because in 1950 self-employment income was not covered by Social Security.

Example: Eve was paid $800 in January 1978, but did not earn anything the rest of the year. Based on the earnings test in effect in 1978, she got three credits for the year—one for each $250 in earnings—based on her earnings for January alone.

Example: Rebecca was paid $500 a month in 2000 at her part-time job, for total earnings for the year of $6,000. Since her earnings of $6,000 divided by $780 (the amount needed to earn one credit in 2000) is more than 4, she received the maximum four credits for 2000.

Special Rule for Military Service 1940 to 1956

Before 1957, Social Security taxes were not paid by members of the military. However, Congress passed a rule that permits members of the military during those years to earn work credits for active duty service.

If you are receiving a military retirement pension for active duty, however, you cannot also receive Social Security credit for the same period. Your Social Security record can be credited with $160 per month in earnings for active military service between September 16, 1940, and December 31, 1956, if:

- you served 90 or more days active service and were honorably discharged
- you were discharged because of a disability or injury which occurred in the line of duty, or
- you are applying for Social Security survivors benefits based on the record of a veteran who died on active service.

E. Determining Your Benefit Amount

If you are eligible for a Social Security benefit, the amount of that benefit is determined by a formula based on the average of your yearly reported earnings in covered employment since you began working. Wages before 1937 are not counted, however. And self-employment income before 1951 is not counted, either.

1. Effect of Age

Social Security computes the average of earnings differently depending on your age. If you reached age 62 or became disabled on or before December 31, 1978, the computation is simple: Social Security averages the actual dollar value of your total past earnings.

If you turned 62 or became disabled on or after January 1, 1979, Social Security divides your earnings into two categories: earnings from before 1951 are credited with their actual dollar amount, up to a maximum of $3,000 per year; and from 1951 on, yearly limits are placed on earnings credits as shown in the chart at right, no matter how much you actually earned in those years.

Yearly Dollar Limit on Earnings Credits

1951 - 1954	3,600
1955 - 1958	4,200
1959 - 1965	4,800
1966 - 1967	6,600
1968 - 1971	7,800
1972	9,000
1973	10,800
1974	13,200
1975	14,100
1976	15,300
1977	16,500
1978	17,700
1979	22,900
1980	25,900
1981	29,700
1982	32,400
1983	35,700
1984	37,800
1985	39,600
1986	42,000
1987	43,800
1988	45,000
1989	48,000
1990	50,400
1991	53,400
1992	55,500
1993	57,600
1994	60,600
1995	61,200
1996	62,700
1997	65,400
1998	68,400
1999	72,600
2000	76,200

2. Benefit Formula

Based on a worker's earnings record, the Social Security Administration computes what is called the worker's Primary Insurance Amount, or PIA. This is the amount a worker would receive if he or she claims retirement benefits at full retirement age, which is 65 for everyone born in 1937 or earlier. The full retirement age is 67 for those born in 1960 or later. (If you were born between 1938 and 1960 see the chart Retirement Age for Those Born After 1937 in Chapter 2.) The exact formula applied to each worker's earnings record depends on the year the worker was born.

Social Security benefits for a disabled worker (Chapter 3), or for a worker's dependents (Chapter 4) or survivors (Chapter 5), are based on a percentage of the worker's PIA. You can get an estimate of your future retirement or disability benefits, or those of a worker on whose earnings record you will receive dependents or survivors benefits. (See Section F.)

3. Taxes on Your Benefits

A certain amount of Social Security benefits may be taxable, depending on your total income. In determining whether you owe any income tax on your benefits, the Internal Revenue Service looks at what it calls your provisional income. This is a combination of your adjusted gross income, as reported in your tax return, plus 50% of your interest from tax-exempt investments, plus 50% of your Social Security benefits. If the total of this provisional income is over $34,000 ($44,000 for couples filing jointly), up to 85% of your Social Security benefits are taxed, although the percentage is smaller for most people.

The way to calculate any income taxes you may owe on your Social Security benefits is explained in the instruction booklet that accompanies Form 1040 federal tax return. The IRS also publishes an information booklet explaining numerous tax rules pertaining to older people. It is called the "Older Americans' Tax Guide," Publication 554. You can get the booklet free of charge by calling the IRS at: 800-829-3676.

Special Rules for Veterans

Veterans receive extra earnings credit, up to the yearly limits listed above: an extra $160 per month for active duty between September 1, 1940, and December 31, 1956; an extra $300 per quarter for active duty from 1957 to 1977. After 1977, veterans receive $100 of credit for each $300 of actual military pay, up to a maximum extra credit of $1,200 per year.

F. Your Social Security Record

The Social Security Administration keeps a running computer account of your earnings record and the work credits it reflects, tracking both through your Social Security number. Based on those figures, Social Security can give you an estimate of what your retirement benefits would be if you took them at age 62, 65 or 70. It can also estimate benefits for your dependents or survivors, or for your disability benefits, should you need them.

In planning for the future, it makes good sense to find out what your Social Security retirement benefits will be several years before you actually consider claiming them. (See Chapter 2, Section B.) And since so much is riding on your official earnings record, it is important to check the accuracy of that record every few years to make sure that all your covered earnings are credited to you.

1. Checking Earnings Record and Estimated Benefits

Understanding how important it is for people to keep track of their earnings record and estimate of benefits, the Social Security Administration mails out copies of individual Social Security records on a Personal Earnings and Benefit Estimate Statement (PEBES).

A PEBES is supposed to be mailed to everyone age 40 and over who is not currently receiving Social Security benefits.

If you have not received a PEBES—or received one more than a year ago and want a more recent estimate—you may request one by filling out a simple form, SSA 7004, called a Request for Earnings and Benefit Estimate Statement. This form is available in English and Spanish.

The form is available at your local Social Security office. Or call Social Security toll-free at 800-772-1213 to request one by mail. If you have access to a computer connected to the Internet, you can request a PEBES from the Social Security Administration Website at http://www.ssa.gov. Once you are connected to the site, look under Online Direct Services, where you will find the heading Request a Personal Earnings and Benefit Estimate Statement. Click on that heading and fill out the form. The PEBES itself will be sent to you by regular mail in about four weeks. If you do not have access to a computer, check your local library. A librarian should be able to assist you if you are not familiar with online services. You may also fill out a copy of the request form reproduced at the end of this chapter and send it to:

Social Security Administration
Wilkes Barre Data Operations Center
P.O. Box 7004
Wilkes Barre, PA 18767-7004

2. Completing the Request Form

There are only a few questions you need to consider carefully when filling out the request form. Make sure you fill in your name exactly as it is on your Social Security card. That will allow Social Security more easily to track down missing or misplaced records in case your earnings were ever mistakenly reported.

As to Part 6, which requests your earnings, do not worry about providing exact income figures. They are only used to provide you with an estimate of your benefits; your benefits will be based on your actual earnings as reported on your tax returns, not on the estimate you provide on this form. Even if you are off by a couple of thousand dollars on the income estimate you give here, it will have only a slight effect on your benefit estimate.

Part 7 asks you to indicate the age at which you plan to stop working. Again, this is just so that Social Security can estimate the number of years of earnings you still have before you can claim your retirement benefits. In no way does it commit you to anything. If you are not certain when you will stop working, put down age 65, which is currently considered full retirement age. If at any time you consider stopping work earlier or later than age 65, you can request another statement estimating your benefits.

Part 8 asks you to estimate your average yearly earnings between now and the time you think you will retire. Remember that this estimate only includes income from wages, salary or self-employment and does not include investment income, capital gains, gifts or inheritance. If you are more than a few years away from claiming retirement benefits, this is a very difficult question to answer accurately. Unless you know that you are in line for a significant jump or decrease in earned income in the next few years, it is best to fill in your current income here.

Social Security will adjust the figure for inflation and will give you your benefit estimate in current dollars. If you are still a long way away from claiming retirement, the current income estimate and retirement figure Social Security provides will give you a more accurate picture of your benefits than if you try to speculate about what your inflated salary might be years from now. You can judge what it would be like to live at today's cost of living on the amount Social Security estimates in today's dollars.

Once you have sent in your completed request form, it takes several weeks for the Social Security Administration to process it and mail you a copy of your earnings record.

G. Reading Your Earnings Record

The Personal Earnings and Benefit Estimate Statement you will receive from Social Security consists of six pages. The first three pages contain the information on your personal earnings record and benefit estimates. The last three pages of the statement merely give you a general overview of Social Security programs and provide personal information.

The first three pages of a sample benefit statement are reproduced here, and the crucial parts of these pages are explained. If, upon examining your own statement, you believe any of the information is incorrect, you can take steps to set the record straight. (See Section H.)

Page 1. There is little of significance on page 1. It is simply an introductory page with a bit of blather from the Social Security Commissioner. On the bottom right of the page is your name as it appears on your Social Security card, your Social Security number and your date of birth; make sure they are correct. Also listed are your earnings for the previous year, an estimate of your earnings for the current year, and your estimated future yearly earnings. These are the figures you provided to Social Security on the request form for obtaining a PEBES.

Also listed on the bottom right is the age you gave to Social Security as the age when you expect to stop working. What this really means is the year you expect to claim your retirement benefits. This tells Social Security to give you an estimate for that year, but it does not commit you to claim your benefits in that year; it is only for estimating purposes. Even if you continue working past the age stated on this form, you may still claim your benefits—although they may be limited, depending on how much you continue to earn. (See Chapter 2, Section D.)

Earnings and Benefit Statement (page 1 of 3)

Your Personal Earnings and Benefit Estimate Statement
from the SOCIAL SECURITY ADMINISTRATION

A Message from the Commissioner

We are pleased to send you the Personal Earnings and Benefit Estimate Statement you requested. We hope it will help you to better understand the Social Security program and what it means to you and your family. The statement shows the estimated amount of benefits, under current law, that you and your family may be eligible for now and in the future. It also lists the earnings that your employers (or you, if you're self-employed) have reported to Social Security. We hope you will use this information along with other information you may have about your savings, pensions and investments to help you plan for a secure financial future.

Remember, Social Security can be an important part of your financial future whether you're young or old, male or female, single or married. It can help you when you need it most by paying you benefits when you retire or if you become severely disabled. Social Security also can help support your family when you die.

Some people are concerned that Social Security won't be there in the future. The program has changed in the past to meet the demands of the times, and it must do so again. Today we are working to resolve long-range financing issues and to ensure that future generations of Americans can count on the same financial protections from Social Security as past generations did.

Kenneth S. Apfel
Kenneth S. Apfel
Commissioner of Social Security

The Facts You Gave Us

Your Name ....
Your Social Security Number ....
Your Date of Birth ....
1997 Earnings ....
1998 Earnings ....
Your Estimated Future Average Yearly Earnings ....
Age You Plan To Stop Working ....
Other Social Security Numbers You've Used ....

Page 2. This page shows your entire official earnings history, according to Social Security's records. The second column, Maximum Taxable Earnings, shows the maximum amount of earnings you can be credited with for any given year. The third column, Your Reported Earnings, is the most important one, listing your earnings from covered employment. For the years 1937 to 1950, only a summary of your earnings is provided. And if you earned more than the maximum taxable earnings for any particular year, your record will show only that year's maximum. You cannot get Social Security credit for income over that amount.

Notice that the earnings column for the last year on the sample is blank. This is because Social Security recordkeeping is a year behind. The estimate of your benefits provided on Page 3 is based on your highest 35 years of earnings, so having an exact figure for your latest year's earnings is not crucial to a reasonably accurate figure. And your record is updated every year, so the closer you come to retirement, the more accurate the benefits estimate will be.

Carefully check your own earnings records—income tax returns, pay stubs, payroll records at work—against the figures in column three. You can get discrepancies corrected. (See Section H.) Failing to correct mistakes may cost you $10 or $15 per month per mistake, and more in some cases, for as long as you and your family collect benefits. Over all the years you collect benefits, that can amount to a lot of money.

Earnings and Benefit Statement (page 2 of 3)

Your Social Security Earnings

On page 4, we explain more about covered earnings and Social Security and Medicare taxes. The following chart shows your reported earnings. It may not show some or all of your earnings from last year because they are not yet recorded. This year's earnings will not be reported to us until next year.

If your own records do not agree with the earnings amounts shown, please contact us right away. If possible, have your W-2 or tax return for those years available.

	Social Security			Medicare		
Years	Maximum Taxable Earnings	Your Reported Earnings	Estimated Taxes You Paid	Maximum Taxable Earnings	Your Reported Earnings	Estimated Taxes You Paid
1937-50	$3,000	$ 0	$ 0	Medicare did not start until 1966.		
1951	3,600	0	0			
1952	3,600	0	0			
1953	3,600	0	0			
1954	3,600	0	0			
1955	4,200	0	0			
1956	4,200	0	0			
1957	4,200	0	0			
1958	4,200	0	0			
1959	4,800	0	0			
1960	4,800	0	0			
1961	4,800	0	0			
1962	4,800	0	0			
1963	4,800	0	0			
1964	4,800	479	17			
1965	4,800	672	24			
1966	6,600	1,026	39	$6,600	$ 1,026	$ 3
1967	6,600	987	38	6,600	987	4
1968	7,800	0	0	7,800	0	0
1969	7,800	140	5	7,800	140	0
1970	7,800	3,036	127	7,800	3,036	18
1971	7,800	0	0	7,800	0	0
1972	9,000	9,000	414	9,000	9,000	54
1973	10,800	5,904	286	10,800	5,904	59
1974	13,200	2,300	113	13,200	2,300	20
1975	14,100	4,818	337	14,100	4,818	43
1976	15,300	0	0	15,300	0	0
1977	16,500	1,305	64	16,500	1,305	11
1978	17,700	1,525	77	17,700	1,525	15
1979	22,900	0	0	22,900	0	0
1980	25,900	4,467	314	25,900	4,467	46
1981	29,700	2,947	235	29,700	2,947	38
1982	32,400	4,604	370	32,400	4,604	59
1983	35,700	3,949	317	35,700	3,949	51
1984	37,800	6,150	535	37,800	6,150	159
1985	39,600	12,084	1,099	39,600	12,084	326
1986	42,000	17,578	1,652	42,000	17,578	509
1987	43,800	16,407	1,542	43,800	16,407	475
1988	45,000	13,545	1,370	45,000	13,545	392
1989	48,000	0	0	48,000	0	0
1990	51,300	10,978	1,361	51,300	10,978	318
1991	53,400	2,334	289	125,000	2,334	67
1992	55,500	983	121	130,200	983	28
1993	57,600	0	0	135,000	0	0
1994	60,600	5,224	647	No Limit	5,224	151
1995	61,200	11,481	1,423	No Limit	11,481	332
1996	62,700	16,226	2,012	No Limit	16,226	470
1997	65,400	13,522	1,676	No Limit	13,522	392
1998	68,400			No Limit		
Total estimated Social Security taxes paid			$ 16,504	Total estimated Medicare taxes paid		$ 4,040

2

Page 3. On this page, Social Security gives you the numbers in which you are most interested: estimates of your benefits and those for your family. The second section, next to the title Retirement Benefits, provides you with several key pieces of information. First, it tells you whether you have enough work credits to qualify for Social Security retirement benefits and for Medicare. If you do not have enough credits, it shows you how many more credits you need to qualify. (See Section D.)

This section also gives you estimates of how much your retirement benefits would be if you claimed them:

- at the age you told Social Security in your PEBES request form that you planned to retire
- at what Social Security considers full retirement age—65 for people born in 1938 or earlier, gradually increasing to 67 for people born after 1938, and
- at age 70.

If you are within two or three years of claiming benefits at any of these ages, the benefit estimate will be extremely accurate, probably within $25 per month of your actual benefits. The further you are away from these ages when you receive your estimate, however, the less accurate the estimate is likely to be. That is because the amount of your benefits depends on the amount of your covered earnings, and your earnings over the years before your retirement may move your benefits up or down.

The Importance of Keeping Track

Your benefits estimate is based on the average of your earnings over your entire lifetime. Your earnings in the last few years before you claim retirement may be higher than most of your earlier working years, and if so will increase your average, and your benefits, significantly. For that reason, it is important to request an official statement every few years, to keep track of your changing benefits estimate.

The third section of page 3, Disability Benefits, indicates how many work credits you need to qualify for Social Security disability benefits. (See Chapter 3, Section A.) There is also an estimate for the disability benefits you would receive if you were to become disabled right now. If you continue to work in covered employment and you become disabled later, your disability benefits might be higher than the estimate shown. That is because your continued earnings would boost your earnings record on which all benefit amounts are based.

The fourth section, entitled Family Benefits, does not give specific estimates. That is because family benefits—also known as dependents benefits—vary not only with the amount of your retirement benefits but also with the number of your minor children. (See Chapter 4.)

Survivors benefits are estimated in the fifth section. If you have a spouse who has reached qualifying age, or minor or disabled children, they would be covered by survivors benefits when you die. (See Chapter 5.)

Earnings and Benefit Statement (page 3 of 3)

Your Estimated Social Security Benefits

Your work under Social Security helps you and your family to qualify for benefit payments. The kinds of benefits you might get are described below. For each benefit, you need a certain number of work credits (see page 5). Once you have enough credits, your benefit amount depends on your average earnings over your working lifetime. We used the earnings in the chart on page 2 to figure your credits and estimate your benefits. We included any and earnings and any estimated future earnings you told us about.

Retirement Benefits

To get Social Security retirement benefits, you need 40 credits of work. That is also how many you need for Medicare at age 65. Your record shows that you have enough credits.

On page 5, we explain about different ages when you can retire. If you worked at your present rate up to each retirement age, your monthly amount would be about:

At age 65 (reduced benefit) . . . . $

At full-retirement age (years of age) . . . . $

At age 70 . . . . $

Disability Benefits

On page 6, we tell you about disability benefits. If you become disabled right now, you need credits to qualify for disability benefits. You had to earn 20 of these credits in the last 10 years. Your record shows that you have earned enough credits within the right time.

Right now, your monthly disability amount would be about . . . . $

Family Benefits

If you get retirement or disability benefits, your spouse and young children may also qualify for benefits. See page 6 for more information about family benefits.

Survivor Benefits

If you die, certain members of your family may qualify for survivor benefits on your record. See page 6 for an explanation of who may qualify.

If you die right now, you need credits for your survivors to get benefits. Your record shows you have enough. If they met all other requirements, monthly benefit amounts would be about:

For your child . . . . $

For your spouse who is caring for your child . . . . $

When your spouse reaches full-retirement age . . . . $

For all your family members, if others also qualify (more children, for example) . . . . $

We may also be able to pay your spouse or children a one-time death benefit of $255

Medicare

Medicare hospital and medical insurance is a two-part benefit program that helps protect you from the high costs of medical care. Hospital insurance benefits (Part A) help pay the cost when you are in the hospital and for certain kinds of follow-up care. Medical insurance benefits (Part B) help pay the costs of doctors' services.

If you have enough work credits, you may qualify for Medicare hospital insurance at age 65, even if you are still working. You may qualify before age 65 if you are disabled or have permanent kidney failure. Your spouse may also qualify for hospital insurance at 65 on your record.

Almost anyone who is 65 or older or who qualifies for Medicare hospital insurance can enroll for medical insurance. You must pay a monthly premium for it.

For More Information or To Correct Your Record

After you read this statement, if you have questions, want to apply for benefits or want to request a Statement in Spanish, please call 1-800-772-1213* or visit our Website at www.ssa.gov/mystatement. If you are reporting missing or wrong earnings, have your W-2 or tax return for those years available, if possible. This Statement is just an estimate of your potential benefits. You do not qualify for Social Security or Medicare until you apply and meet all the requirements. Meanwhile, your record is updated each year and you can request a new statement to make sure it stays correct.

*Social Security treats all calls confidentially--whether they are made to our toll-free number or to one of our local offices. But we also want to be sure that you receive accurate and courteous service. That is why we have a second Social Security representative listen to some incoming and outgoing telephone calls.

3

The section on page 3 marked Medicare provides only brief general statements about the program. The key piece of personal information about you and Medicare is whether you have enough work credits to qualify for Medicare when you reach age 65. That information, which is the same as whether you qualify for retirement benefits, is included in section two.

H. Correcting Your Earnings and Benefit Statement

Mistakes do occur in official earnings records. Social Security estimates that employers make mistakes in wage reports about 4% of the time. Social Security easily clears up most of these errors—misspelled names, transposed numbers. But one dollar of every $100 reported to Social Security fails to be credited to the correct worker's record.

The problem of unreported earnings occurs more frequently with people who have used more than one name—usually women who have changed their names when they married, or married and divorced, and who may have had their earnings reported under both unmarried and married names.

The problem also appears to be more common for people whose family names the Social Security computer may have trouble identifying properly. Examples include:

- hyphenated names, such as Watson-Jones
- names with spaces between one part and another, such as de la France, and
- names in which the identifying family portion does not come at the end as in Anglo constructions, such as Park Chee Ho or Martina Rosales Rincon.

In recent years, the Social Security Administration has been taking steps to make it easier to correct mistakes. If you believe a mistake has been made on your record, you can do something about it even if it concerns wages from many years past.

First, check the Social Security number on the earnings statement to make sure it is your earnings that are being calculated.

Next, check the amounts listed in column three of page two with your own records of earnings. You may have records of your earnings in your income tax forms or pay stubs. Your place of work may also have pay records for a number of years. (See below.) Note that the amounts of your reported income listed in this column include only earned income from covered employment and do not include any income which is not wages, salary or self-employment and does not count any self-employment income before 1951. Nor does it include any income over the amount listed in the second column under the heading Maximum Taxable Earnings. Even if you made more than that figure during the year, you only got credit for the maximum earnings amount listed.

Locating Your Earnings Records

If you find what you believe is an error that relates to work for your current employer, ask the payroll person at your workplace to verify your Social Security earnings for the year in question and to give you a copy of paperwork showing those earnings.

If the earnings were for a previous employer, ask the personnel office there for records of your earnings. If it no longer has your records, or if the earnings were from self-employment, try to locate among your own records some written evidence of what you contend was your actual covered income for that year—tax returns, W-2 forms, pay stubs, bank deposit statements.

When you have evidence of your covered earnings in the year or years for which you think Social Security has made an error, call Social Security's helpline at: 800-772-1213, Monday through Friday from 7 a.m. to 7 p.m. This is the line that takes all kinds of Social Security questions, and it is often swamped, so be patient. It is best to call early in the morning or late in the afternoon, late in the week and late in the month. Have all your documents handy when you speak with a representative.

If you would rather speak with someone in person, call your local Social Security office and make an appointment to see someone there, or drop into the office during regular business hours. If you drop in, be prepared to wait, perhaps as long as an hour or two, before you get to see a representative. Bring with you two copies of your benefits statement and the evidence that supports your claim of higher income. That way, you can leave one copy with the Social Security worker. Write down the name of the person with whom you speak so that you can reach the same person when you follow up.

The process to correct errors is slow. It may take several months to have the changes made in your record. And once Social Security confirms that it has corrected your record, go through the process of requesting another benefits statement to double check.

One Year Correction Without Evidence of Income

The Social Security Administration has enacted a policy that allows you to get credit for one year's earnings—in certain limited circumstances—even if you cannot come up with written evidence of those earnings. The rule applies only to earnings from 1978 on.

The rule applies if Social Security has a record of your earnings from an employer in a year immediately before or after the year you want corrected, and the earnings you are claiming for that year are consistent with the year just before or after it. In such cases, Social Security can give you credit for earnings in the amount you claim for that year even though neither you nor the employer has written evidence of those earnings.

Request for Earnings and Benefit Estimate Statement

Form Approved
OMB No. 0960-0466

☐ SP

Request for Earnings and Benefit Estimate Statement

☐ Please check this box if you want to get your statement in Spanish instead of English.

Please print or type your answers. When you have completed the form, fold it and mail it to us. (If you prefer to send your request using the Internet, contact us at http://www.ssa.gov)

1. Name shown on your Social Security card:

First Name ______ Middle Initial ______

Last Name Only ______

2. Your Social Security number as shown on your card:

☐☐☐-☐☐-☐☐☐☐

3. Your date of birth (Mo.-Day-Yr.)

☐☐-☐☐-☐☐☐☐

4. Other Social Security numbers you have used:

☐☐☐-☐☐-☐☐☐☐

☐☐☐-☐☐-☐☐☐☐

5. Your sex: ☐ Male ☐ Female

For items 6 and 8 show only earnings covered by Social Security. Do NOT include wages from State, local or Federal Government employment that are NOT covered for Social Security or that are covered ONLY by Medicare.

6. Show your actual earnings (wages and/or net self-employment income) for last year and your estimated earnings for this year.

   A. Last year's actual earnings: *(Dollars Only)*

   $ ☐☐☐,☐☐☐.0 0

   B. This year's estimated earnings: *(Dollars Only)*

   $ ☐☐☐,☐☐☐.0 0

7. Show the age at which you plan to stop working.

   ☐☐ *(Show only one age)*

8. Below, show the average yearly amount (not your total future lifetime earnings) that you think you will earn between now and when you plan to stop working. Include performance or scheduled pay increases or bonuses, but not cost-of-living increases.

   If you expect to earn significantly more or less in the future due to promotions, job changes, part-time work, or an absence from the work force, enter the amount that most closely reflects your future average yearly earnings.

   If you don't expect any significant changes, show the same amount you are earning now (the amount in 6B).

   Future average yearly earnings: *(Dollars Only)*

   $ ☐☐☐,☐☐☐.0 0

9. Do you want us to send the statement:
   - To you? Enter your name and mailing address.
   - To someone else (your accountant, pension plan, etc.)? Enter your name with "c/o" and the name and address of that person or organization.

Name ______

Street Address (Include Apt. No., P.O. Box, or Rural Route) ______

City ______ State ______ Zip Code ______

Notice:
I am asking for information about my own Social Security record or the record of a person I am authorized to represent. I understand that if I deliberately request information under false pretenses, I may be guilty of a Federal crime and could be fined and/or imprisoned. I authorize you to use a contractor to send the statement of earnings and benefit estimates to the person named in item 9.

▶ ______

Please sign your name (Do Not Print)

Date ______ (Area Code) Daytime Telephone No. ______

Form SSA-7004-SM Internet (6-98) Destroy prior editions

Social Security Retirement Benefits

Many people look forward to retirement as a time of contentedness and quiet, a new time for old friendships, a period of calm sufficiency. They imagine they will be able to do things they always wanted to do but could not because they were caught up in working and tending to the needs of others. While this may prove to be a true picture for some people, many others find a far different reality. It is difficult to enjoy retirement life without the financial resources to cope with a high-priced world. In a society that has forgotten how to revere and succor its elders, retirement too often becomes yet another difficult siege in the same old battle for survival.

The reality for many Americans is that after what they had hoped would be retirement age—usually anticipated as age 65—they must continue working to make ends meet. And often they must do so at lower-paying work than they had before retirement age. The Social Security retirement benefit program, as well as private pension and other retirement plans, helps with some of the financial strain of retirement years. But Social Security retirement benefits alone are not sufficient for most people to live at anything near the standard of living they had during their working years. So, unless people have considerable assets or investment income, they must continue to work after reaching retirement age.

Under Social Security rules, retirement does not necessarily mean you have reached age 65, or that you have stopped working altogether. It merely refers to the time you claim and start collecting Social Security retirement benefits. If you continue to work while receiving benefits, the amount of your benefits will be reduced if you earn more than a specific amount of income. Once you reach age 70, however, you will collect the full amount of your retirement benefits no matter how much you continue to earn.

This chapter explains how Social Security figures your eligibility for retirement benefits, when you may and when you should claim the benefits and what the rules are regarding earnings after you have begun to claim your retirement benefits.

A. Work Credits Required

To be eligible for Social Security retirement benefits, you must have earned the required number of work credits over your working years. (See Chapter 1, Section D.) You are fully insured—the term Social Security uses to indicate that you are eligible for retirement benefits—if, when you apply for benefits, you have the number of work credits listed below.

Work Credits Required for Social Security Retirement Eligibility

Year You Were Born	Work Credits Required
1929 or later	40
1928	39
1927	38
1926	37
1925	36
1924	35
1923	34
1922	33
1921	32
1920	31

1. Checking Your Earnings Record

Even if you have not worked for many years, and you did not make much money in the few years you did work, check your earnings record. (See Chapter 1, Sections F and G.) You may be surprised to find that you have quite a few credits from years gone by, since the rules for getting work credits were pretty easy to comply with before 1978.

If you find that you do not have enough work credits to be eligible for retirement benefits now, you may be able to work part-time for a while and earn enough new credits to become eligible. And once you qualify for retirement benefits, you are eligible to receive them for the rest of your life. That could mean a lot of money for you over the years to come.

Example: When Millie got out of school in 1944, she worked in a millinery shop. After several years there, she married and stopped working outside the home. Her husband was in business for himself and supported them both quite well, but he died in 1955. Millie was able to live carefully on their savings and investments, but over the years she found herself slowly going through all her assets. She decided to go back to work but could only find part-time employment.

In 1991, at age 64, Millie checked her Social Security record and found that she had 34 work credits from her time at the millinery shop over 40 years before. With 34 credits, she needed only four more to be eligible for retirement benefits; born in 1927, she needed a total of 38 credits. With her new part-time job, in only one year she was able to get her four additional work credits and qualify for Social Security retirement benefits.

2. Eligibility Rules for Employees of Nonprofits

Before January 1, 1984, nonprofit organizations did not have to participate in Social Security. Some organizations did participate, and their employees' work was covered by Social Security, earning the employees credits just as if they worked for private profit-making employers. Nonprofit organizations that did not participate, however, paid no Social Security taxes on behalf of their employees, and the employees paid no Social Security taxes out of their wages. As a result, during all their work years before 1984, employees of these nonprofit organizations did not earn any Social Security work credits for their labors.

To help make up for these lost years of work, the Social Security laws permit certain employees of nonprofit organizations to qualify for Social Security benefits with less than the standard number of work credits. If you were at least 55 years old on January 1, 1984, and on that date were employed by a nonprofit organization that had not been participating in Social Security, you can qualify for retirement benefits with the amounts of work credits, earned after January 1, 1984, listed below.

These special rules do not apply to you if the nonprofit organization gave you the opportunity of participating in Social Security before 1984 but you declined.

Workers in Nonprofits: Work Credits Required for Social Security Retirement Eligibility

Your Age on January 1, 1984	Work Credits Required
55 or 56	20
57	16
58	12
59	8
60 or older	6

B. Timing Your Retirement

Two factors determine the amount of your retirement benefits. The first is your earnings record—how much you have earned over your working life; the higher your earnings, the higher your benefits. The second is the age at which you claim your retirement benefits. You are allowed to claim benefits as early as age 62, but the earlier you claim them—up to age 70—the permanently lower the benefits will be. This section explains how the timing of your claim affects the amount of your retirement benefits.

1. Claiming Benefits Before Age 65

You become eligible to claim retirement benefits when you turn 62. But if you have just had your 62nd birthday, do not reach too fast for your application form. If you claim benefits at 62, your monthly payment will be considerably less than if you wait until what Social Security considers your full retirement age. (See Section B2.)

Monthly Social Security benefits for retiring at age 62 are about 20% less than if you wait until age 65; about 13% less if you retire at 63; 6.6% less at age 64. And the reduction in monthly benefits is permanent. Benefits do not increase to the full amount when you turn 65. If you claim early retirement, your benefits will be reduced for as long as you live.

Of course, claiming retirement benefits at less than full retirement age means you will collect benefits for a longer time. But the permanent reduction in the amount of your monthly benefits means that if you live to your late 70s or beyond, you will wind up collecting less in total lifetime benefits than if you had waited until full retirement age.

Full retirement age will be going up gradually, from 65 to 67, for people who were born after 1937. For these people, retirement benefits will still be available as early as age 62, although the amount will again be reduced. Woefully, those born in 1960 or later who retire at 62 will see their benefits shrink as much as 30%.

To get a picture of your reduced benefits, request from Social Security a Personal Earnings and Benefits Estimate Statement. That statement will include a comparison of your retirement benefits at age 62 and your full retirement age benefits. (See Chapter 1, Sections F and G.)

Early Retirement and Ill Health

Some people are forced to stop working before full retirement age because of ill health. If you are under 65 and in that position, consider applying for Social Security Disability benefits rather than early retirement. (See Chapter 3.) The reason is that disability benefits are the same as full retirement benefits and the amount does not depend solely on the age at which you qualify for them.

Investing Your Early Retirement Money

Some financial planners suggest that when people reach age 64, they should claim early retirement benefits, which are reduced by 6.6%, and then invest them in certificates of deposit or other safe investments that have a return of 6.6% or more. This not only offsets the year's reduction but also makes the retirement money accessible, which would not happen if they died before claiming benefits.

The advisability of this approach depends on a person's broad financial picture. First, if a person is going to continue to work after reaching age 64, and will earn more than the amounts permitted under Social Security rules, the actual amount of monthly benefits collected will be reduced. (See Section D.) The working person claiming early retirement would then be trading a lifetime of lower benefits for what is probably a small amount of savings. However, for a person who will have substantial income or assets throughout his or her 60s and 70s, without working, this is not a concern.

The permanent reduction in benefits can add up to a tremendous amount over a lifetime. So, if a person who claims early retirement lives a long time and becomes dependent for living expenses on Social Security, the early savings will not have compensated for the long-term drop in monthly benefits, and banking early retirement amounts will not have been a good idea.

Switching From Retirement to Survivors Benefit

Financial straits force many widows to claim their retirement benefits at age 62, even though they would become eligible for a higher monthly retirement amount if they waited longer. Although claiming early retirement benefits permanently reduces their retirement benefits based on their own earnings record, Social Security rules permit widows who have previously claimed early retirement to switch to survivors benefits at age 65. And for many people, these full survivors benefits are higher than their own reduced retirement benefits. (See Chapter 5.)

The same rules apply to widowers, although the disparity in earnings between men and women means this ability to switch benefits is used almost exclusively by women.

2. Claiming Benefits at Full Retirement Age

Since its inception in 1936, Social Security has considered 65 to be full or normal retirement age. Benefit amounts have been calculated on the assumption that most workers will stop working full-time and will claim retirement benefits when they reach age 65. However, the system has long provided for early retirement. (See Section B1.) And to give incentive for people to delay making their retirement claims, Social Security offers higher benefits for people who wait to make their claims after reaching full retirement age. (See Section B3.)

Now that people are generally living longer, the Social Security rules for what is considered full retirement age are changing. Age 65 is still considered full retirement age for anyone born before 1938. However, full retirement age gradually increases from age 65 to 67 for people born in 1938 or later.

Retirement Age for Those Born After 1937

Year Born	Full Retirement Age
1938	65 years, 2 months
1939	65 years, 4 months
1940	65 years, 6 months
1941	65 years, 8 months
1942	65 years, 10 months
1943 - 1954	66 years
1955	66 years, 2 months
1956	66 years, 4 months
1957	66 years, 6 months
1958	66 years, 8 months
1959	66 years, 10 months
1960 or later	67 years

3. Delaying Retirement

If you wait until after your full retirement age to claim Social Security retirement benefits, your benefit amounts will be permanently higher. Your benefit amount is increased by a certain percentage each year you wait up to age 70. After age 70, there is no longer any increase and no reason to delay claiming benefits. This is true even if you keep working after you reach age 70, since reductions in Social Security benefits because of earned income end when you reach age 70. The amount of the yearly percentage increase in benefits depends on when you were born.

Increase Per Year in Benefits for Delayed Retirement

Year Born	Percentage Increase
1927 - 1928	4.0
1929 - 1930	4.5
1931 - 1932	5.0
1933 - 1934	5.5
1935 - 1936	6.0
1937 - 1938	6.5
1939 - 1940	7.0
1941 - 1942	7.5
1943 or later	8.0

If you continue to work after full retirement age and up to age 70, your monthly Social Security benefits will be reduced by any amounts you earn over the yearly limit for your age. (See Section D.) So if you earn over the limit, you will collect small monthly benefits at the same time you are permanently getting lower benefit levels than if you wait to claim retirement. And the increase in benefits you would get by delaying retirement is permanent. If you give up that increase, you will be locking yourself into lower monthly payments for ten, 20 or 30 years to come, depending on how long you live.

Delayed Retirement and Medicare

Even if you do not claim retirement benefits at age 65, you are eligible for Medicare benefits at 65 and must sign up for them then. Signing up for Medicare does not affect the amount of your retirement benefits. You can sign up for Medicare at any local Social Security office. You should do so three or four months before your 65th birthday. (See Chapter 12.)

C. The Amount of Your Retirement Check

Your Social Security retirement benefits depend on how much you earned in covered employment over all your working years. Social Security calculates your benefits based on the amounts in your highest-earning 35 years. Then it applies a set of formulas to these earnings; the exact figures depend on the year you were born. The process is complex and the results are less than bountiful. In 2000, for example, the average retirement benefit for a single person who turns 65 was only about $804 per month. Once you claim your benefits, there is a small cost of living increase each year.

Under Social Security's benefit calculation system, the lower your average lifetime earnings, the higher a percentage of those earnings you'll receive in benefits. If your earnings have averaged in the middle range—the equivalent of around $30,000 in today's dollars—you can expect full retirement benefits of about 40% of your average earnings for the last few years before you reach full retirement age. If your average earnings have been on the low side—around $20,000 a year in current dollars—then your benefits will be about 50% of your earnings in the years just before you claim retirement benefits. If your earnings have always been at or near the maximum credited earnings for each year (see Chapter 1), then your retirement benefits will be about 20% of the maximum amount for the year in which you retire.

But these figures are just averages. To get a much more precise picture of how much your retirement benefits will be, request an official estimate from Social Security. The closer you are to claiming your benefits, the more accurate Social Security's estimate will be. (See Chapter 1, Sections F and G.)

Benefits for Notch Babies: People Born 1917 to 1921

People born between 1917 and 1921—a period referred to as the "notch"—receive slightly smaller benefits than some people with comparable earnings records who were born before 1917.

For a few years in the 1970s people born earlier—1910 to 1916—were actually given benefits that were too high. When the mistake was corrected, the people born in that period were just retiring. Congress did not want to reduce the benefits of the 1910 to 1916 people too abruptly, so they permitted them to keep the extra high benefits. People born in the notch, however, had their future benefit amounts reduced to the correct levels, the same levels as applied to people born later.

While notch people may get a little less than people born slightly earlier, they are not being deprived of their proper benefit amounts. Rather, the people born earlier are receiving a small windfall amount.

1. Increases for Cost of Living

Whatever the amount of your retirement benefit, you receive an automatic cost of living increase on January 1 of each year. This increase is tied to the rise in the Consumer Price Index—the cost of basic goods and services. In the late 1970s, this Consumer Price Index rose more than 10% each year, causing Social Security benefits to rise more than 10% per year. In the 1980s, however, the yearly cost of living increase began to drop. In 2000, for example, the increase was only 2.4%. You cannot be sure that your benefit amounts will increase at any set pace, although they will be increased by some amount every year, no matter how long you continue to collect benefits.

2. Reductions for Government Pensions

Many people have worked both at government agency jobs and at those covered by Social Security. And some have worked long enough in each that they have earned the right not only to Social Security retirement benefits, but also a public employee retirement system pension.

Social Security calculates its benefits based on an average of earnings over 35 years. However, if you had many years in employment with low wages, Social Security artificially adjusts your benefits upward. Also, if you spent years in public employment, Social Security used to consider these as non-income years, which made you eligible for the artificially raised retirement benefits.

Social Security has now decided that if you earned a government pension during those years, your artificially raised benefit amount was an unfair windfall to you. And so your benefits have been reduced.

a. Those covered

If your age and work history fit certain categories, your Social Security check will be reduced by 10% to 35% because of this windfall. You may be affected by this reduction if:

- you were born in 1924 or after
- you first became eligible in 1986 or after for a government pension, and
- you have less than 30 years in work covered by Social Security.

b. Those not covered

The windfall reduction does not apply to you if:

- your only work for an employer not covered by Social Security was before 1957
- your only government pension is based solely on work for the railroad, or
- you were a federal government employee hired on January 1, 1984, or after.

Spouse's Benefits and Government Pensions

Another rule limits benefits to people who collect both Social Security benefits as the spouse of a retired or deceased worker and a public employment pension based on their own work records. (See Chapter 4, Section E, and Chapter 5, Section F.)

D. Working After Claiming Retirement Benefits

Since Social Security retirement benefits plus savings and other investments are often not enough to live on comfortably, many people keep working for at least a few years after they claim Social Security retirement benefits. Other people keep their jobs or take new ones to stay active and involved in the world of work.

If you plan on working after retirement, be aware that the money you earn may cause a reduction in the amount of your Social Security retirement benefits.

1. Reductions Based on Earned Income

Until you reach age 70, Social Security will subtract money from your retirement check if you exceed a specific amount of earned income for the year. The term earned income refers only to money received for work you currently do. Earned income does not include:

- interest on savings or investments
- capital gains
- IRA or 401(k) withdrawals
- insurance cash-ins
- rental income, and
- pensions.

This rule favors the well-to-do who have significant income from these sources, as opposed to wages or salary from current work. Those who need to keep on working, on the other hand, are penalized by having their retirement benefit reduced if they earn over the specific limits.

Special payments are money you receive after retirement from work you performed before. Social Security does not count the following special payments as earned income:

- bonuses
- accumulated vacation pay or sick leave compensation
- retirement funds
- deferred compensation, and
- accumulated commissions.

If you are self-employed, Social Security does not count special payments you receive more than one year after retirement for services performed before retiring.

2. Earned Income Without Penalty

The amount of earned income you are permitted without loss of Social Security retirement benefits depends on your age and changes each year. In 2000, for example, the limits on earned income are $10,000 per year if you were age 62 to 64; $17,000 if age 65 to 69. Once you turn age 70, there is no limit at all on the amount you can earn and still receive your full Social Security retirement benefit.

If you are age 62 to 64 and you earn income over the year's limit, your Social Security retirement benefits are reduced by one dollar for every two dollars over the limit. If you are 65 to 69, you lose one dollar in benefits for every three dollars of earned income over the limit.

3. Break for Your First Year of Retirement

During the first year you receive retirement benefits, you can get your full retirement amount for any month you do not earn more than the maximum allowed. This monthly maximum amount is calculated by taking the yearly limit and dividing it by 12. In 2000, for example, the monthly allowable limit is $840 ($10,080 divided by 12) for age 62 to 65, and $1,417 ($17,000 divided by 12) for age 65 to 69.

If you are self-employed, you may receive full benefits for any month during this first year in which you did not perform what Social Security considers substantial services. The usual test for substantial services is whether you worked in your business more than 45 hours during the month.

Change in How You Report Earnings

The Social Security Administration recently changed its rules about when and how benefit recipients under age 70 must report yearly earnings. The Social Security Administration now bases its benefit calculations on earnings reported on W-2 forms or self-employment tax payments. Individual benefit recipients are no longer required to send in an estimate of earnings by April 15 of each year.

The Social Security Administration still requests earnings estimates from some beneficiaries—those with substantial self-employment income, or whose reported earnings have varied widely from month to month, including people who work on commission. Toward the end of each year, Social Security sends those people a form asking for an earnings estimate for the following year. The agency uses the information to calculate benefits for the first months of the following year. It will then adjust the amounts, if necessary, after it receives actual W-2 or self-employment tax information in the current year.

Once a beneficiary reaches age 70, his or her income will no longer be checked. Since there is no Social Security limit on how much a person can earn after reaching age 70, there is nothing to report.

■

Social Security Disability Benefits

Over five million disabled workers and their families receive Social Security disability benefits. Some people have drawn disability benefits for many years, based on severe injuries and illnesses that were obviously and substantially disabling as soon as they struck. Other people, however, have chronic injuries that only become acute with age, or progressive conditions that deteriorate over the years. They may slowly notice that work is becoming more difficult and feel very much that they cannot do their jobs any longer.

If people develop disabilities in their 50s or early 60s, they are not quite old enough to collect retirement benefits. Or if they have reached retirement age, they may not have enough work credits to qualify for retirement benefits. In both situations, Social Security disability benefits may provide an answer.

If you have serious difficulty working because of a physical or emotional condition that is not likely to resolve itself within a year—and you are short of retirement age—read this chapter carefully. If you have enough work credits for your age, you may be eligible for monthly disability benefits. And if you are eligible to receive disability benefits, your spouse and minor or disabled children may also be eligible to collect benefits. (See Chapter 4, Section A.)

A. Who Is Eligible

Social Security disability benefits are only paid to workers and their families when the worker has enough work credits to qualify. Work credits for disability benefits are calculated in the same way as for retirement benefits, although fewer credits are required to qualify for the disability program. A person can earn up to four work credits per year, and anyone who works full-time, even at a very low-paying job, easily accumulates them. (See Chapter 1, Section D.)

1. Work Credits Required

The number of work credits needed to qualify for disability benefits depends on your age when you become disabled.

There are two ways to qualify for disability benefits—or be fully insured, in Social Security lingo. You must:

- have one or more work credits for each year between 1950 and the year you become disabled or reached age 62, or
- have one or more work credits each year from the year you turned 21—if that was after 1950— until you became disabled or turned 62.

At least six credits are always required, and no one is required to have more than 40.

Example: Eunice was born in 1940 and became disabled in 1999. To qualify for disability benefits she needs one work credit for each of the 38 years between 1961 (the year she turned 21) and 1999, the year she became disabled.

The charts below provide a quick reference to see how many work credits you need to qualify for disability benefits.

There are also rules that make it easier for younger workers and people who become blind to qualify for disability benefits. (See Sections A3 and A4.)

Work Credits Required to Qualify for Disability Benefits

If you were born before 1930 and you became disabled before age 62 in:	You need this many work credits:
1980	29
1981	30
1982	31
1983	32
1984	33
1985	34
1987	36
1989	38
1991 or later	40

If you were born after 1929 and you became disabled at age:	You need this many work credits:
42 or younger	20
44	22
46	24
48	26
50	28
52	30
54	32
56	34
58	36
60	38
62 or older	40

Help From the Americans with Disabilities Act

A federal law, the Americans with Disabilities Act, or ADA, prohibits employment discrimination on the basis of a worker's disability. The ADA is intended to help people with disabilities who want to work but are frustrated by employers.

In general, the ADA prohibits employers from discriminating against disabled people in hiring, promoting and other job decisions. It also precludes employers from maintaining a workplace that has substantial physical barriers to people with disabilities. The ADA requires that employers make reasonable accommodations for qualified workers with disabilities, unless that would cause the employers undue hardship.

Unfortunately, the ADA is full of vague language. Disability rights advocates, lawyers, employers and courts are still wrangling over precisely what terms like "reasonable accommodations" and "undue hardship" mean. And given the current anti-regulation climate in government, it is not clear how strenuously the government or the courts will enforce the law. All in all, it is difficult to say how effective the law will be in the coming years in assisting people to keep working despite their disabilities.

For information about how the ADA is being enforced and where you can go for help in seeking its protection, contact the Office on the Americans with Disabilities Act in the Civil Rights Division of the U.S. Department of Justice at: 800-514-0301 (voice) or 800-514-0381 (TDD). The Justice Department also has an ADA Website at http://www.usdoj.gov/crt/ada/adahom1.htm. For help and referrals from an activist disabled citizens action group, contact the Center for Independent Living in Berkeley, California at: 510-841-4776 or 510-848-3101 (TDD) or at its Website on the Internet at http://www.cilberkeley.org.

2. Requirement of Recent Work

You must have earned at least 20 of the required work credits within the ten years just before you became disabled, unless you qualify under one of the special rules for young or blind disabled workers.

Example: Monica worked for ten years before she had children, earning 40 work credits during that time. After her children were in high school, she went back to work. That was in 1995, and at the beginning of 1999, she became disabled with a back injury.

Although she had more than the 40 total credits required for disability benefits, she could not collect them at the beginning of the year because she had only worked four years—earning 16 credits—within the ten previous years. She needed to work long enough to earn four more credits before she could qualify for disability benefits. In 2000, that meant she had to earn $3,120 during the year (four credits at $780 per credit) before she could qualify.

3. Young Workers

If you were disabled between the ages of 24 and 31, you only need half of the work credits you could have earned between age 21 and the time you became disabled. And if you were disabled before age 24, you would only need six credits in the three-year period immediately before you became disabled. These special rules exist because workers who become disabled at a young age obviously do not have the opportunity to acquire many work credits.

Example: Boris became disabled at age 29. There were eight years between when he was age 21 and the time he became disabled. During those years he could have earned 32 work credits—4 per year. Under the special rule for young workers, however, Boris needs only half, or 16 credits to qualify for disability benefits.

4. Blind Workers

If you are disabled by blindness, you must have the same number of work credits as anyone else your age. (See Section A.) However, you need not have earned your work credits within the years immediately preceding your disability, as required for other workers. Your work credits can be from any time after 1936—the year the Social Security law went into effect.

For purposes of Social Security disability benefits, being blind means having no better than 20/200 vision in your better eye with glasses or other corrective lens, or having a visual field of 20 degrees or less. (See Section B.)

5. Disabled Widows and Widowers

If you are a widow or widower age 50 or older and disabled, you may receive disability benefits even though you do not have enough work credits to qualify. The amount of these benefits depends entirely upon your deceased spouse's average earnings and work record. Because they are based on a spouse's work record, these benefits will end if you remarry.

You must also meet a number of qualifications.

- You must be disabled, as defined by Social Security rules. (See Section B.)
- Your spouse, at death, must have been fully insured—meaning he or she had enough work credits to qualify for disability benefits, based on his or her age.
- Your disability must have started no later than seven years after your spouse's death.
- If you already receive Social Security benefits as a surviving widow or widower with children, your disability must have begun no later than seven years after those benefits end. (See Chapter 5, Section A.)
- If you divorced before your former spouse died, you will be eligible for these benefits only if the two of you were married for ten years or more.

B. What Is a Disability

To receive Social Security disability benefits, you must have a physical or mental disability that both:

- is expected to last, or has lasted, at least one year or to result in death, and
- prevents you from doing any substantial gainful work.

Of course, several of the terms within these definitions are subject to different interpretations. This section explains some guidelines developed by Social Security and the courts regarding qualifications for disability.

1. Conditions That May Qualify

Social Security has a listing of common conditions it considers disabling. (See Section B2.) And the medical community has a tendency to treat more seriously the things it can easily name. But every person's physical and mental state is different, and the human mind and body can be very complex. So you may well have a condition that disables you from work but it is difficult to get doctors to name and describe it precisely. Don't let that discourage you from filing for disability benefits.

The only absolute rule regarding disability is that the condition which prevents you from working at gainful employment must be a "medical" one, meaning that it can be discovered and verified by doctors. It does not have to be a simple one that can be immediately given a name. If you are considering making a claim for disability benefits, examine the requirement that the disability must prevent you from performing substantial gainful work. (See Section B4.) Discuss the matter thoroughly with your doctor or doctors. If the people who have treated you for your condition do a good job of describing it, with the substantial gainful employment rule in mind, any physical or mental medical condition can qualify you for benefits if it is truly disabling. (How to organize and present your application is discussed in Chapter 7.)

2. Listed Impairments

To simplify the process of determining whether a disability makes a person eligible for benefits, Social Security has developed a list of common serious conditions that it usually considers disabling. If you prove, through medical records and doctors' reports, that you have one of the listed conditions—paralysis of both an arm and a leg, for example—Social Security will likely consider you eligible for benefits without making you prove that you cannot perform substantial gainful work and that the condition will last a year. (See Sections B3 and B4.) If you have one of the listed conditions, Social Security will simply assume that you are eligible.

The more common serious conditions that Social Security normally considers disabling are listed below. Each claim for disability is considered individually, however, and having a condition on this list does not automatically qualify you for disability benefits. You must have medical verification—from a doctor or hospital that has treated you—of the condition that appears on the list. If you do, your application for disability benefits is likely to be approved unless you have been working since you became disabled. If you have been working, Social Security will determine whether your condition prevents you from performing what it defines as substantial gainful work. (See Section B4.)

The conditions Social Security lists as being disabilities include:

- diseases of the heart, lung or blood vessels resulting in a serious loss of heart or lung reserves as shown by X-ray, electrocardiogram or other tests—and, in spite of medical treatment, there is breathlessness, pain or fatigue
- severe arthritis causing recurrent inflammation, pain, swelling and deformity in major joints so that the ability to get about or use the hands is severely limited
- mental illness resulting in marked constriction of activities and interests, deterioration in personal habits and seriously impaired ability to get along with other people, such

that it prevents substantial gainful employment

- damage to the brain or brain abnormality resulting in severe loss of judgment, intellect, orientation or memory
- cancer which is progressive and has not been controlled or cured
- Acquired Immune Deficiency Syndrome or any of its related secondary diseases resulting in an inability to perform substantial gainful employment
- diseases of the digestive system which result in severe malnutrition, weakness and anemia
- loss of a leg or a disease or injury that has made one leg completely useless
- loss of major function of both arms, both legs, or a leg and an arm
- serious loss of function of the kidneys, and
- total inability to speak.

3. Must Be Expected to Last One Year

No matter how seriously disabling a condition or injury is, it will not make you eligible for disability benefits unless it has lasted, or is expected to last, one year. The disability will also qualify if it is expected to cause death within a year.

Apply for Benefits Upon Diagnosis

Even though the disability must be expected to last at least a year, you do not have to wait the year to apply for benefits. As soon as the condition is disabling and a doctor can predict that it is expected to last a year, you may qualify. (The application process is described in Chapter 7.)

Example: Ladonna fell down some stairs and dislocated her hip. She was placed in a body cast and was told by her doctor to stay in bed for three to four weeks. The cast would stay on for four months. After that, Ladonna would need a cane for another two or three months. In six to nine months, she would be walking normally again, although a little bit more cautiously, particularly around stairs. She would be off work for a total of seven or eight months.

Despite the seriousness of her injury and her total inability to work while she recovered, Ladonna cannot claim Social Security disability benefits. The reason is that her disability was not expected to last for a year. However, she might qualify for her company's disability benefits, if the company provides them, or for unemployment or state disability compensation through her state's employment or disability office.

If, after you begin receiving benefits, it turns out that your disability does not actually last a year, Social Security cannot ask for its money back. You are not penalized for recovering sooner than expected, as long as the original expectation that the disability would last a year was expressed in writing by your doctor and accepted by the Social Security review process.

Example: Ravi had a stroke, leaving most of his left side paralyzed. He was unable to walk on his own, unable to speak clearly and needed help with most simple daily life tasks. He began physical and speech therapy, but his doctors predicted that he was unlikely to recover full use of his left arm and leg. Ravi was found eligible for disability benefits because his condition was totally disabling and it was not expected that within a year he would recover sufficiently to return to work. However, through hard work, Ravi recovered both his speech and enough of the use of his arm and leg to return to work in ten months.

Although his total disability did not last the required year, he was able to keep the disability payments he had already received because the doctors had expected that his condition would be totally disabling for at least a year and the Social Security disability review process had accepted that prognosis.

4. No Substantial Gainful Work

To be eligible for Social Security disability benefits, you must be unable to perform any substantial gainful work—considered to be any work from which you earn $700 per month or more.

In determining whether your condition prevents you from doing substantial gainful work, Social Security will first consider whether it prevents you from doing the job you had when you became disabled, or the last job you had before becoming disabled. If your disability prevents you from performing your usual job, Social Security will next decide whether you are able to do any other kind of substantial gainful work—that is, any job in which you could earn $700 per month or more.

As part of this determination, Social Security considers your education, training and work experience. For example, a highly trained professional, whose work does not require any physical exertion but which is highly compensated, may still be able to earn $700 a month despite a certain physical disability. However, someone whose entire working life has been in lower skilled, lower paying work that requires considerable physical labor might have a harder time earning $700 per month with exactly the same physical disability

Age is also taken into consideration. Social Security does not commit to as great an outlay of money when it grants disability benefits to people nearing retirement age as it does to younger workers. Since older workers could collect retirement benefits anyway as early as age 62, and since no one can collect more than one benefit at a time, Social Security is not likely to pay much more money to an older worker than it would have without granting the disability. For this reason, and because it is more difficult for them to find new employment or to retrain for other kinds of work, older workers filing disability claims tend to have them approved more readily than younger workers do.

Finally, Social Security will determine whether you are able to perform any kind of work for pay existing anywhere in the economy, whether or not there are actually any such jobs available in the area in which you live. However, it is up to Social Security to prove that there is gainful employment you can perform. It is not up to you to prove there is no work you can do. Once you have shown that you are unable to do your usual work, the shoe is on Social Security's foot.

5. Blindness

If your vision is no better than 20/200 with correction, or if your field of vision is limited to 20 degrees or less, you are considered blind under Social Security disability rules. Assuming that you have worked long enough to have earned the required work credits for your age, you and your family can receive disability benefits. This is true even though you may actually be working, because if you are blind you can earn up to $1,110 per month—the amount increases from year to year—before your job is considered substantial gainful work which would disqualify you from benefits.

If you are between ages 55 and 65 and blind, it is easier to qualify for disability benefits. If you are unable to perform work requiring skills or abilities comparable to those required by the work you did before you turned 55, or before you became blind, whichever is later, you can qualify for benefits. This level of performance is measured by whether you work at the kind of job you previously had and you earn more than $1,110 every month. If you earn that much occasionally but not every month, you can still qualify for benefits. Checks will be withheld, however, for any month in which you do perform substantial gainful work—that is, earn over $1,110.

Applying Protects Your Retirement Benefits

If you are legally blind but are earning too much money to qualify for disability benefits, you may want to apply for them anyway if your earnings are significantly lower than they were before you became blind. If your earnings are over the limit but are much lower than before your blindness, Social Security can put what is called a disability freeze on your earnings record.

The amount of your retirement benefits, or of your disability benefits if you later qualify, is determined by your average income over the years. (See Chapter 1, Section E.) If, because of your disability, you are now making considerably less than you were before, these lower earnings will pull your average income lower, resulting in a lower ultimate Social Security payment. The disability freeze permits you to work and collect your lower income without having it figured into your lifetime average earnings.

6. Examples of Disability Determinations

The following examples help illustrate Social Security's reasoning in applying its guidelines and making disability determinations.

a. Unsuitability for other work

Example: Arnold has been a longshoreman for most of his life. At age 58, his back has been getting progressively worse. His doctor has told him that his back won't get better, and that continuing to do longshore work won't be possible much longer. The doctor also says that sitting for any length of time will aggravate the condition. Arnold applies for disability.

Since there is no question that Arnold's condition will last more than a year, Social Security will next ask whether it prevents Arnold from performing substantial gainful employment. Arnold's back prevents him not only from doing his regular job or other physical labor but also from sitting for long periods of time. Unless Social Security can describe a job which requires neither physical labor nor sitting, Arnold would probably get disability payments. And because Arnold has done physical labor all his life, he may not have the training, work experience or education to do many other jobs. Considering his age and the difficulty finding any type of work for which he could be retrained, it is likely that Social Security would find him eligible for disability benefits.

b. Two conditions combined

Example: Ernestine has been a music teacher for many years. She is now 60 years old and is losing her hearing. She has also developed phlebitis, which makes it difficult for her to walk very far or to stand for long periods of time; she has to elevate her legs for a while every few hours. When her hearing loss makes it impossible for her to continue teaching music, she applies for disability benefits.

The combination of her two conditions may make her unable to perform any gainful employment. She would have to find a job which required neither good hearing nor standing, and permitted her to put her legs up for a half hour several times a day. Since such jobs are scarce, Social Security would very likely find Ernestine eligible for disability, particularly in light of her age.

c. Mild disability

Example: Rebecca is 52 and has a mild heart condition. Despite medication, she has intermittent fatigue and shortness of breath, especially at her job as a waitress. Her doctor says that her work is too physically demanding and stressful for her heart. Rebecca applies for disability benefits.

While Rebecca's condition—disease of the heart leading to breathlessness and fatigue despite medication—is on Social Security's listing of impairments, she is not automatically eligible for disability benefits. Her condition is mild enough that she could probably find new and different work. If Rebecca had training or experience doing any other kind of work, she would almost certainly be required to look for a job elsewhere. Even if she had no other developed job skills, because of her relatively young age, she probably would be required to train for some other type of work.

C. Amount of Disability Benefit Payments

Disability benefits are available both for individual disabled workers and for the families—spouse and minor or disabled children—of disabled workers. The maximum amount for worker and family combined is either 85% of what the disabled worker was earning before becoming disabled, or 150% of what the individual disabled worker's benefit would be, whichever is lower. But this is the maximum, and like other Social Security benefits, the amount of your actual disability check is determined by your age and your personal earnings record—your average earnings for all the years you have been working, not just the salary you were making most recently.

Example: Manu was making $3,200 a month when he was disabled at age 56. When he became disabled, Manu's Social Security earnings record would have given him an individual disability benefit of $900 a month. But Manu's wife and teenage daughter are also eligible to collect dependents benefits. Their total family benefits would be the lower of 85% of Manu's $3,200 monthly salary, which comes out to $2,720, or 150% of what Manu's individual disability benefit ($900) would be, which comes out to $1,350. The family would receive $1,350 a month, the lower of the two amounts.

1. Estimating Benefit Amounts

There is no simple formula for what your actual disability payments will be. Although some books and magazines print tidy charts matching age and income with disability benefit amounts, more often than not these charts mislead people, frequently causing them to overestimate their benefits. The charts all base their figures on your current earnings, and assume that you have had a consistent earnings pattern during your entire working life. Since most people do not have such a perfect curve of earnings, however, the estimates the charts give you based on one year's current earnings are bound to be wrong.

You can get a general idea of disability benefits amounts by considering average payment amounts from 2000.

Estimated Disability Benefits for 2000

Average Annual Lifetime Income in Current Dollars	Monthly Benefits
$10,000 to $20,000	$500 to $750 (individual) $850 to $1,050 (couple or parent and child)
$20,000 to $30,000	$700 to $1,000 (individual) $1,100 to $1,500 (couple or parent and child)
$30,000 and up	$1,000 to $1,340 (individual) $1,500 to $2,000 (couple or parent and child)

Check Eligibility for Supplemental Benefits

If you receive only a small disability benefit, and you have savings or other cash assets of less than $5,000, you may be eligible for Supplemental Security Income benefits (SSI) in addition to your Social Security disability benefits. (See Chapter 6.)

Stopping with general estimates of disability benefits makes little sense, because you can get a very accurate estimate, based on your exact earnings record, directly from Social Security. You can get this estimate when you apply for benefits at a local Social Security office. Or if you are not currently disabled under Social Security rules but believe that your condition will render you disabled in the future and you want to know how much your disability benefits would be, you can request a Personal Earnings and Benefits Estimate Statement. In a matter of weeks, the agency will send you its estimate of how much your disability benefits would be if you applied now. (See Chapter 1, Sections F and G.)

2. Cost of Living Increases

Monthly disability benefit amounts are based entirely on your personal earnings record, with no consideration given to a minimum amount needed to survive. Whatever your monthly amount, however, there is a yearly cost of living increase based on the rise in the consumer price index; in recent years, the increase has been only 1% to 3%.

Applying for Disability Benefits

Applying for disability benefits and proving your disability can be a slow, sometimes difficult business. You need to organize your paperwork, have the cooperation of your doctors, be patient and persistent. What to expect in the application process and how best to prepare for it is discussed in Chapter 7.

D. Collecting Additional Benefits

Since disability payments are often not enough to live on, it is important for you to collect all the other benefits to which you may be entitled, and even try to supplement your income by working to the extent you can.

1. Disability and Earned Income

Your benefit check will not be reduced if you earn income while collecting Social Security disability benefits. However, if you regularly earn enough income for your work to qualify as gainful employment, you might not be considered disabled any longer and you could become ineligible for any Social Security disability payment.

It is possible, though, to earn a little money and still remain eligible for disability benefits. Social Security usually permits you to earn up to about $700 a month—$1,170 if you are blind—before you will be considered to be performing substantial gainful work. However, in deciding how much you are earning, Social Security is supposed to deduct from your income the amounts of any disability-related work expenses, including medical devices or equipment such as a wheelchair, attendant care, drugs, or services required for you to be able to work. If Social Security contacts you for a review of your disability status because of too high a monthly income, you must show proof of such expenses, or your disability benefits might be ended on the reasoning that you regularly earn over $700.

The $700 per month amount is not a fixed rule. You cannot simply keep your income below this level and expect automatically to continue your disability benefits. Both your physical condition and the amount of your work will be reviewed periodically. (See Section E.) This review will take into account the amount and regularity of your income, your work duties, the number of hours you work, and, if you are self-employed, the extent to which you run or manage your own business.

If you are working long hours or have significant work responsibility, particularly if you are in business for yourself, Social Security will look hard, during its review of your disability status, at whether the $700 income limit is a true measure of your work. If, for example, family members are suddenly earning quite a bit more than they used to from the business, Social Security may suspect that you are doing the work and simply paying them instead. Or, if you are not getting paid much but you are working long hours for a business in which you have an ownership interest, they may look more closely at whether you are still disabled.

2. Other Social Security Benefits

You are not permitted to collect more than one Social Security benefit—retirement, dependents, survivors, disability—at a time. If you are eligible for more than one monthly benefit, based either on your own work record or on that of a spouse or parent, you will receive the higher of the two benefit amounts to which you are entitled, but not both. Supplemental Security Income (SSI) is an exception; you may collect SSI in addition to any other Social Security benefit. (See Chapter 6.)

3. Other Disability Benefits

You are permitted to collect Social Security disability benefits and, at the same time, private disability payments from an insurance policy or coverage from your employer. You may also receive Veterans Administration (VA) disability coverage at the same time as Social Security disability benefits. (See Chapter 10.)

4. Workers' Compensation

You may collect workers' compensation benefits—payments for injuries suffered during the course of employment—at the same time as Social Security disability benefits. Workers' compensation benefits are paid only until you recover, or until your injuries are determined to be permanent, at which time you receive a lump sum compensation payment.

While you are receiving monthly workers' compensation, the total of your disability and workers' compensation payments cannot be greater than 80% of what your average wages were before you became disabled. If they are, your disability benefits will be reduced so that the total of both benefits is 80% of your earnings before you became disabled. If you are still receiving Social Security disability benefits when your workers' compensation coverage runs out, you can again start receiving the full amount of your Social Security benefits.

Example: Maxine became disabled with a back condition while working as a gardener and earning $1,400 a month. Her Social Security disability benefits were $560 a month; because her disability was related to her job, she also received workers' compensation benefits of $625 a month. The total of the two benefits was more than 80% of her prior salary (the combined benefits of $560 and $625 total $1,185, and 80% of $1,400 is $1,120, and she would be getting $1,185), so her disability benefits were reduced by the extra $65 down to $495 a month.

If Maxine were still disabled when her workers' compensation benefits end, her Social Security disability benefits would go back up to $560 a month, plus whatever cost-of-living increases had been granted in the meantime.

5. Medicare

After you have been collecting disability benefits for 24 months—and those months need not be consecutive—you become eligible for Medicare coverage even if you are not age 65, which is otherwise the standard age to qualify for Medicare. Medicare hospitalization coverage is free. However, you must pay a monthly premium if you want to be covered by Medicare medical insurance. (See Chapter 12.)

6. Medicaid and SSI

If you have few or no assets—or your disability and the resulting medical costs deplete your assets and hamper your ability to earn income—you may qualify for Medicaid coverage. Medicaid is a program of government medical coverage available to people based on their low income and assets, excluding their home. You may be eligible for Medicaid coverage as soon as you qualify under its rules, without the 24-month wait Medicare requires. And even when you do qualify for Medicare, Medicaid can continue to pay medical bills that Medicare won't. (See Chapter 16.)

If you qualify for Medicaid assistance, you may also qualify for cash payments from the SSI program, in addition to your Social Security disability benefits. Like Medicaid, SSI is intended to assist people with low income and assets. (See Chapter 6.)

Protecting Your Medicaid Eligibility

You must have very few assets to be eligible for Medicaid to cover your medical expenses. (See Chapter 16.) The same is true for government-assisted housing and other government benefit programs.

But if your disability was caused by an accident that was someone else's fault, you may have a chunk of money coming to you as the result of an insurance claim or a lawsuit. Receiving that money, however, might disqualify you from Medicaid and eligibility for other benefits, which would mean you'd have to spend it all on future medical bills, with nothing left for other living expenses.

Federal law and the laws of many states address this problem by allowing you to set up a "Special Needs Trust" which permits you to accept accident compensation without losing your Medicaid and other benefit eligibility. With such a trust, instead of the accident compensation going to you in a lump sum, it is held for you by a bank or similar institution and is used to pay only certain types of bills—usually medical and basic living expenses. If your situation requires a Special Needs Trust, consult an experienced estate planning lawyer for help.

E. Review of Your Eligibility

Eligibility for disability benefits is not necessarily permanent. Depending on the nature and severity of your condition and on whether doctors expect it to improve, Social Security will periodically review your condition to determine whether you still qualify for benefits.

1. When Your Eligibility Will Be Reviewed

If, when you apply for disability benefits, your doctors and Social Security's medical experts expect that your condition will improve, your eligibility will be reviewed six to 18 months after you applied for benefits. If improvement in your condition is theoretically possible but not predicted by the doctors, Social Security will review your eligibility approximately every three years. If your condition is not expected to improve, Social Security will review your case every five to seven years.

If at any point after you are receiving disability benefits you earn a steady or frequent monthly income of close to $700 a month, Social Security may also call you in for a review. The agency will determine whether you are actually able to perform substantial gainful employment for more than $700 per month. It will do this by comparing the work you are doing with other work, in your geographic area, which you could do and which is available. Social Security will also check to see whether you are arranging to be paid less than $700 per month by having someone close to you receive money for your work, or whether you are being paid in some way other than cash wages or salary.

2. The Review Process

The first step in a review of your eligibility for disability benefits is a letter from Social Security summoning you to a local office for an interview about your medical condition and about any work you are doing. You should bring with you to this interview the names and addresses of the doctors, hospitals and other medical providers you have seen since your original eligibility was established, or since your last review. You should also bring with you information about any income you are currently earning—including where you work, how much you earn and the person to contact at your place of employment.

The local Social Security office service worker will ask you about your condition and work, and will then refer your file to the Disability Determination Services (DDS), the special agency that reviews all disability claims. (See Chapter 7, Section B3.) The DDS will obtain your current medical and employment records and may again ask that you undergo a medical consultation or examination. (See Chapter 7, Section B3b.) The DDS will make a determination about your continued eligibility based on the medical records and reports and on your earned income. Unless your condition has substantially improved, or you have regularly been earning more than $700 per month, or you are found to be doing substantial gainful employment despite being paid less than $700 a month, your benefits will continue. If your eligibility is terminated, you have a right to appeal that decision. (See Chapter 8.) And if you lose your eligibility, benefits can continue for an adjustment period of up to three months while you look for work and wait for a paycheck. (See Section F.)

F. Returning to Work

Most disabled people would rather work than not, and many attempt to find ways of working despite their disabling conditions. Social Security encourages people to try to work despite their disabilities, particularly if their conditions have improved somewhat. And if you have been earning more than $700 per month for several months, Social Security might require that you at least try to return to work, although there is a system in place that allows you easily to start your disability payments again if the return to work does not turn out well. The incentive to return to work takes tangible form in a trial work period, during which you can continue collecting your disability benefits.

1. Trial Work Period

Within any five-year period, you may try out some kind of work—and keep any income you earn—for up to nine months while still getting full disability benefits. Your medical condition must still qualify you as disabled during this trial period. You may try one job for a month or two and, if it doesn't work out, you may attempt another sometime later—up to a total of nine months within any five-year period. The Social Security office can also help you find employment during this trial work period.

Any months in which you earn less than $200, or spend less than 40 hours in self-employment, don't count as trial months for purposes of the nine-month limit. The nine trial work months do not have to be consecutive—you can try working for a month or two, then wait a while, and try again later, as long as it is all within one five-year period. And in any of the trial work months, you may earn as much as you can without losing any of your disability benefits.

After your nine-month trial work period, Social Security reevaluates your ability to do substantial gainful work. If you have not averaged more than $700 per month—$1,170 if you are blind—in earnings during your trial work period, your benefits will continue. In figuring your monthly earnings, Social Security subtracts any work or commuting expenses you had that were directly related to your disability. If you have averaged more than $700 per month and so are considered able to perform substantial gainful employment, your benefits will continue for a three-month grace period, then end.

During the 36 months following a trial work period that has ended with your return to work, you will receive your monthly disability benefit for any month in which you do not earn at least $700. You need only report your earnings for that month to your Social Security disability worker. You do not have to file a new application for benefits or go through the eligibility process again. Also, if you have been receiving Medicare coverage because of your disability, that coverage will continue for 39 months following the end of your trial work period. And after that 39-month period, you may sign up for Medicare and pay for it through a monthly premium.

2. Reinstating Disability Benefits

Some people return to work after having received disability benefits, then later become unable to work again. If you go off disability payments because you have returned to work, but you again become unable to work within 15 months of completing a nine-month trial work period, you can again get disability payments without filing a new claim or going through another application waiting period. (See Chapter 7.) And you can receive benefits for any month during that 15-month period in which you have been unable to do substantial gainful work.

3. A Second Period of Disability

If you once received disability benefits and you again become disabled and unable to work within five years after your benefits stopped, you may receive disability payments again without going through another application waiting period. (See Chapter 7.) This is true whether your payments were originally stopped because your medical condition improved or because you returned to work. Your new period of benefits starts with the first full month of your new disability. This provision also applies if you had received benefits as a disabled widow or widower and have become disabled again within seven years after your benefits ended.

If you had been entitled to Medicare during your earlier disability period and you again become eligible for disability benefits, Medicare coverage will automatically resume when your new benefits start. If you did not qualify for Medicare during the earlier period, the months you were previously on disability will be added to your new disability period until you reach a total of 24 months on disability—qualifying for Medicare coverage.

Example: Charlie received disability payments for 18 months when he was unable to work three years ago due to a heart attack. He returned to work for several months, but then had to leave work once again when his heart condition worsened. He reapplied for disability benefits and they were immediately reinstated. After six months of his new disability period, he had accumulated a total of 24 months of disability eligibility within a five-year period, becoming eligible for Medicare coverage.

■

Social Security Dependents Benefits

A retired or disabled worker with a family cannot live on the same benefit amounts as a retired or disabled person living alone—amounts that currently average about $800 per month. This is particularly true when the retired or disabled worker was the family's primary breadwinner. Social Security woke up to this reality in 1939, four years after it passed the original Social Security retirement law, and provided dependents benefits, paid to the spouse and to minor children of a retired or disabled worker.

A. Who Is Eligible

Family members of a retired or disabled worker are eligible for monthly dependents benefits if the worker has enough work credits to qualify for, and is claiming, his or her own retirement or disability benefits. The amount of benefits paid to dependents is determined by the worker's earnings record. Being a dependent for Social Security purposes does not necessarily mean that a person actually depends on the worker for support.

1. Individuals Who Qualify

To be entitled to benefits, you need to fit one of the following categories:

- a spouse age 62 or older
- a divorced spouse age 62 or older, with certain conditions (see Section A2)
- a spouse under age 62 who is caring for the worker's child under age 16 or disabled before age 22
- unmarried children under age 18. Although benefits to the parents end when the child turns 16, the child continues to receive benefits until age 18
- unmarried children up to age 19 and still in high school
- unmarried children of any age if they were severely disabled before they reached age 22, for as long as they remain disabled. For this purpose, disability is defined by Social Security in the same way as for Supplementary Security Income benefits (see Chapter 6)
- unmarried stepchildren up to age 18 (19 if still in high school) if living with and under the care of the retired or disabled worker, and
- grandchildren of the worker if they live with and are under the actual care of the worker if the parents are deceased or disabled, or the grandparent has adopted them.

2. Effect of Marriage and Divorce

Couples come in many forms other than the traditional married: companions who are not married; couples who are divorced; people who were divorced but have married again. Each status has some ramifications regarding dependents benefits.

a. Divorced spouses

You are eligible for dependents benefits if both you and your former spouse have reached age 62, your marriage lasted ten years and you have been divorced two years. This two-year waiting period does not apply if your former spouse was already collecting retirement benefits before the divorce.

You can collect benefits as soon as your former spouse is eligible for retirement benefits at age 62. He or she does not actually have to be collecting those benefits for you to collect your dependents benefits.

If You Are Divorcing, Try to Stretch It to Ten Years

If you are in the process of getting a divorce and you have been married almost ten years, try to have your spouse agree—or stall the legal paperwork long enough—that the divorce will not become final until after ten years.

Under Social Security rules, the marriage is considered in effect until the divorce legally becomes final, even if you and your spouse have already been living apart, have separated your property and one of you has begun paying spousal or child support. If you anticipate that your spouse might object to the delay, you might remind him or her that your dependents benefits have no effect on the amount he or she may collect in retirement benefits. Nor would your benefits effect the amount of dependents benefits a new spouse could collect in addition to yours.

b. Remarried

If you are collecting dependents benefits on your former spouse's work record and then marry someone else, you lose your right to those benefits. However, you may then be eligible to collect dependents benefits based on your new spouse's work record.

If you divorce again, you can collect benefits again on your first former spouse's record, or on your second spouse's record if you were married for ten years the second time as well.

It does not affect your eligibility if your former spouse remarries. Nor does the fact that you collect dependents benefits on your former spouse's record affect his or her new spouse's right to collect benefits. And there is no reduction in either of your benefits because two spouses are collecting them.

c. Unmarried

For the most part, Social Security laws do not recognize the relationship between two adults who are not officially married. There are two exceptions.

First, if one person in a unmarried couple adopts the minor child of the other person, that child becomes eligible for dependents benefits based on the adoptive parent's work record. The other person in the couple does not, however, become eligible for Social Security benefits.

Second, if you live in a state that recognizes common law marriage and you qualify under that state's rules for such marriages, you may also qualify for dependents benefits. The states that recognize common law marriages are: Alabama, Colorado, District of Columbia, Georgia, Idaho, Iowa, Kansas, Montana, Ohio, Oklahoma, Pennsylvania, Rhode Island, South Carolina, Texas and Utah.

The qualifying rules for a common law marriage vary somewhat from state to state, but all require that you have lived together and have represented yourselves as married by such things as using the same name and owning property together. Common law marriage does not apply, however, to same sex couples or to anyone who is still legally married to someone else.

B. Calculating Dependents Benefits

The amount of benefits available to a retired or disabled worker and dependents are calculated based on the total number of people in the immediate family. Social Security figures that the economies of scale permit two to live more cheaply than one, three to live more cheaply than two, and so on. Therefore, the amount by which benefits increase with each additional dependent is smaller and smaller for each person added.

1. One Dependent

The amount of your dependents benefits is based on the earnings record of the worker of whom you are a dependent. If there is only one person claiming dependent benefits, he or she receives 50% of the worker's retirement or disability benefits. If a divorced spouse and the new spouse of a retirement age worker both receive dependent benefits, each will receive 50%.

A worker who wants to find out what retirement benefits or disability would be can request an Earnings Record and Benefits Estimate Statement. (See Chapter 1, Sections F and G.)

Claiming Before or After Full Retirement Age

Like other retirement benefits, a dependent spouse's benefits are permanently lower if the dependent claims them between age 62 and full retirement age, but permanently increased if not claimed until after full retirement age. (See Chapter 2, Section C.)

At age 65, a dependent spouse is also eligible for Medicare coverage based on the spouse's work record if the spouse is at least age 62. (See Chapter 9.)

2. Family Benefits

If there is more than one dependent—a spouse and one or more children, or no spouse but two or more children—the benefits paid to the worker and the dependents are combined into what is called a family benefit amount. This family benefit is less than the total would be if the worker's benefits and individual dependent benefits were paid separately.

The maximum family benefit is 150% to 180% of the retired worker's benefits—the precise amount depends on a complicated Social

Security formula—or 150% of a disabled worker's benefits. The retired or disabled worker collects 100% of his or her benefits, and the remaining 50% to 80% is divided equally among the dependents. The actual dollar amount depends on the amount to which the worker is entitled. (See Chapter 2, Sections C and D.)

Example: Chiang-Fa is retired. Alone, he would be entitled to $900 per month in retirement benefits. He and his wife Yoka have a 17-year-old daughter. If it were just Chiang-Fa and Yoka, Yoka would be entitled to $450 per month dependents benefit—50% of Chiang-Fa's $900 retirement benefit.

However, because his daughter is also eligible, the three of them together are limited to a maximum family benefit of 180% of Chiang-Fa's benefit, or $1,620. That amount would be divided as follows: Chiang-Fa, $900; Yoka and the daughter, each $360. Once the daughter reaches age 18, however, she is no longer eligible for dependents benefits and Yoka would begin to get a full 50% dependents benefit of $450 per month.

C. Eligibility for More Than One Benefit

Many people are eligible for Social Security retirement or disability benefits based on their own work and earnings records, and also for dependents benefits based on their spouses' work records. As with other Social Security benefits, you are not permitted to collect both your own retirement or disability benefits and dependents benefits.

But if your own earnings record is low and your spouse's earnings record high, you may be entitled to higher benefits as a dependent than you would be collecting retirement or disability benefits on your own work record. You can choose either to wait to claim dependents benefits when your spouse claims retirement or disability, or you can claim your own retirement benefits and then switch to higher dependents benefits when your spouse later claims retirement or becomes eligible for disability benefits.

Possible Perils of Claiming Early: Reduced Benefits

If you claim retirement benefits at less than full retirement age, your retirement benefits are reduced by up to 20%. (See Chapter 2, Section C.) And if you later switch to dependents benefits, those benefits, too, will be reduced by the same amount as your retirement benefits were reduced.

Example: Clare became eligible for retirement benefits of $500 per month at age 65. She decided to claim early retirement benefits at age 62—her full retirement amount of $500 less 20%, for a monthly sum of $400. When her husband turned 65, he applied for retirement benefits and received $1,200 per month. Clare switched from her own retirement claim to dependents benefits, which ordinarily would have been $600, or 50% of her husband's monthly amount. But because Clare had already taken 20% reduced retirement benefits at age 62, her dependents benefits were now reduced by 20% to $480 per month, instead of the $600 per month she would have received had she waited.

D. Working While Receiving Benefits

A dependent's benefit will be reduced by $1 for every $2 of income earned over the yearly maximum, if the dependent is age 62 to 64. For a dependent who is age 65 to 69, the benefit is reduced by $1 for every $3 over the yearly limit. Once a dependent reaches age 70, there is no reduction in benefits, regardless of how much is earned. (See Chapter 2, Section D.)

If several dependents are receiving a combined family benefit amount, one dependent's earnings do not affect the amount the other family members receive.

Example: Grace and Omar and their teenage son receive a combined family retirement and dependents benefit of $1,650 a month. Grace and the son's portions of the family benefit are $350 each. Grace is offered a job for a year as a substitute teacher at a salary that is $6,000 over the yearly earnings limit for her age of 63 years old.

Since Grace's benefit amount is reduced $1 for every $2 she earns over the limit, her benefit would be reduced by half ($1 out of $2) of $6,000. Her benefits would be reduced by $3,000, or $250 per month. Since her own part of the family benefit is $350, that benefit would be reduced to $100 per month. The rest of the family's benefits—Omar's $950 per month and the son's $350—would not be affected.

E. Public Employee Pension Offset

Millions of people have worked for a branch of government or other public agency—federal, state or local government or civil service employment—and have earned a retirement pension based on that work. (See Chapter 9.) However, if you receive Social Security dependents benefits and also a public employment retirement pension based on your own work record, your dependents benefits will be reduced dollar for dollar by two-thirds the amount of your pension.

There is no offset, however, if you receive a dependents benefit from your spouse's public employment pension. If your spouse is collecting a public pension as well as Social Security, you can collect dependents benefits from both programs without affecting your Social Security benefits.

Not only should you be aware of these rules when figuring out how much your combined government pension and dependents benefits are, but it may affect which pension benefit you choose to collect.

Example: Gina is entitled to $500 per month in Social Security dependents benefits. She is also entitled to both a public employee retirement pension of $400 per month and a $250 per month benefit as a dependent on her husband's public employee retirement pension.

Ordinarily, she would choose to claim her own public retirement pension. But her Social Security dependents benefits would be reduced by two-thirds of her government pension ($400); if she claims government pension dependents benefits, her Social Security amounts are not reduced at all. She is better off to collect both her smaller public pension dependents benefits ($250) and her full Social Security dependents benefits ($500) for a total of $750 per month, than her larger public pension retirement benefit ($400) and her reduced Social Security amount ($500 minus $333 offset = $167) for a total of only $567 a month.

Private Employer Pensions Not Affected

The pension offset rule does not apply to pensions paid by private employers. As far as Social Security is concerned, you are entitled to your full Social Security dependents benefits as well as your private pension benefits. However, the rules of a few private pension plans provide that your pension benefits are reduced by what you receive from Social Security. (See Chapter 11.)

Exceptions for Those Who Qualified Earlier

The public pension offset rule does not apply if you were eligible for Social Security dependents or survivors benefits before December 1, 1977.

Nor does the rule apply if you began receiving or were eligible to receive a public employment pension before December 1, 1982, and you meet the requirements for dependents benefits in effect in January 1977.

One major rule difference in January 1977 was that a divorced spouse had to have been married 20 years rather than ten years to collect dependents benefits.

The other rule difference reflected a lingering anachronism. For a man to claim dependents benefits back then, he had to prove actual dependence on his wife for at least one-half of his support. There was no such rule for women, however. So, virtually all women who were eligible to receive a public pension before December 1982 could collect both Social Security dependents benefits and their own public pension, while most men could not.

■

Social Security Survivors Benefits

The Social Security laws recognize that a worker's family will need financial support after the worker dies. Even if the surviving spouse has always worked, the loss of the deceased spouse's income will almost surely be an economic blow to the family. And if the surviving spouse did not work, or earned much less than the deceased spouse, the loss of the deceased worker's income can be financially devastating. Recognizing the family financial burden brought on by the loss of the primary earner, Social Security provides for what are called survivors benefits to be paid to the spouse and children of an eligible worker who has died.

A. Who Is Eligible

A number of surviving family members may be eligible to collect survivors benefits—provided the deceased worker had enough work credits. (See Section B.)

To be eligible for benefits, you must fit into one of the following categories:

- a surviving spouse age 60 or over
- a divorced surviving spouse age 60 or over, if the marriage lasted at least ten years
- a surviving spouse under age 60 if he or she is caring for the worker's child who is under age 16 or disabled; this benefit, sometimes called the mother's benefit or father's benefit, may also be paid to a surviving divorced spouse
- a surviving spouse age 50 or over who becomes disabled within seven years of the worker's death or within seven years after mother's benefits or father's benefits end; if you were divorced, you can collect these disabled survivors benefits only if your marriage lasted at least ten years.
- unmarried children under 18; benefits may continue to age 19, as long as the child is a full-time high school student
- unmarried children of any age who were severely disabled before age 22 and are still disabled, and
- one or both parents of the worker who are at least age 62 and who were dependent on the worker for at least one-half of their financial support; if an unmarried dependent parent remarries after the worker's death, the parent loses the survivors benefits.

1. Length of Marriage Rule

To collect benefits as a surviving spouse, you must have been married to the deceased worker for at least the nine months before the worker's death. However, there are some exceptions to this rule. If you are the biological parent of a child with the worker, or you adopted the worker's child or adopted a child with the worker before the child was 18, the nine-month rule does not apply.

The rule is also waived if you were previously married to the same person and your first marriage lasted more than nine months. And the nine-month rule does not apply if the worker's death was the result of an accident, as opposed to illness, or occurred while he or she was on active military duty.

2. Effect of Remarrying

One of the assumptions behind survivors benefits for spouses is that almost all surviving spouses are women—14% of all Social Security recipients, compared with fewer than 1% men—and that women are financially dependent on their husbands. While things are slowly changing, the fact that there are still fewer women than men in the workforce and women still make only 70 cents to every dollar men earn in wages in comparable jobs proves the assumption true.

Another reality is that if a surviving spouse—usually a woman—remarries, her need for survivors benefits will end because there is a new spouse upon whom to depend financially. So a series of qualifying Social Security rules apply to collecting survivors benefits after remarriage.

- A widow or widower who remarries before age 60 loses the right to collect survivors benefits on the deceased spouse's earnings record, even if he or she still cares for the former spouse's children. The children, however, remain eligible for benefits. At age 62, the remarried spouse may be eligible for dependents benefits based on the new spouse's record.
- A widow or widower who remarries after reaching age 60 does not lose survivors benefits based on the deceased former spouse's work record. He or she may want to transfer—at age 62 or later—to dependents benefits based on the new spouse's earnings record if that benefit would be higher than the survivors benefits.
- If you were divorced from your now deceased former spouse, and you had been married to that spouse for at least ten years, you are eligible for survivors benefits even if you remarried before age 60 but are again widowed or divorced. After age 60, you may remarry without losing your survivors benefits.

Example: Akiko and Yosh were divorced ten years ago after being married 25 years. Three years ago, Yosh died. Akiko and Ben have been together for the past year and are now considering marriage. But Akiko is concerned about the affect their marriage would have on her right to collect Social Security survivors benefits. Akiko is 59 and next year she would be eligible for survivors benefits based on Yosh's work record because their marriage had lasted more than the required ten years.

If she waits one more year, she and Ben can marry and she will still be able to collect survivors benefits based on Yosh's record. If she marries before reaching age 60, she will lose those benefits for good.

B. Requirements for Deceased's Work Record

Surviving family members of a deceased worker are entitled to survivors benefits only if the worker had earned enough work credits before dying. Work credits are accumulated based on earnings from employment covered by Social Security, and the required number of work credits depends on the worker's age at death. (See Chapter 1, Sections C and D.)

1. Work Credits Required

The number of work credits on the worker's Social Security record needed for survivors to collect benefits are listed below.

Credits Required From Deceased's Work Record

If the worker was born after 1929 and died or became disabled at age:	If the worker was born before 1930 and died or became disabled before age 62 in:	Work credits needed:
28 or younger		6
30		8
32		10
34		12
36		
38		16
40		
42		20
44		
46	1975	24
48	1977	
50	1979	28
52	1981	
54	1983	32
56	1985	
58	1987	36
60	1989	
62	1991	40

2. Credits Earned Just Before Death

Even if the deceased worker did not have enough work credits according to the chart above, benefits may still be paid to the surviving spouse and children if the worker had at least one and one-half years of work in covered employment in the three years immediately before dying.

C. Amount of Survivors Benefits

Like all other Social Security benefits, the amounts of survivors benefits are determined by the earnings record of the deceased worker. Social Security determines what the full retirement benefit would have been for the worker had he or she not died, then awards a percentage of that amount to the survivors.

1. Percentage of Benefits Awarded

The percentage of the deceased worker's retirement benefit awarded to a survivor depends on whether you are the spouse or child of the deceased worker. And for a surviving spouse, the amount goes up or down depending on the age between 60 and 65 at which benefits are first claimed.

a. Surviving spouse at 65

A surviving spouse who waits until age 65 to claim benefits will receive 100% of what the deceased worker's full retirement benefit would have been.

b. Surviving spouse at 60

A surviving spouse at age 60 will receive 71.5% of what the worker's full retirement benefits would have been. Each year a surviving spouse delays claiming benefits after age 60, those benefits will rise 5.7% until full benefits are reached if the claim is first made at age 65.

c. Mother's or father's benefits

The full mother's or father's benefit for the surviving spouse who has reached age 65 and is caring for the worker's child under age 16 or disabled is 75% of what the worker's full retirement benefits would have been.

d. Minor or disabled child

A surviving minor or disabled child receives 75% of what the worker's retirement benefits would have been.

e. Dependent parent

A surviving parent who was dependent on the deceased worker for at least half of his or her financial support may be eligible for 75% of what the worker's retirement benefit would have been. For both surviving dependent parents, the total is 82.5%.

f. Surviving spouse and children together

A surviving spouse and children together are not entitled to the full amount each would get alone. A maximum amount is placed on the total one family can receive. The family benefit limit is 150% to 180% of what the deceased worker's retirement benefits would have been. The benefits are divided equally among the surviving spouse and children.

2. Estimating Benefit Amounts

You can get a general idea of survivors benefit amounts by looking at these recent average figures.

a. Low income

The survivor of a worker who had relatively low income most of his or her working life—$10,000 to $20,000 per year in current dollars—will receive monthly benefits of $500 to $800. If there is both a surviving spouse and a minor child receiving benefits, the total for the two would be between about $800 to $1,200.

b. Moderate income

The survivor of a person who had a moderate annual income—$20,000 to $30,000 in current terms—will receive $700 to $1,100 per month. A surviving spouse and child would receive a total of about $1,100 to $1,600.

c. High income

The survivor of a worker who usually had relatively high earnings—$40,000 per year or more in current dollars—can expect between $1,000 to $1,350 per month. The high earner's surviving spouse and child together would receive between $1,300 and $2,000.

d. Getting an estimate

You can get a very accurate personal estimate of your survivors benefits based on a worker's exact earnings record directly from Social Security. As soon as you apply for benefits, you will be given that figure. And if you want an estimate before you are actually eligible, you can request a Personal Earnings and Benefits Estimate Statement from Social Security and receive the figures within weeks. (See Chapter 1, Sections F and G.)

D. Eligibility for More Than One Benefit

Many surviving spouses are eligible for Social Security retirement or disability benefits based on their own work and earnings records, and also for benefits based on their spouses' work records. However, you are permitted to collect only one type of benefit. If your own earnings record is low and your deceased spouse's earnings record was high, as is the case with most widows, you may be entitled to higher benefits as a surviving spouse than as a retired or disabled worker collecting on your own work record.

Even if you will ultimately be eligible for a higher retirement benefit after you turn age 62, you can claim survivors benefits as soon as you are eligible at age 60 and then switch to your own retirement benefits whenever they become higher than your survivors benefits. Claiming survivors benefits before age 65 does not reduce your own retirement benefit.

It also works in reverse. You can claim reduced early retirement benefits—between age 62 and 65—on your own work record, and then switch to full survivors benefits at age 65 if those benefits would be higher.

Example: Francesca would be eligible for full retirement benefits of $600 per month at age 65, based on her own work record; at age 62, she is eligible for reduced retirement benefits of $480 per month. At age 65, she would also be eligible for a full survivors benefit of $800 per month based on her deceased husband's work record; at age 62, she is eligible for a reduced survivors benefit of $660 per month.

Francesca has two choices at age 62. She can claim her early retirement amount of $480 per month and then switch to full survivors benefits of $800 per month at age 65. Or she can claim her reduced survivors benefits of $660 per month at age 62 and collect that amount, plus cost-of-living increases, for the rest of her life. She could switch to full retirement benefits at age 65, but in her case they would be only $600 per month, less than her reduced survivors benefits.

Francesca has to decide whether she can get along well enough with the $480 per month retirement benefits she would receive for three years until she switched to her $800 survivors benefits. If she can manage, then waiting would be better in the long run. Waiting makes particularly good sense if she will also be working during those three years, because her benefits might be reduced because of her earnings. (See Section E.)

One-Time Payment for Funeral or Burial Expenses

In addition to the monthly survivors benefits to which family members may be entitled, a family may also receive a one-time-only payment—currently $255—intended to defray funeral or burial expenses. A surviving spouse can claim the money if the couple was not divorced or legally separated at the time of death.

A divorced widow or widower can still collect the $255 if he or she qualifies for the regular survivors benefits. And if there is no qualifying spouse, the sum may be paid to the surviving minor children, divided equally among them. You must file a claim for the death benefit at your local Social Security office within two years of the worker's death.

E. Working While Receiving Benefits

Many surviving spouses find that despite their survivors benefits, they also have to work to make ends meet. How much a surviving spouse earns, however, can affect the amount of benefits he or she receives.

The benefit for a surviving widow or widower age 60 to 64 will be reduced by $1 for every $2 of income earned over the yearly maximum. For a survivor of age 65 to 69, the benefit is reduced by $1 for every $3 over the yearly limit. Once a dependent reaches age 70, there is no reduction in benefits, regardless of how much is earned. (See Chapter 2, Section D.)

If a widow or widower and children are receiving a combined family benefit amount, the parent's earnings do not affect the amount the children receive.

Example: Manjusha and her teenage son receive a combined family survivors benefit of $1,500 a month, or $750 each. Manjusha is taking a job at a salary that is $6,000 over the yearly earnings limit for her age.

Since Manjusha is 62, her benefit amount is reduced $1 for every $2 she earns over the limit. Her benefits would be reduced by half of $6,000 for a total reduction of $3,000, or $250 per month. Since her own part of the family benefit is $750, that benefit would be reduced to $500 per month. Her son's $750 would not be affected.

F. Offset for Public Employment Pension

If you worked enough years for a local, state or federal government agency, you may be entitled to a civil service retirement pension. However, if you are also entitled to a Social Security survivors benefit based on your deceased spouse's work record, you may lose a portion of that survivors benefit.

If you are entitled to Social Security survivors benefits and also a public employment retirement pension based on your own work record, your survivors benefits are reduced dollar for dollar by two-thirds of the amount of your pension. There is no such offset, however, if the public pension you receive is as a surviving spouse rather than as a retiree on your own work record. You can collect survivors benefits from both programs without affecting your Social Security benefits.

This rule will not only affect how much your combined government pension and dependents benefits are, but it may also cause you to choose to collect your own Social Security retirement benefits, if you are eligible for them, rather than Social Security survivors benefits. The combination of your public employment retirement pension and your own Social Security retirement benefits may total a higher amount than your survivors benefits reduced by two-thirds the amount of your pension.

Example: Alice is entitled to $500 per month in Social Security survivors benefits. She is also entitled to both a public employee retirement pension of $400 per month and a $250 per month benefit as a widow based on her deceased husband's public employee retirement record. Ordinarily, she would choose to claim her own public retirement pension rather than the lower public employee widow's benefit.

But her Social Security survivors benefits would be reduced by two-thirds of her government pension ($400); if she claims government pension dependents benefits, her Social Security amounts are not reduced at all. She is better off to collect both her smaller public pension dependents benefits ($250) and her full Social Security dependents benefits ($500) than her larger public pension retirement benefit ($400) and the reduced Social Security amount which would result ($500 minus $267 offset = $233).

The pension offset rule does not apply to pensions paid by private employers. However, the rules of a few private pension plans provide that your pension benefits are reduced by what you receive from Social Security. (See Chapter 11.)

Also, the public pension offset rule does not apply if you were eligible for Social Security survivors benefits before December 1, 1977, or you were eligible to receive a public employment pension before December 1, 1982, and you meet the pre-1977 rules, which required that a divorced spouse had been married 20 years, rather than ten, to collect survivors benefits.

■

Supplemental Security Income

Over five million people receive some Supplemental Security Income, or SSI, benefits. SSI is a program jointly operated by the federal and state governments and administered by the Social Security Administration. SSI is intended to guarantee a minimum level of income to financially hard-pressed older, blind and disabled people. SSI eligibility is based entirely on your age or disability, and on financial need as determined by both your income and your assets. SSI benefits do not depend on how long you have worked, or on how much you have paid into the Social Security system.

You must be quite financially needy to qualify for SSI payments. Indeed, the level of income and assets required to qualify under SSI rules is so low that many people who have no income other than their Social Security retirement benefits are not eligible for SSI. And those who are eligible for SSI to supplement their Social Security benefits will probably receive just a small amount from the SSI program. Nevertheless, if after reviewing the rules explained in this chapter you think you may be close to meeting the requirements for SSI eligibility, it will be worth your while to apply for it. If you qualify for SSI, you may also be eligible for Medicaid (see Chapter 16) and food stamps, as well as free rehabilitation and home care programs, should you need them.

A. Who Is Eligible

You must meet four basic requirements to be eligible for SSI cash benefits.

- You must be either 65 or over, blind or disabled.
- As of February 1, 1997, a new applicant for SSI benefits must be a citizen of the United States, or meet strict requirements for long-time residency, military service or political asylee or refugee status.

  Some permanent legal residents of the United States may also be eligible for SSI benefits if they are blind or disabled.
- Your monthly income must be less than a certain minimum amount established by the state in which you live.
- Your assets must be worth less than $2,000, or $3,000 for a couple, although there are certain items excepted from this amount, including your car and home.

The rules for each of these requirements are more complicated than they first appear. But the complications in these rules almost always make it easier for you to qualify for SSI benefits than you might first imagine. Generally speaking, you are permitted to have more income and assets than the initial figures indicate, so you may well find that, despite these low figures, you are eligible for SSI benefits.

1. Blind or Disabled

If you are under age 65, you can qualify for SSI payments if you are blind or disabled. Basically, you are considered blind if your vision is no better than 20/200, or your field of vision is limited to 20 degrees or less, even with corrective lenses. You are considered disabled if you have a physical or mental impairment which prevents you from doing any substantial work and which is expected to last at least 12 months, or to result in death. This definition of disabled is similar to the test used for Social Security disability benefits. (See Chapter 3, Section A.) But unlike the Social Security disability program, which looks only at the income you currently earn, SSI looks at income from all sources and measures that income in a more complicated way.

2. Citizens or Longtime Residents

SSI benefits are generally available only to U.S. citizens and longtime residents. Noncitizens must fall within one of the narrow categories described below; their eligibility for benefits was recently restricted.

The restrictions hit the country's neediest people the hardest. These are people, often elderly, who have lawfully immigrated to this country to join their children or siblings, only to be met here by joblessness and poverty. And now these family immigrants are denied subsistence-level government benefits.

As a noncitizen of the United States, you only qualify for federal SSI benefits if:

- you are a legal resident of the U.S. and you were already receiving SSI benefits on August 22, 1996, or
- you were a legal resident of the United States on August 22, 1996, and you are now blind or disabled, or
- you are a legal resident of the United States and you or your spouse have worked for at least ten years in this country, having paid at least the minimum Social Security taxes to qualify for 40 quarters of work credits (see Chapter 1, Section D), or
- you are a legal resident of the United States and you or your spouse was honorably discharged from the U.S. military, or
- you have been granted political asylum or refugee status by the Immigration and Naturalization Service; however, your benefits in this situation will last for only seven years after you have been admitted to the country.

State Benefits May Be Available

Healthy noncitizens who were in the United States but not receiving SSI benefits as of August 22, 1996, are generally not eligible for federal SSI benefits. However, if you fall into this category but you have now reached age 65, your state might provide you with SSI benefits, as well as food stamps. You may also be eligible if you arrived in the United States after August 22, 1996, but your immigration sponsor has since died or become disabled. If you are in one of these categories, apply for both federal and state SSI assistance; you may be entitled to state benefits even if you are denied federal SSI.

3. Income Limits

There are actually two SSI payments:

- the basic federal SSI payment, and
- a supplemental SSI payment which some states pay over and above the federal benefit and which other states pay alone if you qualify for it, even if you do not qualify for the federal payment.

Not all income is counted when deciding whether you qualify for SSI. In fact, more than half of your earned income—wages and self-employment income—is not counted towards SSI limits. And even though you may have counted income over the allowable maximum for federal SSI payments, you may still qualify for your state's supplemental payment. A few states set a higher income limit than the federal SSI program does, making it easier to qualify for those states' supplemental payment than for the federal one. (See Section B.)

The federal SSI limit on counted income is about $450 monthly for an individual, about $690 per month for a couple. In many states, however, you would qualify for the state's SSI supplement payment even if your counted income is more than $450 a month. (See Sections B1 and B2.)

a. Income that is counted

In general, any income you earn in wages or self-employment and any money you receive from investments, pensions, annuities, royalties, gifts, rents or interest on savings is counted toward the SSI limits. Social Security benefits are also considered counted income. In addition, if you receive free housing from friends or relatives, the value of that housing—based on what similar housing would cost in your area if you had to pay for it—may be considered as counted income by SSI. In other states, such arrangements are not considered as income but result in you receiving a lower SSI benefit. (See Section C3.)

b. Income that is not counted

Some specific amounts of money and support are not counted in determining whether you have too much income to qualify for SSI benefits.

When determining your counted income, SSI will not count:

- the first $20 per month you receive from any source—except other public assistance based on need, such as General Assistance
- the first $65 per month of your earned income—wages or self-employment
- one-half of all your earned income over $65 a month
- irregular or infrequent earned income—such as from a one-time-only job—if such income is not more than $10 a month
- irregular or infrequent unearned income—such as a gift or dividend on an investment—up to $20 per month
- food stamps, energy assistance or housing assistance from a federal housing program run by a state or local government agency
- some work-related expenses for blind or disabled people which are paid for through public assistance, or
- some other types of one-time payments, such as tax refunds, reimbursement for financial

losses such as insurance payments for medical bills or compensation for injury to you or your property.

c. Differences in local rules

Keeping in mind that different income limits apply in various states, one general suggestion applies to everyone: if you are age 65, blind or disabled, you are living on a small fixed income and you have relatively few assets (discussed in Section A4), apply for SSI benefits. The local Social Security or social welfare office may consider certain income differently than you do and you may be pleasantly surprised to learn that you are eligible for some help from SSI.

Example: Carmela receives Social Security survivors benefits of $310 a month and a $40 per month private pension payment, for a total of $350 in regular unearned income. She also receives a quarterly dividend check; the most recent was $15.

The dividend check would not be counted at all because it is infrequent income less than $20. The first $20 of income from any source is not counted, so the $350 total of unearned income would be reduced to $330 countable income.

Carmela also earns $210 a month doing part-time work. Since the first $65 a month of earned income is not counted, her earned income amount would be reduced to $145; and since one-half of all earned income over $65 a month is not counted, half of $80 ($145 minus $65) would not be considered for SSI purposes.

This leaves Carmela with $105 countable earned income to be added to the $330 countable unearned income for the month, for a total of $435 countable income. Since this amount is under the federal SSI limit of about $460 per month, Carmela would be eligible for the basic federal SSI payment. Because Carmela lives in New York where there is a state supplemental benefit, she may be eligible for that amount as well. (See Section B1.)

4. Asset Limits

In addition to the limits on your income, SSI rules limit the amount of assets and other resources you may have and still qualify. The general limit is $2,000 in assets for an individual, $3,000 for a married couple living together. But as with the rules regarding income, people are actually allowed more assets than these figures initially indicate.

a. Assets that are counted

The assets or resources that are counted by SSI include money in the bank, investments of any kind, real estate, personal property and household goods.

They also include any money or property in which you have an interest, even if you are not the sole owner. If you have a joint bank account with someone, or hold any property in joint tenancy with someone else, SSI will consider that you own the entire account or property because you have access to all of it. If you have only a partial interest in some property—for example, an ownership interest in a family home along with other family members—SSI will determine how much your individual ownership portion is worth, and count that as an asset.

b. Assets that are not counted

You are allowed to have more property of value than the $2,000 and $3,000 limits first indicate. Several important categories of assets are not counted in determining your eligibility for SSI benefits. They include:

- your home and the land it sits on, regardless of value, as long as you live in it
- your automobile, up to a current market value of $4,500; if your car is used in your work, or getting to and from a job or regular medical treatment, or is specially equipped for the transportation of a handicapped person, the value of your car is not counted, no matter how much it is worth
- your personal property and household goods—such as clothing, furniture, appliances, tools, sporting goods and hobby or craft material—up to a total current value of $2,000; the value is not judged by what the articles cost new, but by what you could sell them for now, less the amounts you still owe on them
- wedding and engagement rings, regardless of value
- property needed for medical reasons, such as wheelchairs, hospital beds, prosthetics
- property essential to self support—such as tools and machines used in your trade—up to a value of $6,000.
- life insurance policies with a total face value of $1,500 or less per person, and term life insurance policies with no cash surrender value, and
- burial spaces for you and your spouse, plus a specially earmarked fund of up to $1,500 for funeral and burial expenses.

c. Selling or spending assets

Even if your countable assets appear to be over the limits, it may still be possible for you to qualify to receive some SSI benefits. You may begin to receive SSI payments if you sell or spend enough property to come under the limits within a certain time period. That time period begins when you apply for benefits and runs six months for real estate, three months for personal property and liquid assets.

However, the sale or transfer must be a real one. Simply transferring title on the property to someone else while you keep control or use of it is not enough; neither is selling something for a token sum.

Example: Rose and Peter are living on Peter's Social Security retirement benefits and on Rose's pension. They qualify under SSI income limits, and have the following assets: their home; a five-year-old car; $1,500 in savings; stocks worth $500; kitchen appliances worth about $300; a TV worth about $100; a stereo worth perhaps $150; Peter's carpentry tools, worth about $500; and Rose's jewelry which, aside from her wedding band, is worth about $200.

Despite the fact Rose and Peter's house is now worth $120,000, it is not counted as an asset. Their car is not worth $4,500, so it is not counted at all. Their personal property and household goods add up to about $1,350, but none of it will be counted because this is below the permissible amounts for personal property.

Their total counted assets would be their savings and stocks worth about $2,000. Since the SSI limit on resources is $3,000 for a couple, Rose and Peter would qualify for SSI benefits.

B. Benefit Amounts

Because supplementary payments vary from state to state, the amount of your SSI check will vary depending on where you live, as well as on the amount of your countable income. The basic federal SSI payment for 2000 is $512 a month for an individual, $769 a month for a couple. These figures go up on January 1 each year; the amount of increase depends on the rise in the cost-of-living index.

1. States With Federally Administered Supplements

A number of states pay supplements to the basic federal SSI amount. In these states, the supplement is added on directly to the federal SSI payment. This means that a person only needs to apply once, to Social Security, to receive both the basic amount and the supplement. Both amounts are included in one payment which is administered by Social Security.

The amount of the supplement differs for a single individual, a couple or a person who is blind. Also, the amount may be affected if the person receiving SSI lives in the home of family friend, in congregate living arrangements or in a nursing facility.

States in which SSI recipients receive a federally administered supplement include:

California
District of Columbia
Hawaii
Iowa
Maine
Massachusetts
Michigan
Nevada
New Jersey
New York
Pennsylvania
Rhode Island
Utah
Vermont
Washington
Wisconsin

Note that Delaware and Montana have federally administered supplements that are available only to people who live in protective care arrangements.

2. States With Their Own Supplements

Just over half of the states provide supplements to the basic federal SSI payment, but the amounts and rules are administered entirely by the states. You must apply for this state supplement separately, to the social welfare agency for the county in which you live. The amounts of these supplements range from a few dollars to a hundred dollars over the basic federal SSI payment. The amounts change frequently, based on the willingness of state legislatures to provide for SSI recipients in their state budgets.

States with their own supplement systems are:

Alabama
Alaska
Arizona
Colorado
Connecticut
Florida
Idaho
Illinois
Indiana
Kentucky
Louisiana
Maryland
Minnesota
Misouri
Nebraska
New Hampshire
New Mexico
North Carolina
North Dakota
Ohio
Oklahoma
Oregon
South Carolina
South Dakota
Virginia
Wyoming

3. States With No Supplements

In the following states, no supplements are paid above the basic federal SSI payment.

Arkansas
Georgia
Kansas
Mississippi
Tennessee
Texas
West Virginia

C. Reductions to Benefits

Maximum benefit amounts are reduced by any income you make over allowable countable limits, as dictated by a number of specific rules.

1. Limit on Earned Income

Your benefits are reduced by one dollar for every two dollars more than $65 per month you earn in wages or self-employment.

Example: Ronda has a part-time job at which she earns $280 a month. She is entitled to the basic federal SSI benefit of $500 per month, but that amount is reduced by $107.50 because of her earnings. The total of $107.50 is arrived at by taking the amount of her earned income over $65 ($215) and dividing it in half—one out of every two dollars over the limit. Her monthly income would then be her earnings of $280 plus her SSI benefit of $392.50, for a total of $672.50.

2. Limit on Unearned Income

Your benefits are reduced dollar for dollar by the amount of any unearned income you receive over $20 a month. This unearned income includes your Social Security benefits, pensions, annuities, interest on savings, dividends or any money from investments or property you own.

Example: Carl lives alone in a home he owns. His only income is his Social Security retirement check of $330 per month. From Carl's $330 Social Security check, $20 is excluded, making his total countable unearned income $310. Since he has no earned income, his total countable income would be the same: $310. In the state in which Carl lives, the basic SSI payment is $520 per month. From this, Carl's total countable income of $310 is subtracted, leaving $210 as Carl's monthly SSI payment, which he receives in addition to his Social Security benefit.

3. Limit on Outside Support

Your basic SSI payment will be reduced by one-third if you live in a friend's or relative's home and receive support in the form of food or clothing from them.

Example: Adam lives in his daughter and son-in-law's house. His only income is his monthly Social Security retirement check of $270, His daughter and son-in-law provide food for Adam, as well as give him a place to live. The basic SSI benefit of $598 in Adam's state would be reduced by one-third because Adam receives food and *lodging from his daughter and son-in-law. This would leave an SSI amount of $399. Adam's only income is his Social Security check of $270; $20 of that amount is not counted, leaving a total countable income of $250. This $250 is subtracted from his SSI amount, leaving a monthly SSI payment to Adam of $149, in addition to his Social Security check.*

4. Limits on Working Couples

A final example shows how SSI amounts are figured for a couple, and how SSI payments change when one person takes a job.

Example: Beverly marries Carl and together they collect a monthly Social Security check of $455. In figuring Carl and Beverly's SSI payment, $20 would be exempted from the $455 Social Security check, for a total countable income of $435 a month. That $435 would be subtracted from the basic SSI benefit for a couple, which in Carl and Beverly's state is $787, leaving a monthly SSI payment of $352.

When Beverly takes a part-time job paying $100 a month, their SSI payment changes. Beverly and Carl's countable unearned income is still the same $435 a month—their Social Security check minus $20. But now they have an earned income of $100 a month. The first $65 of this $100 is not counted under SSI rules. Of the remaining $35 of earned income, only one-half of it, or $17.50, is considered counted income. Only $17.50 is added to the $435 of counted unearned income, making a total countable income of $452.50 a month.

The basic SSI benefit for a couple in Carl and Beverly's state is $787 a month. The $452.50 countable income would be subtracted from this amount, leaving a monthly SSI payment to Carl and Beverly of $334.50. Their monthly income would be their Social Security check of $455, plus their part-time income of $100, plus their SSI check of $334.50, for a total of $889.50.

■

Applying for Benefits

Once you get an accurate estimate of how much your Social Security benefits will be, and you decide when it is best to begin receiving them, applying for those benefits is usually a simple process. Most people will already have all the documents needed, and can complete their application in no more than one or two trips to a local Social Security office. This chapter explains the process.

Section A explains the basics of applying for the main Social Security benefits: retirement benefits (see Chapter 2), dependents benefits (see Chapter 4) and survivors benefits (see Chapter 5).

Section B of this chapter will help you understand the nuances of applying for disability benefits, which has the most complicated procedure and requires greatest preparation. (See Chapter 3.) It explains the important role your doctor can play and will prepare you for the several steps you must go through to qualify for benefits.

Section C explains how to organize the required documents relating to your income and assets when you apply for SSI benefits. (See Chapter 6.)

A. Retirement, Dependents and Survivors Benefits

The application process for retirement benefits, dependents benefits and survivors benefits all involve the same basic documents and procedures. The only part of applying that takes much thought is figuring out the best time to claim benefits—and that requires understanding the relationship between your age and the amount you will receive.

1. When to Claim Benefits

You may be eligible for more than one type of benefit at different ages—for example, survivors benefits at age 60, based on your deceased spouse's work record, and retirement benefits at age 62 based on your own work record. And you are eligible for increased benefits for every month you wait to claim them up to age 70. As a result, your decision about which benefits to claim and when to claim them should be based on how much each benefit would be, measured against the earnings limit for your age, if you intend to continue working. (See Chapter 2, Section D; Chapter 4, Section D, and Chapter 5, Section E.)

To find out what each type of benefit would be at different ages, request a copy of your estimate of benefits statement. (See Chapter 1, Sections F and G.) You should request this estimate about six months before you would become eligible for a particular benefit; it takes several weeks for Social Security to get it to you. This will give you plenty of time to decide whether you want to apply for a particular benefit, and to get the process started if you choose to file immediately.

2. Where to File Claims

All Social Security claims are filed at local Social Security offices. Most sizable cities have at least one local Social Security office, and in major urban areas, there are several offices. You can find the address and telephone number of the office closest to you in your telephone directory under the listing for United States Government, Social Security Administration, or sometimes under United States Government, Department of Health and Human Services, Social Security Administration. If you have trouble finding a local office, call the Social Security at: 800-772-1213 for specific information.

3. Where to Get Information

Questions about Social Security claims or benefits can be answered either at a local office, over the phone through the toll-free number mentioned above (see Section A2), and at the Social Security Website at http://www.ssa.gov.

a. Help over the telephone

Over the phone, Social Security workers answer general questions about benefits and rules, including how to fill out a form and when to file a particular form. The phone service is available between 7 a.m. and 7 p.m. Monday through Friday. The phone lines are busiest early in the week and early in the month, so it is best to call at other times.

Sign Up Three Months Before Your Birthday

If you will need to actually receive a benefit payment as soon as you reach the youngest eligibility age, file your claim three months before the birthday on which you will become eligible. This will give Social Security time to process your claim so that you will receive benefits as soon as you become eligible. If you file a claim later, you cannot get benefits retroactively for months during which you were eligible but before you applied.

Anyone who is eligible for Social Security benefits is also eligible for Medicare coverage at age 65. (See Chapter 12). Even if you are not going to claim Social Security benefits at age 65—because your benefit amount will be higher if you wait—you should sign up for Medicare coverage three months before your 65th birthday. There is no reason to delay signing up for Medicare, and waiting until after your 65th birthday will delay coverage.

b. Help in person

A Social Security worker in your local office is best suited to answer specific questions about your claim. If there are unusual circumstances, the local office will obtain your full records from Washington, D.C., or seek the answer to your question from a regional office. Whenever you consult with someone in a Social Security office, write down the person's name and keep it with your other Social Security papers. That way, when you again contact the office, you can ask to speak with the same person, or you can refer to that person if a question arises about what occurred on your previous visit.

Getting the Best Results: Preparation, Patience, Perseverance

Social Security offices are usually understaffed. Although individual Social Security workers are often helpful, polite and well-versed in the various regulations that govern Social Security programs, the maze of rules, when added to normal human fallibility, inevitably makes for delays, misunderstandings and mistakes.

It's up to you to help yourself. The best way to begin the Social Security application process is to use the first six chapters of this book to understand the workings of the benefit program for which you will apply.

The next most important thing is to keep your papers organized. During the benefit application process, you may send papers and forms to your local Social Security office through the mail. However, it is best to deliver important papers—any original document or certified copy—in person. That way, the papers will not only be sure to get to the local office but also will go directly into your file. This will cut some time off the process and will help to avoid the adventures that sometimes befall papers that go into the incoming mail stack at an office.

Keep copies of any form or document you submit to Social Security. If the local Social Security office asks to see the original or a certified copy, it will usually make a copy on the spot and return the original to you. It's best to keep a copy in your files in case the original gets lost.

4. Documentation Required

The waiting time for service in most local Social Security offices is longer than one would like. Some people suggest the most important things to take with you to Social Security are a sandwich and something to read. But personal needs aside, when you visit a Social Security office to apply for benefits, bring with you all the papers that relate to your claim; that will speed up the process and may save you an extra trip.

Most documents required by Social Security must be originals or certified copies. However, if you want to apply for benefits right away but do not yet have all your documents together, go to the local Social Security office and file your claim anyway. The Social Security office workers will advise you about how to get the documents you need, and in the meantime, the application process can begin.

Everything Is in a Name

On any copy of a document you bring or send to Social Security, write your name as it appears on your benefit application and your Social Security number. Also include the name and Social Security number of the person on whose work record you are claiming benefits. If you bring or send an original document, clip a piece of paper to it with those names and numbers.

When you apply for any type of benefit, bring with you the number of your account at a bank, credit union or other financial institution. Social Security will arrange to have your monthly benefit payment sent directly to your account—a process called direct deposit. Direct deposit is now used for all new Social Security and SSI beneficiaries. It saves money for the Social Security Administration and also avoids the problem of lost or stolen checks.

a. Retirement benefits

Bring the following documents with you when you apply for retirement benefits.

- Your Social Security number. You do not need your actual Social Security card.
- Your birth certificate. If you do not have a birth certificate, bring any other evidence of the date of your birth: baptism record, military papers, immigration papers, driver's license, passport.
- Your military discharge papers, if you served in the military.
- Your most recent W-2 tax form or federal self-employment tax return.

b. Dependents benefits

Bring the following documents with you when you apply for dependents benefits.

- Marriage certificate, if you are applying for benefits based on your spouse's work record.
- Birth certificate of any children claiming benefits. If you do not have a birth certificate, bring any other evidence of the date of your child's birth: baptism record, immigration papers, passport.

c. Survivors benefits

Bring the following documents with you when you apply for survivors benefits.

- Social Security number of the deceased person on whose work record you are claiming benefits, and your own Social Security number.
- Divorce papers, if you are applying as a divorced spouse.
- Death certificate of your deceased spouse.
- Your birth certificate and those of your children who are claiming benefits. If a birth certificate is not available, bring any other evidence of date of birth: baptism record, military papers, immigration papers, passport.
- If your spouse died within the past two years, the most recent W-2 tax form or federal self-employment tax return of your deceased spouse.
- If applying as a surviving dependent parent who was receiving support from your son or daughter who has died, you will need a recent tax return from your deceased child which shows you as a dependent, or proof of expenditures by your deceased child showing how much support was given to you, as well as your own most recent tax returns.

If You Retire From Your Own Business

If you are retiring from your own business, Social Security requires some extra information. This is to ensure that you are really giving up full-time work and not merely shifting your pay, in name only, to someone else.

The reason for this concern is the rule that retirement benefits are reduced if you have earned income over certain limits for your age. (See Chapter 2, Section D.) Some people with their own businesses try to get around this rule by continuing to work and paying a relative instead of themselves, or by continuing to run the business but being paid only for reduced work time.

Social Security is likely to ask for information regarding your continuing involvement with your own business if:

- other family members are involved in the business and a relative is assuming most of your previous duties
- you continue to work for the business at lower pay
- you control the amount you work and how much you are paid, such that you could manipulate either one
- you maintain ownership of the business
- relatives now receive the salary you previously earned.

The specific additional information Social Security may ask for can include the business's pay and personnel records, personal and business tax returns, stock transfer agreements and business expense records. If you are planning to claim retirement benefits from your own business, contact your local Social Security office several months in advance. This extra time will permit you to learn what documents Social Security wants you to provide and to gather the documents.

If Social Security determines that you provide services to the business that exceed the amount you are paid—based on the time you spend, the level of your responsibility and the value of services you provide—the agency may attach a dollar value to those services. If this dollar value exceeds the amount of earned income you are permitted for your age, your benefits may be reduced. (See Chapter 2, Section D).

5. At the Social Security Office

You must apply for benefits at a local Social Security office. (See Section A3.) At some offices, you can phone in advance and make an appointment. Other offices do not set up appointments until you have actually filed an application. Still other offices do not regularly make appointments at all.

At your local Social Security office, you will be interviewed by a case worker who will help you fill out the application form. The worker will open a file for you, which from then on will contain all of the documents pertaining to your application. Write down the name of the worker who talks with you, and his or her direct telephone line if available, so that you can speak with the same person if you need to call in to provide or receive further information. The Social Security worker will make copies of the documents you have brought and will explain what other information is needed to process your application. If additional documents are needed, ask whether you may mail in copies instead of bringing originals in person.

When you first apply for benefits, do not expect to be told precisely how much your benefits will be. Exact benefit amounts are based upon the computerized records kept at the Social Security Administration's national records center. Your precise benefit amount will be calculated there. Applications take six to eight weeks to be processed, but when you receive your first payment, it will include benefits back to the date you first applied, or to the date on which you are first eligible, whichever is later.

6. Withdrawing a Benefits Application

It may happen that you apply for retirement, dependents or survivors benefits but your work situation then changes, altering significantly the amount of benefits to which you are entitled. This can occur if you are offered a new position, new job or increased salary, or you are not laid off from a job you expected to lose, or you are called back to work after a temporary job loss, or you simply change your mind and decide to continue working full-time.

In any of these situations, if the income you earn at your continued work significantly exceeds the earnings limit for your age, it may eat up your benefits. (See Chapter 2, Section D). If so, your decision to claim benefits may prove to be a bad one, because you will receive little or no benefit payments while you continue to work, and your benefit amount will be permanently lower than if you had waited to file your claim at a later age.

For a limited time after you apply for benefits, however, it is possible to withdraw your application. The limit is 60 days from the date Social Security mails you a notice that your benefits application has been approved. If you are still within this time period, you can go to your local Social Security office and ask to withdraw your application for benefits. A Social Security worker will discuss your decision with you. If you still want to withdraw your application, the worker will give you a form on which to make a formal request to do so. However, any benefits already paid on the claim must be returned. And a spouse or adult disabled child whose dependents benefits would be affected must consent in writing to the withdrawal of the application.

B. Disability Benefits

Eligibility for disability benefits depends upon your physical or mental condition, and your inability to work because of that condition. (See Chapter 3.) Because it involves these qualifying standards, the application process is much more complicated and time-consuming than it is for other Social Security benefits. It is therefore even more important in disability claims than in other benefit applications to get and keep your papers organized, and to be thorough and persistent in your contacts both with doctors and with Social Security personnel.

1. When to File Your Claim

You will not be paid any disability benefits until you have been disabled for six full months. This waiting period begins with the first full month after the date your disability began. That date is usually the date you stopped working because of your physical or mental condition.

However, disability claims take between two and six months to be processed. Do not wait for the six month period of disability to elapse before filing your claim. Don't even wait to gather all the necessary information and doctors reports before you file your claim. (See Section A4.) File the claim as soon as your medical condition forces you off work and the doctors expect that it will prevent you from working for a year or more. You can complete the gathering of necessary documents while the claim is being processed, with the help of your local Social Security office.

2. Required Documentation

When you file an application for disability, there are a number of documents you must bring to the Social Security office.

- Your Social Security number and proof of age for yourself and for each person eligible for dependents benefits. (See Section A4 for the documents that can be used for proof of age.)
- Names, addresses and phone numbers of doctors, hospitals, clinics and other health service institutions that have diagnosed your medical condition and have given estimates of the length of time it is expected to keep you disabled, plus the approximate dates of your treatment. Although you are not required to produce medical records of your disability—Social Security can request them directly from doctors and hospitals—you may be able to speed up the process if you bring copies of medical records you already have.
- A list of where you have worked in the past 15 years and a description of the kind of work you did.
- A copy of the past year's W-2 forms, or your last federal income tax return if you are self-employed.
- The dates of any military service.
- Information concerning any other type of disability payment you are receiving.
- If your spouse is applying as a dependent, the dates of any prior marriages. A certified copy of the divorce papers will provide this information.
- If you are applying as a disabled widow or widower, your spouse's Social Security number and a copy of the death certificate.
- If you are applying as a disabled surviving divorced husband or wife, proof that your marriage lasted ten years; marriage and divorce papers will serve this purpose.

If you are physically unable to get to a Social Security office in person, or you are unable to complete the forms or meet other filing requirements, your application can be completed by your spouse, parent, other relative, friend or legal guardian. And once the initial claim has been filed, a service worker in the local Social Security office can assist you by having the Social Security office directly request necessary documents.

3. The Eligibility Process

Applications for disability benefits go through several stages. Initially, you will fill out an application at a local Social Security office and provide documents regarding your age and employment. After that, however, the process becomes more complicated as Social Security determines whether your physical condition is actually disabling according to its standards.

a. Disability Determination Services

When your claim has been completed and the local Social Security office has checked to see that you meet all the general requirements regarding work credits for your age (see Chapter 3), it will forward your claim to a Disability Determination Services (DDS) office in your state. Based on your medical records and on the kind of work you have done, the DDS office will decide whether you are disabled under the rules of the Social Security law.

Enlisting the Help of Your Doctor

The state DDS office will base its determination of your eligibility for disability benefits primarily on your medical records. Therefore, what your doctor puts in your records can be crucial to this decision.

If possible, discuss the matter with your doctor before you file your application for disability benefits. Inform your doctor that you intend to apply and ask him or her to make specific notations in your medical records of how your physical activities—particularly work-related activities such as walking, sitting, lifting, carrying—are limited or how your emotional condition affects your ability regularly to perform work. Ask also for your doctor to make a note of when your disability reached a point that it interfered with your ability to work.

Do not ask the doctor to give an opinion about whether you are disabled according to Social Security guidelines. Doctors will readily describe a specific medical condition, but many are unwilling to give an opinion about your ability to do any work at all. And in any event, the DDS evaluation team would not accept your doctor's opinion on this ultimate question of eligibility. Instead, it will base its determination on its own evaluation of your medical records.

In determining the nature and extent of your disability, the DDS will rely almost exclusively on the diagnoses of medical doctors, to the exclusion of physical therapists, chiropractors and other non-physician healers. This reflects an institutional bias against non-traditional medical treatment. But it also reflects the fact that the decision about eligibility depends on diagnosis of your condition, not on the best way to treat it, and that physicians have diagnostic tools—such as laboratory tests, X-rays and other technological and intrusive procedures—that are not available to non-physician healers.

The decision at DDS is made by a doctor and a disability evaluation specialist. They examine all medical records you have provided with your application and may request more information from you, your doctors and your employers. Based on these records, they determine whether your disability is expected to last more than one year and whether it is severe enough to interfere with your ability to perform any work you have done over the past 15 years. If so, they then determine whether it is also so severe that you cannot perform any substantial gainful employment. (See Chapter 3, Section B4.) If your condition limits you in these ways, you will be found eligible for benefits. If not, those evaluating you may request further medical records and you may be referred for a consultative physical examination.

b. Medical examinations

In some cases, the DDS evaluators do not feel that they can come to a conclusion about your disability based on your existing medical records. They may request further reports from doctors who have examined or treated you. And they may request that you undergo a medical evaluation or test, called a consultative examination. The cost of the additional reports, examinations or tests are paid by Social Security. And if you must travel outside your immediate area to get to this examination, Social Security can pay for the cost of that travel, if you request it.

Fortunately, this extra examination or testing is often done by a physician who has already examined or treated you. This is particularly true if one of your doctors is a specialist in the area of medicine that deals directly with your disability. In other words, if you have seen an orthopedic surgeon for your back problem, Social Security is likely to have that same doctor perform the consultative examination. However, if you have not been treated by a specialist in the field—for example, if only your internist or general practitioner has treated you for a particular medical problem—Social Security may send you to another doctor for this examination.

Consultative examinations are limited to specific issues the DDS needs to clarify regarding your ability to work. It often involves certain kinds of tests—a range of motion test, for example, if your disability involves restricted movement—that have not been recently performed by your doctor but which give DDS specific information on the extent of your disability. The DDS will set up the examination and send the doctor a written request for the information needed and any specific tests it wants performed. The doctor will not conduct a general examination and will not prescribe any treatment for you. On occasion, a representative from DDS will attend the examination to record specific test results. The doctor will send a report to DDS describing the results of the examination, but he or she will not take part in the final decision about whether you are eligible for disability benefits.

Even though you may not be thrilled by the idea of going through another medical examination, especially if it is by a doctor you do not know, you must cooperate with the DDS to successfully process your disability claim.

c. Vocational rehabilitative services

When you apply for disability benefits, you may be referred to your state's vocational rehabilitation agency for a determination of whether any of its services might be of help to you. These free services can include job counseling, job retraining and placement, and specialized medical assistance. The services can also train you to use devices—such as a modified computer keyboard—that may enable you to work despite your disability.

Even if you do not believe that any of these services can help you, it may be necessary for you to cooperate with the vocational rehabilitation agency before you can receive disability benefits from Social Security. Of course, if you have good reason not to participate in a particular rehabilitative service offered to you, inform Social Security and do not participate in the particular service.

C. Supplemental Security Income (SSI)

You may file a claim for SSI benefits at your local Social Security office at the same time you file for retirement, disability, dependents or survivors benefits. (See Chapter 6.) However, SSI is not automatically included in these other applications, and so you must tell the Social Security worker that you wish to file for SSI benefits as well. If you believe you might be close to the qualifying income and asset limits for SSI benefits, be sure to apply for SSI benefits, too. If your state offers a separate state-administered supplementary payment in addition to the basic federal SSI payment, you will have to apply for that supplement at your local county social welfare office. (See Chapter 6, Section B.)

The process of applying for SSI benefits is very similar to applying for Social Security benefits. You will need to provide the same general documents. (See Sections A1 and A2.) However, unlike Social Security benefit applications, SSI benefit applications also require that you show records of your income and assets.

1. Proof of Income and Assets

Regardless of whether you are applying for SSI payments as disabled or over age 65, you must also bring information regarding your income and assets. This includes:

- information about where you live: for homeowners—a copy of your mortgage papers or tax bill; for renters—a copy of your rental agreement or lease and the name and address of the landlord
- documents indicating your current earned income, such as pay stubs and income tax returns
- papers showing all your financial assets, such as bankbooks, insurance policies, stock certificates, car registration, burial fund records, and
- information about your spouse's income and assets, if the two of you live together.

Even if you do not have all these papers available, go to your local Social Security office and file your application for SSI as soon as you think you may qualify for assistance. The Social Security workers can tell you how to get whatever papers and records are necessary, and in some instances will get copies of the required records for you.

2. Proof of Age If 65 or Over

If you are age 65 or over, bring your Social Security number and proof of your age, such as a birth certificate. If you do not have a birth certificate, bring any other evidence of the date of your birth: baptism record, military papers, immigration papers, driver's license, passport. If you are already receiving any kind of Social Security benefit, you do not have to bring proof of your age.

3. Proof of Blindness or Disability

The process for proving that you are blind or disabled for purposes of SSI benefits is the same as the process for establishing that you are blind or disabled when qualifying for Social Security disability benefits. (See Chapter 3, Section B.) The information you need to gather and the process of applying for disability benefits is discussed in this chapter. (See Section B.)

4. Proof of Citizenship or Legal Residence

To qualify for federal SSI benefits, you must be:

- a U.S. citizen, or
- a legal resident of the United States who was already receiving SSI benefits on August 22, 1996, or
- a legal resident of the United States on August 22, 1996, who is now blind or disabled, or
- a legal resident of the U.S. who has worked, or whose spouse has worked, for at least ten years in the United States and has paid at least the minimum Social Security taxes to qualify for 40 quarters of work credits (see Chapter 1, Section D), or
- a legal resident of the United States who was honorably discharged from the U.S. military, or whose spouse—whether alive or deceased—was honorably discharged from military service, or
- a political refugee or someone granted asylum by the Immigration and Naturalization Service. However, your benefits only last for seven years after you have been admitted to the country.

You can prove your citizenship by showing copies of your birth certificate, baptismal records or U.S. passport or naturalization papers. If you are a noncitizen legal resident, bring proof of your qualifications under one of the categories listed above.

For proof of work for ten years, bring your legal resident alien card and Social Security numbers for yourself and your spouse; the Social Security or local welfare office will use the numbers to check your reported Social Security taxes.

If you seek to qualify as a veteran of the U.S. armed forces, bring evidence of honorable discharge from the military. You will also need a copy of your marriage certificate if you are seeking SSI as the spouse of a veteran.

Periodic Review of SSI Eligibility

Social Security periodically reviews your SSI eligibility and the amounts you receive. These reviews take place at least once every three years, although there may be a brief review of your finances annually. When you receive a notice of review, you will have to produce the same kinds of information as you did for the original application: your income, assets, living arrangements and, if claiming based on a disability, updated medical information. Often, most of this process can be handled by mail or telephone, although you may have to make a trip to the Social Security office for an interview.

D. Finding Out What Happens to Your Claim

You will not find out from your local Social Security office whether your claim for benefits has been approved; that word has to come from the Social Security Administration in Washington, D.C. If your claim is approved, you will have several methods of payment from which to choose.

1. Notification of Eligibility

Social Security will notify you in writing whether your claim has been approved, how much your benefits will be and when you will get your first check. From the time the application is filed, a retirement, dependents or survivors claim usually takes from four to eight weeks. A disability claim can take up to six months. For all types of claims, you will receive benefits dating back to the date you first applied, or first became eligible if you applied before you reached an age of eligibility.

SSI benefits usually begin four to eight weeks after you have completed the necessary paperwork. If your claim is based on a disability that has not already been established for Social Security disability payments, it may take three to six months. When you do finally get your money, however, it will cover the entire period from the time you file your claim until the time you receive your first check.

If you were unable to work more than six months before applying for disability benefits, you might be eligible for back benefits. If Social Security determines that your disability actually began more than six months before your application, based on when you actually stopped work, it can grant up to 12 months of back benefits.

If your claim for any Social Security or SSI benefit is denied, the written notice of denial will state the reasons why. You have a right to appeal a denial of your claim. The appeal process must be started within 60 days from the date you receive written notice of the denial or other decision. (See Chapter 8, Section A.)

When You Need Money in a Hurry

It is possible to get some SSI payments even before your claim is finally approved. If you appear to be eligible for SSI and you need immediate cash to meet a financial emergency, the Social Security office can issue you an advance payment. The amount of this emergency payment will be deducted from your first regular SSI check.

Similarly, if you have already qualified for Social Security disability benefits and you appear financially eligible, you may be approved for and begin receiving SSI benefits immediately, without medical review.

If you are financially eligible, and appear to meet the disability requirements but your disability application has not yet been approved by Social Security, you can receive SSI payments for up to three months while your claim is being reviewed by the disability office.

2. Methods of Receiving Payment

As of January 1, 1999, all new beneficiaries will receive their Social Security and SSI benefits by direct deposit into their bank accounts. However, it is possible to receive payment by government check sent directly to you through the mail, or to someone who handles the money for you, called a substitute payee. You must indicate on the application if you want these options.

You may change your method of payment any time after you begin to receive benefits.

a. Direct deposit

Direct deposit has a number of advantages. You do not have to wait for your check to arrive in the mail, nor do you have to travel to your bank to make the deposit. And you do not have to worry about your check being lost or stolen.

When you first sign up for benefits at your local Social Security, workers there will ask for the name and address of your bank branch and the number of the account where you want the funds deposited. The bank where you have your account can help you fill out the form to request direct deposit.

If you change banks—or want to close one account and open another—you must fill out a new direct deposit form. The bank where you open your new account will assist you with the form. But do not close your old account until you see that your benefit has appeared in your new one. If your benefit continues to be deposited in the old account, contact your local Social Security office.

b. Checks through the mail

Social Security now strongly urges everyone to use direct deposit. But you may not want to receive your payment this way, either temporarily or for the long term. For example, you may not want to pay the bank charge to maintain an account. Or, you may be moving and temporarily will not have a local bank account. If, for any reason, you do not want to receive your benefit payment by direct deposit, you may arrange with your local Social Security office to have your payments mailed in the form of a check.

All Social Security and SSI checks sent through the mail arrive at about the same time—close to the third day of every month. If your check does not arrive on or near its usual day, call your local Social Security office right away to report it lost. The local office can then start the process of getting you a replacement check. This usually takes 20 to 30 days.

c. Substitute payee

If you are unable to handle your own banking and check writing, you may have a family member, close friend or legal representative receive the benefit payments on your behalf. That person should spend the money according to your wishes or directions. This may be done informally, by simply adding the other person as a joint account holder on the bank account where Social Security deposits your check; the bank can make this arrangement for you.

If you feel more comfortable with some oversight on how that person spends your benefits, you can have this other person officially appointed by Social Security as a substitute or representative payee. That person would then personally receive the benefit payments on your behalf. Anyone proposing to be a substitute payee must bring to the local Social Security office medical proof—for example, a letter from the original payee's doctor—that you are unable to care for yourself. The substitute payee must sign a sworn affidavit at the Social Security office stating that he or she will use the Social Security check for your benefit. The Social Security office will then verify your medical condition and the identity of the substitute payee.

If a person has already been appointed by a court to serve as legal guardian or conservator, proof of that court appointment is all that is required to be appointed representative payee. But people who are named to act in powers of attorney do not automatically qualify as representative payees; they must still apply for representative payee status at the local Social Security office.

The rules require that a substitute payee deposit and keep the money belonging to the person entitled to Social Security in a separate bank account, and periodically file an accounting with Social Security to show how the money has been spent to care for the beneficiary. The substitute payee should keep all bills and receipts in a systematic and organized way so they can be produced easily.

■

Appealing Social Security Decisions

No matter how carefully you follow Social Security rules and regulations, you may be denied a benefit to which you believe you are entitled. This is most often the case with disability claims, where questions about medical conditions and ability to work are subjective and susceptible to different interpretations.

But if your application for benefits is initially denied, or is granted but you are awarded less than you had hoped, that need not be the end of the matter. Virtually all decisions of the Social Security Administration may be appealed. Whether a new benefit has been denied or an existing benefit reduced or ended, you may appeal the decision as long as you follow some fairly simple rules.

This chapter explains the four possible levels of appeal following any Social Security decision. The first is called reconsideration; it is an informal review that takes place in the local Social Security office where your claim was filed. The second level is a hearing before an administrative law judge; this is an independent review of what the local Social Security office has decided, made by someone outside the local office. The third level is an appeal to the Social Security national Appeals Council in Washington, D.C. And the final level is filing a lawsuit in federal court.

Time Limit for Filing Appeals

The same time limit applies to each step of the appeals process. From the date on the written notice of Social Security's decision—whether denying or granting a benefit—you have 60 days within which to file a written notice that you are appealing that decision to the next stage in the process. If you receive the notice by mail, you have an additional five days within which to file your notice of appeal.

A. Reconsideration of Decision

When a claim for any type of Social Security benefit—retirement, disability, dependents or survivors—is denied, or an existing benefit is ended, or you receive an amount you feel is less than that to which you are entitled, the first step taken to appeal that decision is to request reconsideration.

The procedure for requesting reconsideration of these denials of benefit claims is discussed in Sections A1 through A3. The procedure for requesting reconsideration of a decision ending existing disability benefits is explained in Section A4. And the slightly different procedure for appealing denial of an SSI claim is discussed in Section A5.

Is an Appeal Worth the Effort?

The first question that may occur to you when considering an appeal is whether it is worth the effort.

Keep in mind that a substantial percentage of decisions are changed on appeal. Almost half of all disability appeals, which are by far the most common, are favorably changed in the appeal process.

And appealing a Social Security claim need not be as difficult as you might imagine. If you have properly organized and prepared your original claim, most of your work for the appeal is already done. In many situations, the appeal will require little more from you than taking another opportunity to explain why the information you already presented should qualify you for a benefit. In other cases, it will simply involve presenting one or two more pieces of information that better explain your situation to Social Security personnel.

The Social Security decision that you think is incorrect may affect your rights for many years. Because it is so important, and because the appeal process is relatively simple, it is almost always worth the effort to appeal a negative decision.

1. Reconsideration of Decision on Initial Claim

The first formal step in appealing the denial of a claim for retirement, disability, dependents or survivors benefits is to file a written request for review of the decision, called a Request for Reconsideration.

This is also the step you take if you are allotted benefits less than the amount to which you believe you are entitled. Your local Social Security office has the required form. Or you can order the form by calling the Social Security office at: 800-772-1213. A sample of the form follows.

The form is in duplicate: the top copy for the Claims Folder (the Social Security office's copy) and a bottom Claimant's Copy (for you). You only fill in the top part of the form, and the information requested is straightforward: name, address, Social Security number, type of claim—retirement, disability, dependents, survivors. If you cannot get the actual form in time to file it within the 60-day limit, copy the form in this book and submit it to your local Social Security office. Be sure to keep a copy of the completed form for your records.

2. Completing the Form

The first few lines of the Request for Reconsideration form are fairly simple. On the top left, fill in your own name, exactly as it appears on your Social Security card. Use the box on the top right only if you are claiming dependents or survivors benefits; if so, you put the name of your spouse or parent on whose work record you are claiming benefits. On the second line to the left is the box for the Social Security claim number. Copy that number from the written denial of your claim which you received from Social Security.

The remaining boxes on the top three lines apply only if you are appealing the denial of SSI benefits. If so, you must fill in your spouse's name and Social Security number so that the agency can check his or her earnings. And on the middle line to the right, you must note your SSI claim number, which you will find on the written denial of your SSI claim.

The most important part of the form comes on the lines following the words: "I do not agree with the determination made on the above claim and request reconsideration. My reasons are: …" On those lines, state briefly and simply why you think you were unfairly denied your benefits. You need not go into great detail, because on reconsideration, your entire file will be examined—including any additional materials you want to submit that were not in your file when the original decision was made. Your statement should simply identify the problem, such as: "The decision that I am not disabled was based on insufficient evidence about my condition. I am submitting an additional letter from my doctor about my condition." Or: "The DDS evaluation of my disability did not take into account my inability to sit for prolonged periods."

Along with your completed Request for Reconsideration form, you can submit a letter describing in more detail why you think Social Security's decision was incorrect. You can also submit other materials you want added to your file, such as recent medical records or a letter from a doctor or employer about your ability to work. This additional information does not have to be submitted by the 65th day after the written decision. But if you are going to submit additional information after your Request for Reconsideration, indicate on the form—along with the reasons you disagree with the decision—that you will be submitting additional information.

Be sure to include your Social Security number and your claim number, in addition to your full name and the date on all material you send in. And keep a copy for your records.

3. The Reconsideration Process

Your claim will be reconsidered by someone in the Social Security office other than the person who made the decision on it the first time around. He or she will consider everything that was in your file when the decision was made, plus anything you have submitted to the office since the original decision. Generally, you do not appear in person at this review; you do not have the right to speak face to face with the person making the decision, although you can request a chance to do so. The person doing the review may request more information and may ask you to come in for a further informal interview.

Request for Reconsideration

DEPARTMENT OF HEALTH AND HUMAN SERVICES
SOCIAL SECURITY ADMINISTRATION

TOE 710

(Do not wirte in this space)

REQUEST FOR RECONSIDERATION

The information on this form is authorized by regulation (20 CFR 404.907 – 404.921 and 416.1407 – 416.1421). While your responses to these questions is voluntary, the Social Security Administration cannot reconsider the decision on this claim unless the information is furnished.

NAME OF CLAIMANT	NAME OF WAGE EARNER OR SELF-EMPLOYED PERSON *(If different from claimant.)*
SOCIAL SECURITY CLAIM NUMBER	SUPPLEMENTAL SECURITY INCOME (SSI) CLAIM NUMBER
SPOUSE'S NAME *(Complete ONLY in SSI cases)*	SPOUSE'S SOCIAL SECURITY NUMBER *(Complete ONLY in SSI cases)*

CLAIM FOR *(Specify type, e.g., retirement, disability, hospital insurance, SSI, etc.)*

I do not agree with the determination made on the above claim and request reconsideration. My reasons are:

SUPPLEMENTAL SECURITY INCOME RECONSIDERATION ONLY *(See reverse of claimant's copy)*

"I want to appeal your decision about my claim for supplemental security income, SSI. I've read the back of this form about the three ways to appeal. I've checked the box below."

☐ Case Review ☐ Informal Conference ☐ Formal Conference

EITHER THE CLAIMANT OR REPRESENTATIVE SHOULD SIGN – ENTER ADDRESSES FOR BOTH

SIGNATURE OR NAME OF CLAIMANT'S REPRESENTATIVE ☐ NON-ATTORNEY ☐ ATTORNEY			CLAIMANT SIGNATURE		
STREET ADDRESS			STREET ADDRESS		
CITY	STATE	ZIP CODE	CITY	STATE	ZIP CODE
TELEPHONE NUMBER *(Include area code)* (— — —)		DATE	TELEPHONE NUMBER *(Include area code)* (— — —)		DATE

TO BE COMPLETED BY SOCIAL SECURITY ADMINISTRATION

See reverse of claim folder copy for list of initial determinations

1. HAS INITIAL DETERMINATION BEEN MADE? ☐ YES ☐ NO
2. CLAIMANT INSISTS ON FILING ☐ YES ☐ NO
3. IS THIS REQUEST FILED TIMELY? ☐ YES ☐ NO
(If "NO", attach claimant's explanation for delay and attach only pertinent letter, material, or information in social security office.)

RETIREMENT AND SURVIVORS RECONSIDERATIONS ONLY (CHECK ONE) REFER TO (GN 03102.125)

SOCIAL SECURITY OFFICE ADDRESS

☐ NO FURTHER DEVELOPMENT REQUIRED (GN 03102.125)

☐ REQUIRED DEVELOPMENT ATTACHED

☐ REQUIRED DEVELOPMENT PENDING, WILL FORWARD OR ADVISE STATUS WITHIN 30 DAYS

ROUTING INSTRUCTIONS (CHECK ONE) →

☐ DISABILITY DETERMINATION SERVICES *(ROUTE WITH DISABILITY FOLDER)*
☐ ODO, BALTIMORE
☐ PROGRAM SERVICE CENTER
☐ INTPSC, BALTIMORE
☐ DISTRICT OFFICE RECONSIDERATION
☐ OCRO BALTIMORE

NOTE: TAKE OR MAIL COMPLETED COPIES TO YOUR SOCIAL SECURITY OFFICE

FORM **SSA-561-U2** (9-85)

CLAIMS FOLDER

You will receive a written notice of the decision made on your request for reconsideration—usually within 30 days. If you have not received a written notice within 30 days after giving all the new information regarding reconsideration, contact the local Social Security office and ask about the delay. Reconsideration of a disability claim often takes two to three months, particularly if new medical information has been provided during the course of the appeal.

Once you receive written notice of decision following reconsideration, you again have 65 days from the date of that decision within which to file a request for an administrative hearing if you want one. (See Section B.)

4. Reconsideration of End to Existing Disability Benefits

If you are already receiving disability benefits, but Social Security decides that your condition has improved and you no longer qualify, the reconsideration process is slightly different than described above. (See Section A3.) If you file a Request for Reconsideration following Social Security's decision to end your existing disability benefits, you do have a right to meet in person with a disability officer to explain why you believe you still qualify for those benefits.

If you want to meet with a Social Security representative face to face instead of simply relying on the papers in your file, you must request the meeting, called a Disability Hearing. You can do so by indicating on your Request for Reconsideration form (under "My reasons are: ...") that you want to meet in person. Or you can inform the local Social Security office when you file your Request for Reconsideration form. You can also write or call your local Social Security office to request and schedule the meeting after you file your Request for Reconsideration form. This hearing is in addition to, not instead of, the hearing in front of an administrative law judge to which you are later entitled if your claim is still denied after reconsideration. (See Section B.)

The Importance of Reviewing Your File

Sometimes a Social Security or SSI claim is denied because a document or other piece of information that should be in your file is not there. Or perhaps some misinformation has gotten into your file without your knowledge. This happens most often on the question of medical condition, where an incomplete medical record is in your file, or the report from the DDS examination includes a mistake based on a misunderstanding with the doctor who did the examination.

The only way for you to find out if such mistakes exist is to look at your file, which is supposed to contain all documents related to your claim. After you have filed your Request for Reconsideration, call your local Social Security office to set up an appointment to see your file if you wish to check its accuracy.

If you find a mistake in the file, write a letter to Social Security explaining the mistake. Send the letter to your local Social Security office, asking that it be made part of your file for reconsideration. And, as always, keep a copy of the letter.

Continuing Your Benefits During an Appeal

In some circumstances, you can continue to receive Social Security disability benefits and SSI benefits while Social Security is deciding your appeal. This can happen if:

- you have been collecting Social Security disability benefits and you are now appealing Social Security's decision to end your benefits because it has determined that your condition has improved, or
- you have been collecting SSI benefits and Social Security has decided that you are no longer eligible, or that you are eligible for lower benefits.

If you want your benefits to continue during the appeal process, you must make the request to your local Social Security office within ten days of the date you receive a written notice ending or reducing your benefits.

It May Not Be for Keeps

If you continue to collect benefits while appealing Social Security's decision to end those benefits, and Social Security denies your appeal, you may have to pay back the benefits you received during the appeal.

5. Reconsideration of SSI Decisions

If you request a reconsideration of a decision regarding a claim for SSI benefits, different situations lead to different reconsideration procedures.

- If you request reconsideration of a decision denying a new SSI claim because Social Security has decided that you are not disabled, you can have your case file reviewed, but you do not have any right to meet with Social Security representatives. (See Sections A1 to A3.)
- If you have been turned down for SSI because you do not qualify under the income or assets limits, you may request an informal face to face meeting with the person reviewing your claim. At that meeting, you can explain why you think the decision should be changed and you can bring along anyone you want to help explain your situation. (See Section A4.)
- If you have been receiving SSI benefits but Social Security has decided to end or reduce them, you can request what is called a Formal Conference. This is actually an informal meeting at which you can present whatever written materials you want, have people come to the meeting and give whatever information they have, and also explain your situation in your own words. It is only formal in the sense that the Social Security office can issue a legal summons for people to show up at the hearing and answer questions if you want them there but they refuse to come voluntarily. If you want Social Security to force someone to appear, you must notify

your local office several weeks before the hearing date.

B. Administrative Hearing

If your claim is again denied after reconsideration, you may request a formal administrative hearing. Because the hearing is held in front of an independent administrative law judge rather than someone who works in the same office as the person who originally denied your claim, you have a good chance to have the denial of your claim reversed at this hearing, even if you have no new information to present.

1. Requesting a Hearing

As with other steps in the appeal process, you must file a request for this hearing with your local Social Security office within 65 days of the date on the written notice of the decision after reconsideration.

The request for administrative hearing is filed on a form available at your local Social Security office or from the Social Security office at: 800-772-1213. A copy of the form, Request for Hearing by Administrative Law Judge, is reproduced below. There are five copies of this form, separated by carbon paper, so when you fill it out, make sure the information can be easily read on all five copies. Although one of the copies is for you, make several extra copies to keep in your file, especially if you are going to mail the form to your local Social Security office rather than take it in person. If you have questions about the form, your local Social Security office can help you fill it out.

Representation at Administrative Hearing
Although you may not have had any assistance in preparing your original claim or for the reconsideration stage of your appeal, consider getting assistance from an outside professional, such as a lawyer or other counselor specializing in Social Security matters, if you intend to carry on through an administrative hearing. (See Section E.) This is particularly true if the issue is whether your physical or emotional condition qualifies you as disabled. Your best chance of reversing Social Security's decision comes at the administrative hearing, and so you will want to be as well prepared as possible at this stage.

Informal Hearings at Social Security

When Social Security decides to end your disability benefits or to end or reduce your SSI payments, you have a right to meet in person with a Social Security hearing officer to discuss the decision. The hearing itself is very informal, without any courtroom-style rules. You are given the opportunity to explain in your own words why you believe the decision ending your benefits is wrong. If you feel that you can explain yourself better in person than you can in writing, you might want to take advantage of this opportunity.

There are several things to bear in mind during the hearings.

- Do not expect to be able to tell your whole life story. The hearing officer will only want you to discuss the specific reason Social Security has given for ending your benefits—a change in your physical condition, increased work hours or income—and you should do your best to stick to that specific matter.
- The hearing officer will have seen all the documents in your file, so do not try to go over them all or read them aloud except to point out what you believe are errors, or to focus on something in a document that you believe is important but that seemed to have been ignored in the original decision.
- A hearing officer who asks a question is probably doing so to focus in on what Social Security considers important. Do not dismiss or ignore the question; try to answer it as best you can, and if there is other information—from your doctor or employer, for example, that you believe might help answer the question, tell the hearing officer and ask that you be allowed to provide the information before the hearing officer makes a decision.
- Be calm and polite. Hearing officers understand that the ending of benefits is an emotional matter for you, but they are not the person who made the initial decision, and they are human, so you will not do yourself any good by taking out your frustration on them.

2. Completing the Form

The first four sections of the form, along the same top line, are straightforward. Your name goes in box number 1, as Claimant.

If you are seeking dependents or survivors benefits, then you must also fill in box number 2 with the name of the spouse or parent on whose earnings record you are claiming benefits. Box 3 simply asks for your claim number and Box 4 for that of your spouse, if this is an SSI claim.

Section 5 of the Request for Hearing by Administrative Law Judge form asks for you to state the reasons you disagree with the determination made on your claim. State your reasons here simply and briefly, for example: "The decision that I am not disabled was based on incorrect statements about the number of hours I regularly work. I am submitting letters from my co-workers explaining that I actually work fewer hours than stated in the decision ending my benefits." Or: "The DDS evaluation of my disability did not take into account my inability to travel to and from work."

After you and your representative have organized your papers and spoken with your doctor, employer or other person who can provide additional or clarifying information about your claim, you, or you and your representative, can write a detailed statement about your claim. You can then send that statement to your local Social Security office to be placed in your file, and also directly to the administrative law judge who will hear your claim. You should send in that additional information at least two weeks before your hearing date so that the administrative law judge will have a chance to read it before the hearing. If you do not prepare it in advance, bring it with you to the hearing and present it there.

Section 6 includes two boxes to indicate whether you have additional evidence to submit. You should always check the second box—the one that says you do have additional evidence. This will allow you to submit a new written statement to the judge, as well as any letters or documents that were not already in your file. If it turns out that you do not have any additional letters or documents to submit, at the hearing you can inform the judge that you have no new written materials but would like an opportunity to speak.

In Section 7 on the hearing request form, you must indicate whether you want to attend the hearing or instead have the judge make a decision based on the papers in your file. It is almost always to your advantage to be present at the hearing. Your presence puts a human face on your claim and shows the judge that you are truly concerned about the outcome. It also allows the judge to ask you questions that might not get answered if you were not there. If you choose to attend your hearing but later decide not to, you must notify the hearing judge's office beforehand. If, on the other hand, you have stated on the form that you do not want to attend the hearing but later decide you do, the hearing will have to be rescheduled to a later date. That is because hearings with the claimant present are usually scheduled at different times and places than hearings consisting solely of a review of the file.

Section 9 asks you to write the name and address of your representative. If you do not have a representative by the time limit for filing your request for hearing, file the request without naming anyone. If later you obtain a representative, you can supply that information then.

Request for Hearing by Administrative Law Judge

DEPARTMENT OF HEALTH AND HUMAN SERVICES
SOCIAL SECURITY ADMINISTRATION
OFFICE OF HEARINGS AND APPEALS

Form Approved
OMB No. 0960-0269

REQUEST FOR HEARING BY ADMINISTRATIVE LAW JUDGE
[Take or mail original and all copies to your local Social Security Office]

PRIVACY ACT NOTICE ON REVERSE SIDE OF FORM.

1. CLAIMANT	2. WAGE EARNER, IF DIFFERENT	3. SOC. SEC. CLAIM NUMBER	SPOUSE's CLAIM NUMBER

5. **I REQUEST A HEARING BEFORE AN ADMINISTRATIVE LAW JUDGE.** I disagree with the determination made on my claim because:

You have a right to be represented at the hearing. If you are not represented but would like to be, your Social Security Office will give you a list of legal referral and service organizations. (If you are represented, complete form SSA-1696.)

An Administrative Law Judge of the Office of Hearings and Appeals will be appointed to conduct the hearing or other proceedings in your case. You will receive notice of the time and place of a hearing at least 20 days before the day set for a hearing.

6. Check one of these blocks.

☐ I have no additional evidence to submit.

☐ I have additional evidence to submit. (Please submit it to the Social Security Office within 10 days.)

7. Check one of the blocks:

☐ I wish to appear at a hearing.

☐ I do not wish to appear and I request that a decision be made based on the evidence in my case (Complete Waiver Form HA-4608)

[You should complete No. 8 and your representative (if any) should complete No. 9. If you are represented and your representative is not available to complete this form, you should also print his or her name, address, etc. in No. 9.]

8. (CLAIMANT'S SIGNATURE)	9. (REPRESENTATIVE'S SIGNATURE/NAME)
ADDRESS	(ADDRESS) ☐ ATTORNEY; ☐ NON ATTORNEY
CITY STATE ZIP CODE	CITY STATE ZIP CODE
DATE AREA CODE AND TELEPHONE NUMBER	DATE AREA CODE AND TELEPHONE NUMBER

TO BE COMPLETED BY SOCIAL SECURITY ADMINISTRATION—ACKNOWLEDGMENT OF REQUEST FOR HEARING

10. **equest for Hearing RECEIVED for the Social Security Administration on ______________ by: ______________**

(TITLE) ADDRESS Servicing FO Code PC Code

11. ☐ Request timely filed

☐ Request not timely filed-Attach (1) claimant's explanation for delay, (2) any pertinent letter, material, or information in the Social/Security Office.

12. Claimant not represented – ☐ list of legal referral and service organizations provided

13. Interpreter needed – ☐ enter language (including sign language): ______________

14. Check one: ☐ Initial Entitlement Case
☐ Disability Cessation Case
☐ Other Postentitlement Case

15. Check claim type(s):

- ☐ RSI only .... (RSI)
- ☐ Disability—worker or child only .... (DIWC)
- ☐ Disability—Widow(er) only .... (DIWW)
- ☐ SSI Aged only .... (SSIA)
- ☐ SSI Blind only .... (SSIB)
- ☐ Disability only .... (SSID)
- ☐ SSI Aged/Title II .... (SSAC)
- ☐ SSI Blind/Title II .... (SSBC)
- ☐ SSI Disability/Title II .... (SSDC)
- ☐ HI Entitlement .... (HIE)
- ☐ Other—Specify: (______________)

16. **HO COPY SENT TO:** ______ HO on ______.
☐ CF Attached: ☐ Title II; ☐ Title XVI; or
☐ Title II CF held in FO to establish CAPS ORBIT; or
☐ CF requested: ☐ Title II; ☐ Title XVI
(Copy of teletype or phone report attached).

17. **CF COPY SENT TO:** ______ HO on ______.
☐ CF attached: ☐ Title II; ☐ Title XVI
☐ Other attached ______________

FORM **HA-501-U5** (5-88)
Issue old stock

CLAIMS FOLDER

Timing May Be Important

To make sure that all your evidence gets in your file and to the administrative law judge in time for your hearing, you must submit all new evidence—letters, documents, records that were not previously given to Social Security—within ten days of filing your request for a hearing. So, even if you are ready to file a request for an administrative hearing immediately after you receive written notice of the reconsideration decision, it is a good idea to wait until you have gathered whatever additional information you want the hearing judge to see. This may delay slightly the date of your hearing, but it will allow you to make sure all your evidence will be considered there.

3. The Hearing

After you file the request for hearing, you will be notified by mail of the date and place of the hearing. This notice will come at least three or four weeks before the hearing. If you cannot attend the hearing on that date, contact the office of the administrative law judge and arrange for a new date. Make a request for a change in schedule as soon as you know you need a change. Most offices of administrative law judges are reasonable about rescheduling, but if you wait until the last week to request a change, and you do not have a medical or other valid emergency, the judge could refuse to postpone your hearing and hold the hearing without you.

The hearing itself is conducted in a style less rigid than a courtroom but a bit more formal than a hearing at the local Social Security office. An administrative law judge presides, and everything said or done in the hearing is recorded. You may be represented or assisted at the hearing by a friend or relative or by a lawyer or other advocate. (See Section E.) You may present any evidence you would like the judge to consider—including documents, reports and letters. And you may present the testimony of any witnesses you would like to have help prove your claim. This testimony is also informal. The person simply gives information regarding your employment or medical condition to the judge and answers any questions the judge may ask. The judge will give you an opportunity to explain your claim in your own words, and may also ask you some questions.

The administrative law judge who presides at your hearing is a lawyer who works for the Social Security Administration, but has not taken part in the original claim decision or in reconsidering your claim. The judge will follow certain rules of procedure and may ask you questions about your claim that are not easy to answer, but in general, the judges try to be as helpful as possible to claimants during the hearings. If you are not sure how to present certain information to the judge, explain the problem and the judge should help you get the information into the official record of the case.

The judge will issue a written decision on your appeal, usually within four to six weeks of the hearing. You will receive a copy of this decision in the mail. If your claim has been denied by the administrative law judge, you have 65 days from the date on the written notice of the denial to file a further appeal. If your claim is approved, you may be entitled to receive benefits dating all the way back to the time you filed your original claim.

Preparing for the Hearing

During the time between filing your request for a hearing and the hearing date, you should take several steps.

First, discuss your claim with the attorney or representative who will assist or represent you at the hearing. (See Section E.) It is particularly important to make sure that your representative understands what you believe to be the most important part of your claim and that he or she has thoroughly reviewed any documents that you believe support your position on that point.

Second, examine your file either at your local Social Security office or at the hearing office. This allows you to see that all the papers you have given to Social Security have found their way into your file and it also allows you to review all of both the positive and negative information that Social Security has collected, such as a report on your disability from a DDS examination. Call your local Social Security office to see when and where you can examine your file.

Finally, obtain letters or records from medical providers or employers establishing your claim and responding to the reasons expressed by the Social Security office or DDS examiners for rejecting your claim. If you get additional written materials, submit copies to your local Social Security office and directly to the administrative law judge, while keeping the original and at least one more copy.

C. Appeal to the National Appeals Council

If your appeal has been denied after an administrative hearing, your next step is to file a written appeal with the Social Security Administration Appeals Council in Arlington, Virginia. A written request must be filed within 65 days from the date on the written notice of the administrative law judge's decision.

1. Completing the Form

Forms for requesting this appeal are available at your local Social Security office and must be filed there. There is a sample form on the following page.

There are two sets of boxes on the top right of the form. The first asks you to check either Initial Entitlement or Termination or Other Postentitlement Action. Initial Entitlement means the claim that was denied was your first attempt to obtain a particular benefit. Termination or Other Postentitlement Action refers to when you were already receiving a benefit but Social Security decided to end it or to reduce the amount you receive.

Also notice the explanation in the middle of the form under the heading Additional Evidence. Any documents you wish to submit to the Appeals Council that are not already in your file must be either attached to the form or sent directly to the Appeals Council within 15 days after filing your request for review.

When to See a Lawyer

If you are not yet represented by a lawyer who specializes in Social Security matters, you had better hire one now. The Appeals Council usually reverses an administrative law judge's decision only when a technical argument can be made as to why the administrative law judge made a legal mistake. Simply arguing to the Appeals Council that the judge was wrong in deciding your case will not be enough. (See Section E.)

2. Appeal Procedure

Unfortunately, your appeal to the Appeals Council is not likely to meet much success. The Appeals Council usually reviews a case based on the written documents in your file only. It very rarely accepts a case for a hearing, and when it does, the Council meets only in Washington, DC. If you want to appear at the hearing, you have to go or send a representative to the hearing in Washington.

More often, if the Appeals Council believes there is some merit to the appeal, it sends the case back to the administrative law judge with the direction that the judge hold a new hearing and reconsider something the Appeals Council will point out in its written decision.

Although the success rate of having claims denials overturned by the Appeals Council is very low, filing an appeal may be important. You are required to file this appeal before you can move on to the next step, which is filing a lawsuit in federal court.

Request for Review of Hearing Decision/Order

DEPARTMENT OF HEALTH AND HUMAN SERVICES
SOCIAL SECURITY ADMINISTRATION/OFFICE OF HEARINGS AND APPEALS

Form Approved
OMB No. 0960-0277

REQUEST FOR REVIEW OF HEARING DECISION/ORDER
(Take or mail original and all copies to your local Social Security office)

See Privacy Act Notice on Reverse

CLAIMANT

(Check ONE) Initial Entitlement ☐ Termination or other Postentitlement Action ☐

WAGE EARNER (Leave blank if same as above)

SOCIAL SECURITY NUMBER

SPOUSE'S NAME AND SOCIAL SECURITY NUMBER
(Complete ONLY in Supplemental Security Income Case)

NAME | SSN

Type Claim (Check ONE)

- Retirement or Survivors . . . . Only ☐ (RSI)
- Disability, Worker or Child . . . . Only ☐ (DIWC)
- Disability, Widow or Widower . . . . Only ☐ (DIWW)
- Health Insurance, Part A . . . . Only ☐ (HIA)
- SSI, Aged . . . . . . Only ☐ (SSIA) With Title II Claim ☐ (SSAC)
- SSI, Blind . . . . . . Only ☐ (SSIB) With Title II Claim ☐ (SSBC)
- SSI, Disability . . . Only ☐ (SSID) With Title II Claim ☐ (SSDC)
- Other (Specify) ____________

I disagree with the action taken on the above claim and request review of such action by the Appeals Council of the Office of Hearings and Appeals. My reasons for disagreement are:

____

____

ADDITIONAL EVIDENCE

Any additional evidence which you wish to submit must be either attached to this form or forwarded within 15 days to the Appeals Council at the address shown below. It is important that you write your Social Security number on any letter or material you send us. Where the evidence is not submitted within 15 days of this date, or within any extension of time granted by the Appeals Council, the Council will proceed to take its action based on the evidence of record.

Knowing that anyone making a false statement or representation of a material fact for use in determining the right to payment under the Social Security Act commits a crime punishable under Federal law, I certify that the above statements are true.

Signed by: (Either the claimant or representatives should sign—Enter addresses for both)

SIGNATURE OR NAME OF CLAIMANT'S REPRESENTATIVE ☐ ATTORNEY ☐ NON-ATTORNEY	CLAIMANT SIGNATURE
STREET ADDRESS	STREET ADDRESS
CITY, STATE, AND ZIP CODE	CITY, STATE, AND ZIP CODE
AREA CODE AND TELEPHONE NUMBER	DATE	AREA CODE AND TELEPHONE NUMBER

Claimant should not fill in below this line

TO BE COMPLETED BY SOCIAL SECURITY ADMINISTRATION

Is this request filed timely? ☐ Yes ☐ No

If "NO" is checked: (1) attach claimant's explanation for delay; (2) attach any pertinent letter, material or information in Social Security Office.

ACKNOWLEDGEMENT OF RECEIPT OF REQUEST FOR REVIEW OF HEARING DECISION/ORDER

This request for Review of Hearing Decision/Order was filed on ____________ at ____________
The APPEALS COUNCIL will notify you of its action on your request.

For the Social Security Administration:

SIGNATURE BY:

TITLE

STREET ADDRESS

CITY

STATE | ZIP CODE

SERVICING SOCIAL SECURITY OFFICE CODE

APPEALS COUNCIL
OFFICE OF HEARINGS AND APPEALS, SSA
P.O. BOX 3200
ARLINGTON, VA 22203

Form HA-520-U5 (6/88)
Destroy old stock

CLAIMS FOLDER

D. Lawsuit in Federal Court

If your claim has been denied and you have unsuccessfully exhausted all the Social Security Administration appeals procedures, you are entitled to bring a lawsuit against the Social Security Administration in federal district court. You must file the initial papers of this lawsuit within 60 days after the Appeals Council's decision is mailed.

A federal court lawsuit is a complicated, time-consuming and expensive procedure. However, it may be worth it. When you add up the total amount of benefits you might receive in your lifetime should your claim be approved, there may be a lot of money at stake. If the amount seems worth the time and effort to you, then you should at least investigate the possibility of filing a lawsuit by consulting with attorneys who specialize in Social Security appeals.

While you may want to get legal assistance at some earlier stage of the appeal process, you certainly need expert legal assistance to file a lawsuit in federal court. (See Section E.) Your odds of winning there depend almost entirely on convincing a court that the administrative law judge who heard your appeal made a mistake in interpreting the Social Security law. Simply asking a court to take another look at the facts of your case is almost never enough to win a federal lawsuit.

The main things to weigh in deciding whether to file a lawsuit are your chances of winning as explained to you by an attorney specializing in such cases, the money it will cost you to fight the legal battle and the amount of money in benefits that you stand to gain. If you balance all these things and it still seems like a good idea to go ahead with the lawsuit, then you should consider hiring an attorney to help you proceed.

E. Lawyers and Other Assistance

Under Social Security rules, you have a right to be represented at every stage of the appeal process by someone who understands the Social Security rules. This person may be a lawyer who specializes in Social Security matters, it may be a non-lawyer from one of the many organizations that help people with Social Security claims, or it may be a family member or friend who may be better than you are at organizing documents, writing letters or speaking.

1. Deciding Whether You Need Assistance

It is not usually necessary to get assistance in preparing or presenting your appeal at the reconsideration stage. After reconsideration, however, and particularly if your appeal involves medical issues, it is often wise to seek assistance. This assistance can take several forms: talking over your appeal with a knowledgeable friend or relative; having a person who specializes in Social Security problems go over your papers with you, make suggestions, and assist you at hearings; or having a lawyer or other specialist prepare and present the appeal on your behalf.

Deciding whether to hire a lawyer or to seek an experienced non-lawyer representative depends on several things.

- The complications of your case. The more complicated the issues—particularly those involving physical or emotional condition as it relates to qualification for disability benefits—the more likely that you need expert help.
- How much money is at stake. For example, if your appeal is only about whether your disability began in March or April, it is probably not worth hiring an attorney to represent you; the most you stand to win or lose is one month's benefits. On the other hand, if your benefits have been reduced significantly or denied entirely, it may well be worth the money to hire an attorney.
- How comfortable you feel handling the matter yourself. Particularly in the reconsideration stage of the appeal process, many people feel confident obtaining their own records and documents and discussing their claim with a local Social Security office worker. However, many other people are uncomfortable about explaining things adequately, and so would like assistance even at this early stage. And most people become somewhat uncomfortable at the prospect of an administrative hearing because they have never been through such a procedure before. If so, it is a good idea at least to get some advice, and perhaps representation, before this stage of the appeal process.

What a Representative Can Do to Help

If you decide to have someone represent you during the course of your appeal—either a lawyer or other specialist—he or she can handle as much or as little of the process as you want. A representative can:

- look at and copy information from your Social Security file
- file a request for reconsideration, hearing or Appeals Council review, and schedule or reschedule hearings
- provide Social Security with information on your behalf
- accompany you, or appear instead of you, and speak on your behalf at any interview, conference or hearing, and
- receive copies of any written decisions or other notices sent by Social Security.

2. Where to Find Assistance

Assistance with Social Security or SSI appeals can come from a lawyer or from another type of specialist who is experienced in Social Security matters. Non-lawyers who are experienced in Social Security matters frequently offer their assistance free or for a nominal charge. (See Section 2a.) Although lawyers charge for their services, those fees are kept low by laws which restrict how much they can be paid for representing people in Social Security matters. (See Section 2b.)

Whether you should seek assistance from a lawyer or other specialist depends on whether one or the other is easily available to you, and with which one you are most comfortable. If you reach the stage of considering going to federal court, however, you should consult with an attorney who is experienced in similar cases.

Appointment of Representative Must Be in Writing

Once you decide on someone to represent you and that person has agreed to become your representative for the appeal, you must give the name of the representative on a Social Security form entitled Appointment of Representative. If the representative is not a lawyer, he or she also has to sign the form, agreeing to serve as your representative. If your representative is a lawyer, he or she only needs to be named on the form. The form is available at your local Social Security office, which is also where the completed form is to be filed.

a. Hiring specialists other than lawyers

The first place to look for a source of assistance with your Social Security appeal may be Social Security itself. Every written notice denying a claim is accompanied by a written list of local community groups and legal services organizations—such as disability rights groups, legal aid offices, senior counseling services—that either assist with appeals or refer claimants to appeal representatives.

The fact that you find someone through one of these groups or organizations does not guarantee that you will want that person to represent you; that will depend on how well you and the person communicate and whether you feel confident in his or her advice. But finding someone to assist or represent you through one of these organizations at least assures you that the person has experience in Social Security appeals and has backing from a legitimate organization.

Senior centers are good resources, too. Many have regularly scheduled sessions during which trained advocates can give you advice on your Social Security problems. Whether or not a particular senior center has such a program, it can usually refer you to a Social Security advocacy group that includes people trained to assist in Social Security matters. You can usually make use of these referrals if you have a disability claim, even if you are not a senior citizen.

Each state has its own agency or department handling problems of older people, including Social Security disputes. They are referred to, variously, as the Office, Department, Bureau, Division, Agency, Commission, Council, Administration or Center on Aging. In most cases, this state agency will be able to refer you to some place close to your home where you can obtain assistance in preparing and presenting your Social Security appeal. (See the Appendix for contact details.) Call your state's agency and explain that you are looking for someone to assist you with a problem concerning Social Security. The agency should steer you to a Social Security advocate or legal aid office handling Social Security matters.

Other sources of assistance with Social Security matters are religious and social groups, business and fraternal associations and unions. If you belong to such a group, it may have a referral service that can put you in touch with Social Security advocates.

Although many non-lawyer assistants and representatives provide free services, some charge a nominal fee and a few charge a substantial fee, although the amount is limited by Social Security rules. (See Section E3.) If you are considering having anyone assist or represent you, ask about fees and get any fee agreement in writing before you agree to have that person act as your representative.

b. Hiring lawyers

A lawyer may be available to assist or represent you through a legal services organization that has specialists in Social Security appeals. Legal services offices provide advice and representation for little or no money. The first place to look for legal services offices is on the list of references provided by Social Security along with its notice denying your claim. You can also find legal services offices—sometimes listed as Legal Aid—in the white pages of your telephone directory.

Beware, however, that in the steady campaign by the federal government over the past 15 years to slash public services for low-income people, many legal services offices have suffered staff cutbacks or have been eliminated altogether. So it may not be easy to find a legal aid lawyer who can help you with your appeal.

You may also find an attorney in private practice. Be aware, though, that most private lawyers know very little about Social Security; you need to find one who specializes in Social Security claims. The Social Security referral list will either give you the names of local attorneys who specialize in Social Security appeals or give you the name of an organization that gives referrals to such private attorneys.

Your local county bar association will also have a reference list of lawyers who specialize in Social Security appeals. And while in general these bar association referral lists do not always include the best lawyers, in Social Security appeal matters they usually do have the best people. That is because very few lawyers specialize in Social Security appeals, and the few who are expert in the field usually list themselves with the bar association.

Normally, lawyers cost a lot of money. However, Social Security rules strictly limit the amount of money a lawyer or anyone else can charge for a Social Security appeal, which may explain why so few lawyers specialize in the field.

3. Legal Limits on Charges

Whether your representative is a lawyer or other specialist, Social Security rules limit the fees he or she can charge. And not only are fees limited, but they must be approved by Social Security in each individual case.

a. Fee agreements

Many lawyers and some non-lawyers charge a fee only if, with their help, you win your appeal. If you win your appeal at any stage of the process, you will be entitled to benefits from the date you first applied for them—referred to as past due benefits. The lawyers take their fees as a percentage of your past due benefits. Social Security rules say that a lawyer or other representative can take as a fee 25% of your past due benefits, or $4,000—whichever is less. If the lawyer pursues a lawsuit for you in federal court, the court will allow attorney fees of 25% of all past due benefits, but without the $4,000 maximum.

Get It in Writing

If you come to a fee agreement arrangement with your lawyer or other representative, the representative must put it in writing, you both must sign it and the representative must submit it to Social Security for approval. This can be done at any time before your claim is approved.

Once the fee agreement is approved, the lawyer or other representative cannot charge you any more than the amount approved, except for out-of-pocket expenses incurred during the course of your appeal—for example, the cost of getting copies of medical records, or long-distance phone calls to former employers or medical providers.

b. Fee petitions

Some lawyers do not want to depend on winning your appeal and so instead will submit to Social Security a kind of bill called a fee petition. The petition is filed when the appeal is finished, regardless of whether you win or lose. This petition lists in detail each service the lawyer provided for your appeal and the amount of time the lawyer spent on each such service. The lawyer must provide you with a copy of the petition. If you disagree with any of the information on the petition, you must notify your local Social Security office within 20 days of the date you receive it.

Social Security examines the petition and determines a reasonable fee for the services. The fee almost never exceeds 25% of what your past due benefits are if your appeal succeeds, or 25% of what those benefits would have been if your appeal does not succeed. The lawyer or other representative cannot charge you any more than the fee Social Security decides on, except for out-of-pocket expenses incurred during your appeal. Social Security will send you a written notice of the amount it has approved under the fee petition.

■

Federal Civil Service Retirement Benefits

More than three million people are employed by federal government agencies and departments; millions more have previously been employed by the federal government. And while the salaries of these government jobs are not always as high as some of those offered in the private sector, a comprehensive retirement system is one of the benefits that makes federal government employment attractive to many people.

This chapter discusses the two different federal retirement systems—the Civil Service Retirement System and the Federal Employees' Retirement System—and explains the benefits available under each.

Employees of State and Local Governments

Each state government has its own retirement system for its employees, and there are more than 6,000 local government retirement systems, called Public Agency Retirement Systems (PARS). It isn't possible here to discuss the rules of all these plans, but most of them work very much like the federal government's Civil Service Retirement System (CSRS), described in this chapter.

The amount of the pension to which an employee may be entitled is based not on total payroll contributions, as with the Social Security system, but on the highest average salary the employee reached and the number of years of employment. The age at which the employee can claim retirement benefits also depends on the number of years of employment.

As of July 1, 1991, work by employees of state or local governments who are not covered by an employer pension plan is covered by Social Security. These are usually part-time, temporary or probationary workers.

To find out what retirement plan covers your work for a state or local government agency and to determine the rules of that plan, contact the personnel or retirement plan office at that government agency, or the pension office of the public employees' union if you belong to one.

On request, the pension office should provide you with an estimate of how much your pension benefits would be if you claimed those benefits at the various retirement ages permitted by the plan.

A. Two Retirement Systems: CSRS and FERS

There are two entirely separate retirement systems for federal workers, depending on the date the worker was first hired. Until 1984, all federal government workers were part of the Civil Service Retirement System, or CSRS. Workers covered by the CSRS are not also covered by the Social Security system for the same work; the CSRS provides the only benefits those workers will receive for their years of federal government employment.

All federal workers hired from January 1, 1984, on were made part of a different plan called the Federal Employees' Retirement System, or FERS. Workers hired by the federal government after January 1, 1984, are also covered by Social Security, which means that work for the government simultaneously builds toward both FERS and Social Security benefits. (See Chapters 1 through 5.)

Employees already working for the federal government on January 1, 1984, had the choice of remaining in the CSRS or switching over to the FERS. For those who switched, years of employment under the CSRS were credited to the FERS.

The rules for both systems are quite similar, and both are administered by the federal government's Office of Personnel Management (OPM). Both the CSRS and the FERS are funded by automatic payroll deductions from federal employees and by contributions made by the particular federal agency for which the employee works. Under both systems, an employee can receive benefits if disabled, take early retirement, provide for a survivor, take a lump sum retirement amount instead of monthly benefits and can participate in a special savings program called the Thrift Savings Plan.

However, the rules about eligibility and benefit amounts are unlike those of the Social Security system. In particular, benefits are based on the highest average salary for any three years of employment but do not depend on the total amount contributed in payroll deductions. And while benefits may be paid to retirees and to survivors, they are not increased if the retiree has dependents.

This chapter discusses each of these benefits and the slightly different ways in which each retirement system administers them.

B. Retirement Benefits

The CSRS and FERS offer retirement benefits that are easy to qualify for and that can be paid out in any one of several ways. Both programs also permit retirement benefits to be structured so that they provide for a survivor after the retired worker has died. And both offer a special savings plan that provides tax benefits and, in the case of the FERS, includes contributions by the government.

Employees Who Left Federal Work, Then Returned

Some people worked for the federal government before 1984—when the CSRS was their only option for retirement benefits—then left their jobs, and rejoined the federal government after 1984. Those people may be entitled to retirement benefits under both systems.

If you worked for the federal government for at least five years but left that job before 1984, you may return to the CSRS if you start a new job with the federal government after January 1, 1984. If you do not choose to reenter the CSRS, you will work under the FERS and you may qualify for retirement benefits under both the CSRS and the FERS once you have more than five years of employment under each system.

If you were out of federal employment for at least a year and you choose to reenter CSRS, you will also be covered by the Social Security system, as are FERS employees. (See Section B1.) However, once you collect both Social Security benefits and a CSRS retirement annuity, your CSRS payment will be reduced by the amount of your Social Security benefits attributable to your federal government employment.

This prevents double payment, since most CSRS recipients do not receive Social Security benefits from their federal employment and the amount of CSRS benefits is calculated as if there were no additional retirement money from Social Security.

1. Who Is Eligible

If you have worked at least five years for the federal government as a civilian employee, you can qualify for a pension, referred to as a retirement annuity. And if you have worked at least five years at a federal civilian job, you can also get retirement credit for years of military service after 1956 if you pay a premium based on the amount of your military pay. However, you cannot get credit for military service if you are collecting a military retirement pension.

There are two types of retirement annuity under the CSRS and FERS: an immediate annuity and a deferred annuity.

a. Immediate annuity

You can retire at age 62 and immediately begin receiving an annuity if you worked for the federal government a total of five years. The years do not have to be consecutive, nor do they have to be for the same federal agency or department; any combination of jobs totaling five years of work will qualify you. If you have 20 years of service with the federal government, you can claim your immediate annuity at age 60.

With 30 years of service, a CSRS-covered worker can retire with a pension at age 55. A worker covered by FERS with 30 years of service can retire with a pension at what is called the minimum retirement age (MRA). That age is currently 55, but beginning in the year 2002, it is scheduled to rise two months per year. This rise in the MRA is coordinated with the similar rise in the age at which a person may take full Social Security retirement benefits.

If You Are Laid Off Before Becoming Eligible for Your Pension

CSRS and FERS rules allow some long-term workers to collect an immediate annuity even though they have been laid off from their jobs before reaching normal eligibility age for an immediate retirement annuity.

Under CSRS, a worker who has been employed for at least one year in the two years immediately before being laid off, and who is age 50 with 20 years of service, or any age with 25 years of service, may be eligible for an immediate annuity. Under FERS, the eligibility for this immediate annuity is the same, except that you need not have been employed within the past two years. The amount of the immediate annuity is reduced from its full amount by 2% per year for every year you are under age 55 when claiming this immediate annuity.

There are two circumstances in which you may not be entitled to an immediate annuity after losing your job. The first is if you have been fired for cause—misconduct, delinquency, poor job performance. The second is if you have been offered another job in the same agency, in the same geographic area, which is not more than two grades or pay levels below the current job, but you refuse to take it.

Rules for Law Enforcement, Firefighters, Air Traffic Controllers

There are special retirement eligibility rules for people who have worked for the federal government under the CSRS as law enforcement or firefighter personnel, or as air traffic controllers. Recognizing the high stress of these jobs, the government has set early retirement years and lower requirements for years of service. If you have been a law enforcement officer or firefighter under the CSRS, you can claim retirement benefits at age 50 with 20 years of service. If you have been an air traffic controller, you may be able to retire at age 50 with 20 years of employment, or at any age once you have 25 years of service.

b. Deferred annuity

If you end your federal employment before retirement age, you have a choice of leaving your payroll contributions in the CSRS or FERS, or withdrawing them in a lump sum when you leave employment. If you leave the contributions in the system when you end your federal job, you can claim a retirement annuity when you reach age 62. If you leave the money in the retirement system but later decide you want it without waiting for retirement, you can collect it in a lump sum at any time before you reach age 62.

Depending on the amount of your salary and your years of service with the government, it may be to your benefit to leave your money in the retirement system if you switch jobs. The amount of your federal retirement annuity would be based on your length of service and the highest levels of pay you received. (See Section B2.)

If you have worked for a long time and have reached a relatively high salary, you will be eligible for a high pension when you reach age 62. That pension will probably amount to much more money than the lump sum you could withdraw when leaving your federal job.

Before deciding which course of action to take, find out from the OPM exactly how much your lump sum withdrawal would be, and get an estimate of what your annuity would be at age 62. Of course, your decision will also depend on how badly you need the cash immediately upon leaving your federal job.

Example: Kazuo worked for the federal government from 1965 through 1992. In 1984, he decided to remain in the CSRS rather than switch to the FERS. By the time he left his government job, he had contributed over $10,000 to the CSRS retirement fund. Kazuo moved to another job outside the government, and did not immediately need the money in his retirement fund, so he left his contributions in the CSRS.

When he turns 62, he could collect a deferred annuity, which would then add to his monthly income from his job, or to Social Security retirement benefits if he had qualified for them by working long enough in the private sector both before and after his government job.

Example: Angela worked for the federal government from 1975 through 1995. In 1984, she switched her pension coverage from the CSRS to the FERS. By the time she left her job, she had contributed almost $8,000 to the retirement fund. When Angela left the federal government, she did not immediately need the money in her retirement fund, so she left her contributions in the FERS.

When she turns 62, she can collect her FERS deferred annuity, in addition to whatever she is making on a non-federal job, or to Social Security retirement benefits which she also earned from her years of FERS-covered government employment.

2. Calculating Benefits

Two factors are used to figure the amount of your federal CSRS or FERS retirement annuity.

The first factor is the number of years you have been employed by the federal government, contributing to the retirement fund. This can include years of military service if you also have at least five years of civilian service. Military service cannot be counted, however, if you are receiving a military retirement pension.

The second factor used to determine the amount of your annuity is what the retirement program refers to as your high-three average salary—your average salary for the three consecutive years in which you have had your highest earnings. High-three average salary is figured by adding together the three consecutive years in which you had the highest government salary—for example, $35,000, $35,000 and $38,000—and dividing the total by three. In this case, the total would be $108,000, which divided by three equals a high-three average of $36,000.

Both CSRS and FERS base the retirement annuity on the high-three average, but each computes the benefit differently.

Cost of Living Increase

Both CSRS and FERS benefits are increased annually to keep pace with the rising cost of living. As with Social Security benefits, these cost of living increases are tied to the rise in the Consumer Price Index, a yearly indicator of the cost of goods and services.

a. CSRS benefits

Once your high-three average is calculated, CSRS computes your pension benefits by adding:

- 1.5% of your high-three average pay, multiplied by your first five years of service; plus
- 1.75% of your high-three average pay, multiplied by the number of your years of employment over five, up to ten, plus
- 2% of your high-three average pay, multiplied by the number of years of service over ten.

Example: John put in 25 years working for a federal government agency. His highest three consecutive years of pay were $28,000, $30,000 and $32,000. His high-three average pay was $30,000. After 25 years, John's retirement pension would be figured like this:

- *1.5% of the $30,000 average is $450; that $450 is multiplied by the first five years of service, for a total for the first five years of service of $2,250; plus*
- *1.75% of the $30,000 average is $525; that $525 is multiplied by the second five years of service, for a total for the second five years of $2,625; plus*
- *2% of the $30,000 is $600; that $600 is multiplied by the remaining 15 years of service, for a total for the last 15 years of service of $9,000.*

Together, the three parts of John's pension would add up to a yearly benefit of $13,875.

One Worker With Separate CSRS and FERS Benefits

If you had years of service under the CSRS, left that job and later returned to work for the federal government under the FERS, you will receive two separate annuities, one using your high-three earnings under CSRS and the other your high-three earnings under FERS. (See Section A.)

CSRS Benefits and Social Security

If your federal employment is covered by CSRS, it is not also covered by the Social Security system. However, most people who worked for the federal government under CSRS also have worked, or will work, at some other jobs during their lifetimes. If that other work is covered by Social Security and you have enough work credits to qualify for Social Security retirement benefits, you can collect both your retirement benefits and your CSRS annuity.

If you receive a CSRS pension and also Social Security dependents or survivors benefits based on your spouse's work record—rather than Social Security retirement benefits based on your own work record—those benefits will be severely reduced. This is known as the pension offset rule. (See Chapter 4, Section E, and Chapter 5, Section F.) If you are receiving a CSRS annuity as the survivor of a CSRS worker, this rule does not apply.

b. FERS benefits

FERS has several different retirement benefits: full benefits, reduced early retirement benefits, deferred benefits for people who left their federal jobs before retiring and a supplement for long-time employees.

Full retirement annuity. Full FERS pension benefits are figured by taking 1% of the high-three average and multiplying it by the number of your years of service.

Example: Elvira worked 25 years for the federal government, switching to FERS in 1984. Her highest three consecutive years of pay were $38,000, $40,000 and $42,000. Her high-three average pay was $40,000. Elvira's retirement pension would be figured like this: 1% of $40,000 = $400; $400 x 25 (years of service) = $10,000, which would be her yearly pension annuity. And under FERS, Elvira would also collect Social Security retirement benefits as soon as she reaches eligible age for them.

Reduced benefits for early retirement. If you have accumulated enough years of service under the FERS, you can take early retirement with lower benefits. With ten years of service, you can take early retirement at the minimum retirement age (MRA), which until the year 2002 is age 55. (See Section B1.) Your benefits are reduced from the full retirement amount by 5% for each year under age 62 at which you claim retirement.

Deferred benefits if you leave. If you leave your federal job after at least five years service but before reaching retirement status, you can claim retirement benefits when you reach a certain retirement age, which depends on your years of service. With five years of service, you can claim retirement benefits at age 62. With ten years or more, you can claim retirement at the minimum retirement age, currently 55, but the benefit will be reduced by 5% per year for every year earlier than age 62 at which you claim benefits.

Reduced Benefits May Make Financial Sense

Although your deferred retirement benefits will be reduced 5% for every year under age 62 at which you claim them, it may still be to your advantage to claim as early as age 55. Since you are not adding any more years of service and your high-three salary remains the same, the base amount of your benefit will be the same whenever you take it. The 5% per year reduction may be offset by the cost of living increases you will receive each year, plus interest you can get by investing the money.

Annuity Supplement for Long-Term Employees. A special supplement to the retirement annuity is available at age 55 to people with 30 years service, at age 60 with 20 years service. The supplemental amount is based on total earnings and years of service, and is figured using a complex set of calculations. To determine how much your annuity supplement would be, contact the OPM office at the agency where you work.

3. Survivors Benefits

Unlike Social Security retirement benefits, the surviving spouse or other survivor of a federal CSRS retiree does not necessarily receive survivors benefits after the retiree dies. Instead, the federal worker has several choices at retirement. He or she can choose to:

- take a full retirement annuity—if so, no benefits will be paid to any survivors after the retiree dies
- elect a full survivor benefit for a current spouse, in which case the retiree's own annuity will be less
- have survivor benefits paid to someone other than a current spouse, or
- choose to provide a reduced survivor benefit, which means his or her own annuity will be lower than a full retirement annuity but higher than if a full survivor annuity were provided.

Supplement Reduced by Earnings

Unlike the standard FERS annuity, if you are under age 62, your annuity supplement is reduced by $1 for every $2 over a certain yearly amount in earnings from other employment after you retire from federal government work. This earnings limit rule works the same as the earnings limit for Social Security benefits. (See Chapter 2, Section D.)

a. Annuity without survivor benefits

At retirement, a CSRS or FERS employee can choose to take full retirement benefits without any provision for survivors. This makes particular sense if the retiree is unmarried and has no one who is likely to be in great need of financial assistance after the retired worker dies. It also makes good sense if the retiree, or retiree and spouse, have extremely limited income and immediately need the full retirement annuity to get by. Finally, it is a wise choice if the retired worker is married but his or her spouse is not likely to outlive the worker.

A worker who is married at retirement must specifically choose this no-survivor-benefit option by filing a form with the Office of Personnel Management (OPM). The worker's spouse must sign and notarize this form, which acknowledges that the retiree has given up the right to a survivor annuity. If the spouse's whereabouts are unknown, or the spouse is unable to understand the waiver and knowingly sign the form, a petition can be filed with the OPM to waive the requirement of a written consent form.

b. Annuity with full survivor benefits

If you are married when you retire from federal employment, and you and your spouse do not waive your right to a survivor annuity (see Section 3a), your retirement annuity will be reduced slightly to provide a lifetime annuity for your spouse if you die first. This full survivor annuity can also be provided for a former spouse, although if the worker has remarried, the current spouse must consent. A survivor benefit ends when the surviving spouse dies, or when the surviving spouse remarries before age 55. After age 55, the surviving spouse is free to remarry without losing the survivor annuity. The amount of full survivor annuity is slightly different for CSRS and FERS employees.

CSRS full survivor benefits. A CSRS retirement annuity is reduced, to provide full survivor benefits, by 2.5% of the first $3,600 per year, plus 10% of any amount over $3,600. The surviving spouse's annuity will be 55% of the full retirement annuity—that is, 55% of the amount before the 2.5% and 10% reductions are taken. And the 55% will include any yearly cost of living raises the retiree has received since the pension began.

Example: Ethel is eligible to receive a pension of $9,250 a year. She provides a full survivor benefit for Dante, her husband, so her own retirement annuity is reduced.

The first $3,600 is reduced by 2.5%, which means Ethel receives $3,510 of that first $3,600. The remaining $5,650 is reduced by 10%, leaving $5,085. Ethel's total pension is $8,595 a year instead of $9,250, a reduction of $655 a year. For that reduction, Dante is entitled to receive a surviving spouse's pension of 55% of the original $9,250, which works out to $5,087.50 a year if Ethel dies before Dante.

FERS full survivor benefits. An FERS full retirement pension is reduced by 10% to provide an annuity for the surviving spouse. The surviving spouse's annuity will be 50% of the retiree's full pension amount—that is, 50% of the amount before the 10% reduction. A retiring FERS worker can also choose a 5% reduction in his or her annuity, which will provide for a 25% annuity for a survivor. The survivor annuity will include any yearly cost of living raises the retiree receives after the pension begins.

Example: Rigoberto is eligible to receive a pension of $12,000 a year. He provides for a full survivor benefit for Doris, his wife, reducing his own retirement annuity by 10%, or $1,200. So instead of $12,000 per year, Rigoberto receives $10,800—$12,000 minus the $1,200 reduction. In exchange for that reduction, Doris will be entitled to receive a surviving spouse's pension of 50% of the original $12,000, which works out to $6,000 a year if Rigoberto dies before she does.

c. Survivor annuity to other than spouse

Both the CSRS and FERS provide for a 55% survivor annuity that can be paid to a person other than a current spouse. The amount your own retirement annuity is reduced to pay for this annuity depends on the difference in age between you and the named beneficiary.

If the beneficiary you name is older than you or no more than five years younger than you, your annuity is reduced by 10%. Your annuity is reduced 5% for every additional five years the beneficiary is younger than you—15% reduced if five to ten years younger, 20% if ten to 15 years younger, and so on.

If the person you name as beneficiary dies before you do, you can have your own annuity restored to the full amount for the rest of your life by simply notifying the OPM. Once you have chosen to name a beneficiary, however, you cannot change your mind and restore yourself to a full pension as long as that person lives.

d. Reduced survivor benefits

Both CSRS and FERS rules allow a retiring employee to divide up his or her annuity, taking the full amount of one part and using the rest to set up a survivor annuity. You can split up your annuity into survivor and non-survivor parts in any proportions you want.

For example, if you are entitled to a $10,000 per year annuity, you can choose to keep $5,000 as fully your own, and direct that the other $5,000 to be reduced for a survivor benefit. That second $5,000 would be reduced by the normal survivor percentages—2.5% of the first $3,600, and 10% of the remaining $1,400—leaving you $4,770 plus the untouched $5,000. This arrangement would provide a survivor with 55% of the $5,000 you assigned to the survivor annuity, which amounts to a yearly benefit of $2,750 after your death.

Deciding Whether to Reduce Your Annuity

It is not easy to decide whether to take a reduced pension to provide for another person. Each retiree and spouse, or other person who would be named as beneficiary, must decide for themselves. There are several things to consider in arriving at a decision.

Age. If your spouse or other potential beneficiary is considerably younger than you are and likely to outlive you by many years, taking a reduced pension now probably makes good sense. The 55% pension could go for many years to your beneficiary. On the other hand, if your beneficiary is considerably older than you are, there is little advantage to reducing your own immediate pension.

Health. If you are in poor health and may not survive for many years, then it is probably more important to provide a survivor annuity. Conversely, if your beneficiary is in poor health and not likely to survive you, it is probably better to take your full pension.

Income. If your spouse has or will have a substantial retirement pension or other income of his or her own, there is less need to reduce your own pension to protect your beneficiary. On the other hand, if your beneficiary is working now and earning a salary that will enable you to afford taking a reduced pension, that will permit your beneficiary to count on a survivor annuity after you are gone.

4. Thrift Savings Plan

In addition to the annuity pension plan to which both the employee and the employer contribute, the federal employee has the opportunity to build up tax-deferred retirement savings through the Thrift Savings Plan (TSP). The TSP is similar to 401(k) savings plans made available to some employees in the private sector.

a. Contributions to TSP account

The TSP for a CSRS worker is funded solely by the worker; it is a savings account of the worker's own money, which defers tax liability until retirement. For FERS employees, the government also contributes to TSP accounts, so that the TSP is both a tax-deferring savings plan and an additional pension.

CSRS contributions. CSRS-covered workers may put up to 5% of their before-tax wages into a TSP savings account. They pay no income tax on the income, or on interest earned, if they leave the money in the account until retiring from federal service with a CSRS annuity.

FERS contributions. The government automatically contributes an amount equal to 1% of an employee's pay into a TSP account for the employee. A worker who is covered by FERS may also put up to 10% of his or her pre-tax wages into the TSP savings account. If so, the government will match some of the amounts an employee puts in, in addition to its automatic 1% contribution.

The government matches dollar for dollar the first 3% of wages that an employee puts in the TSP account, and matches 50 cents per dollar for the next 2% of pay the employee puts in the TSP account. No income tax is paid on the income put into the TSP account, or on interest the money earns, if the employee leaves the money in the account until retiring from federal service.

b. Withdrawal from TSP account

When an employee retires from federal service with either a deferred or immediate annuity, the employee may take out his or her TSP money in a lump sum or in payments of equal amounts over time. The employee will owe income tax when the amounts are withdrawn. But a person who is no longer working full-time is likely to be in a lower individual income tax bracket and so will owe less in taxes.

The retiring employee also has the option to transfer the money to an Individual Retirement Account (IRA), which continues the money's tax-deferred status. The retiring employee may also use the TSP account funds to purchase an annuity, which is a plan that pays a set amount for life to the retired worker. Some annuities also permit additional payments to the spouse of a retired worker after the worker dies.

An employee who leaves federal service and withdraws the TSP money before being eligible for a retirement annuity will owe a 10% penalty tax on the money in the account. However, the employee has the option of transferring, or rolling over, the money in the TSP account to a non-government Individual Retirement Account (IRA) which will maintain the same tax-exempt status and avoids the tax penalty. The normal limit on yearly contributions to an IRA account does not apply to this one-time transfer of TSP funds.

Penalty for Working After Age 70

If you continue to work for the federal government after you reach age 70, you are not permitted to keep the full tax-deferred amounts in your TSP account. Internal Revenue Service rules require that you begin withdrawing certain minimum amounts from the account at that age. See the personnel administrator where you work to find out the details of this minimum required withdrawal.

C. Disability Benefits to Federal Workers

Both the CSRS and FERS provide benefits for employees who become disabled while working for the government.

1. Who Is Eligible

If you have worked for the federal government for five years or more under CSRS, you may be eligible for benefits if you become disabled before you reach retirement age. If you are covered by FERS, you need only to have been employed for 18 months.

2. Definition of Disability

Under both CSRS and FERS rules, you are considered disabled, if, because of disease or injury, you are unable to perform your job. In deciding whether a worker is disabled, the OPM determines whether:

- the employee can perform useful and efficient service in the specific job
- every reasonable effort to preserve the person's employment, such as making physical modifications to the jobsite, has failed, and
- there is no other vacant position in the same government agency and geographic area and at the same civil service grade or class as the current job that the employee could perform.

Unlike the stricter Social Security disability rules, under federal government disability regulations you may still be able to work at some jobs and qualify for benefits, as long as you cannot work at any vacant government job in the same agency at the level you had attained when you became disabled.

Proof of disability depends on information from two separate but equally important sources. First, your physician must write a letter to the OPM fully describing your disability and the date it began, and explain why he or she believes you are unable to perform your job effectively. You can assist your doctor by carefully explaining what your job entails and why your disability prevents you from performing it.

The second source of information to the OPM is your supervisor at work. He or she must give a written statement explaining your duties at work, how your disability impairs your job performance and whether any other job of comparable rank and pay is available to you. You can help yourself and your supervisor by pointing out the specific ways in which your disability interferes with your job and by noting when your disability began to make efficient work impossible.

3. Review of Disability Status

Your disability does not have to be permanent for you to receive federal employee's disability benefits. But the government, at its expense, will periodically require that you be examined by a physician to determine whether or not the disability is continuing.

As with your original claim for disability benefits, it will be helpful if you can get your own physician to write a letter detailing the specific ways in which your condition continues to be disabling. The letter will assist the government's doctor—who will probably only see you once, for a brief examination—in deciding that you are still disabled. The best approach is to have your own doctor write to the government doctor directly, so that the explanation of your condition and its limitations will already be in his or her file when you undergo your examination.

If your disability is found to be permanent, or if you reach age 60 without recovering from the disability, you will receive permanent disability retirement benefits. You will not be subjected to any further government examinations, and you will receive your disability benefits for life, unless you are later considered to have recovered.

You are officially considered recovered if:

- you voluntarily take any new job with the federal government
- your yearly earnings at jobs or self-employment outside the federal government reach 80% of the current pay for your previous government job, or
- a medical examination determines you are physically able to perform your job.

If any of these types of recovery occur, your disability payments will end either:

- on the date you begin reemployment with the government
- six months from the end of the year in which you earn 80% of your prior salary, or
- one year from the date of the medical exam that determined you had physically recovered.

4. Amount of Benefits

The amount of disability benefits is figured differently by the CSRS and the FERS.

a. CSRS disability benefit amounts

CSRS disability benefits are the lower of either 40% of your high-three average pay (defined in Section B2), or a portion of the regular pension you would have received if you had worked until age 60. This pension figure is computed by adding together the years of service plus the number of years remaining until age 60. Depending on this total, your high-three average salary is multiplied by a certain percentage—slightly more than 16% for ten years total; slightly over 26% for 15 years; slightly over 36% for 20 years; 40% for 22 years or more—to arrive at the disability benefits figure.

Example: Henry went on disability at age 55 after ten years of employment during which he had reached a high-three average pay of $34,000; 40% of his high-three pay would be $14,400. Using the alternate method of computation, the number of years remaining until he reached age 60 is five, which would be added to his number of years of employment for a total of 15 years. At 15 years, the high-three average salary is multiplied by just over 26%, for a total of $8,925. Since Henry is only entitled to the lower of the two computations, he would receive $8,925 per year in benefits.

Example: Alice went on disability at age 50, with 15 years of service. Her high-three average salary was $38,000. There were ten years until she reached age 60, which were added to her 15 years service for a total of 25 years. Because this is more than 22 years, her yearly disability benefit would be 40% of her high-three average salary—which is the same figure as the alternate method of computing benefits—amounting to $15,200.

b. FERS disability benefit amounts

Benefit amounts under FERS change over time. In the first year after disability, the disabled worker receives 60% of the high-three average pay, reduced by any Social Security disability benefits he or she may be receiving. From the second year of FERS disability until age 62, the worker receives 40% of high-three salary, minus 60% of any Social Security disability benefits. These benefits are increased yearly, based on a cost-of-living formula that is 1% lower than the rise in the Consumer Price Index.

At age 62, FERS computes what the disabled worker's retirement annuity would have been had he or she worked until reaching age 62. A benefit figure is determined by taking 1% of the total number of years of employment plus the number of years on disability up to age 62, and multiplying that by the worker's high-three average salary plus all cost of living increases since going on disability. That figure will be the yearly disability benefits for the remainder of the worker's lifetime.

D. Payments to Surviving Family Members

In addition to their retirement pension programs, the CSRS and FERS provide some financial support for the family of a federal worker who dies while still employed by the government.

1. Who Is Eligible

If a federal worker covered by either CSRS or FERS dies while still employed by the government, the surviving spouse and minor children can receive survivor benefits if the worker had been employed by the government for at least 18 months.

a. Benefits for spouse

For the surviving spouse to collect benefits, either the couple must have been married at least a year when the worker died, or the surviving spouse must be the parent of the worker's child. The survivor benefit is paid to the surviving spouse regardless of the spouse's age. A surviving spouse who also works for the federal government can collect both survivor benefits and his or her own retirement pension.

b. Benefits for children

The children of a deceased federal worker also receive benefits until each reaches 18 years of age or gets married. If the child is a full-time high school or college student, benefits can continue until age 22. If a child becomes disabled before reaching age 18, the survivor benefits may continue for as long as the child is incapable of full self-support. A child of an unmarried deceased worker also qualifies for a survivor annuity. If the unmarried worker was the father, the worker must have acknowledged the child or a court must have established paternity. A stepchild may also qualify for benefits if he or she lived with the worker in a parent-child relationship.

2. Amount of Benefits

The amount of survivor benefits depends on whether the deceased employee was covered by CSRS or FERS.

a. CSRS benefits

If a CSRS-covered worker dies while still employed by the government, his or her surviving spouse and qualifying children will each receive an annuity.

Spouse. The surviving spouse's annuity is 55% of the retirement annuity that the worker earned before dying. The survivor is guaranteed a minimum benefit of 55% of whichever is less, either:

- 40% of the worker's high-three average pay (see Section B2), or
- the amount the worker's retirement annuity would have been at age 60.

A surviving spouse loses the annuity if he or she remarries before age 55; after age 55, the annuity continues regardless of remarriage. If the second marriage ends before the surviving spouse turns 55, he or she can have the survivor annuity reinstated.

Children. The amount payable to the surviving children of a CSRS-covered worker depends on whether the other parent is still alive. Each qualifying child receives an annuity based on the following computations:

- If there is a surviving parent who was the spouse of the deceased employee, 60% of the worker's high-three average pay, divided by the number of qualified children, or approximately $350 per month (the figure goes up slightly each year, adjusted for inflation), whichever is less.
- If there is no surviving parent, 75% of the high-three average pay, divided by the number of qualified children, or approximately $400 per month, whichever is less.

b. FERS benefits

FERS benefits payable to a qualified surviving child are the same as for CSRS-covered employees. (See Section a, above.) However, they are reduced by any Social Security survivors benefits the child receives. (See Chapter 5.)

The amount of benefits a surviving spouse may receive depends on the number of years the deceased worker was employed. If the worker was employed for more than 18 months but less than ten years, the surviving spouse is entitled to a lump sum payment. That payment is approximately $22,000 (the figure goes up each year, adjusted for inflation), plus either 50% of the worker's yearly pay at the time of death, or 50% of the worker's high-three average, whichever is higher.

If the worker was employed for more than ten years, the surviving spouse also gets an annuity equal to 50% of what the employee's retirement annuity would have been.

These spouse's survivor benefits are not reduced by any Social Security survivor benefits.

E. Applying for CSRS or FERS Benefits

Decisions about both CSRS and FERS benefit claims are made by the federal government's Office of Personnel Management (OPM). You must file a written application for specific benefits. You may apply at the personnel office within the agency at which you work. If you no longer work for the agency, you may file your application at any OPM office.

You can get general information about benefits, application forms, the application process and appeals from decisions of the OPM by telephone from the OPM's Retirement Information Office. Recorded information is available 24 hours a day at: 202-606-0400. You can get answers to questions that do not depend on your personal employment records by calling: 202-606-0500.

To obtain information about the benefits available to you based on your personal employment record, go in person to your agency's personnel office or put your request in writing and send it to:

U.S. Office of Personnel Management
Employee Services and Records Center
Boyers, PA 16017

This is the office where employee records are maintained, and most questions can be answered by the staff there. If there is some complicated question they cannot answer, they will forward your inquiry to the Washington office of OPM, which will respond.

■

Veterans Benefits

In addition to the pensions and benefits that arise from both public and private civilian employment, many older Americans may be eligible for certain benefits based on their military service.

The Veterans Administration operates a number of programs providing financial, medical and other assistance to veterans. Eligibility may depend on financial need or time of service.

For older veterans, three major benefit programs are of particular value: disability compensation, veterans pensions and, perhaps most significant, free or low-cost medical care through VA hospitals and medical facilities. This chapter explains some of these benefits.

A. Types of Military Service Required

Veterans benefits are available only to people who had active service in a uniformed branch of the military—Army, Navy, Marine Corps, Air Force, Coast Guard, Women's Army Auxiliary Corps (WAAC) or Women's Air Service Pilots (WASP).

Active service is defined as either active duty or active duty for training.

1. Active Duty

Active duty means full-time service in one of the uniformed branches of the military forces mentioned above. It also includes full-time duty in the Commissioned Officer Corps of the Public Health Service or National Oceanic and Atmospheric Administration, formerly Coast and Geodetic Survey. And under some circumstances, full-time members of the Merchant Marine who served during wartime and wartime members of the Flying Tigers may also qualify.

Any length of active duty can qualify a veteran for benefits, with the exception of pensions for financially needy veterans, which require at least 90 days active duty service. (See Section C.)

2. Active Duty for Training

Generally, membership in the National Guard or Reserve Corps does not qualify a person for veterans benefits. However, if a person in the Guard or Reserves is called up for full-time duty in the armed forces, this period of service is called active duty for training. A person who is injured or becomes ill during that period of active duty for training may be eligible for veterans disability benefits if the injury or illness leads to a disability. (See Section B.)

B. Compensation for Service-Connected Disability

The Veterans Administration administers a system of benefits for veterans who have a disability that can be connected in any way to the period of service. More lenient than civil disability benefit programs, a veteran can receive assistance even if he or she is only partially disabled, and almost regardless of the cause, as long as it occurred while performing some duty related to service. And if your injury or illness first arose during a period of wartime, the rules for compensation are even easier to meet.

1. Who Is Eligible

Compensation is available for veterans who have a service-connected disability. Service-connected means that they were wounded, injured or became ill—or aggravated an existing condition—while on active duty, or active duty for training, in the armed forces. (See Section A.)

If your condition arose while you were on active duty during peacetime, your disability must have resulted directly from military duties. In reality, though, this requirement only rules out injuries sustained while on leave, for example, or while AWOL or committing some militarily punishable offense. Virtually all other activities—including playing for the base softball team, eating in the mess, traveling to and from training and authorized leave—are considered part of military duties.

The rules are even more lenient if the condition or injury occurred during time of war or national emergency, as officially designated and listed below. In such cases you may be compensated even though the injury or illness was completely unrelated to military duties, such as while on furlough or leave. These official periods of war or national emergency include:

- *World War I:* April 6, 1917, through November 11, 1918; if you had any active service during this basic period, the time is extended to July 1, 1921.
- *World War II:* December 7, 1941, through December 31, 1946.
- *Korean War:* June 27, 1950, through January 31, 1955.
- *Vietnam War:* August 5, 1964, through May 7, 1975.
- *Persian Gulf War:* August 2, 1990, through a date yet to be set by Congress or Presidential Proclamation.

Note that the periods of time considered part of the Second World War and the Korean War are longer than the time spans normally attributed to those conflicts.

Disabilities From Agent Orange and Radiation

Because of the military use of chemicals and radioactive materials, many veterans have fallen ill with serious, disabling diseases years after their service ended. But these veterans had no way to prove their disease was caused by exposure during military service. After sustained pressure from veterans groups, the Veterans Administration has finally admitted that exposure does indeed cause specific diseases. As a result, if a veteran was exposed to Agent Orange or radiation and later is disabled by certain diseases, the disability is presumed to be service-connected.

Vietnam and Agent Orange: *If you served in Vietnam and have become disabled by one of the following diseases, you are presumed to have contracted the disease through exposure to Agent Orange and may be eligible for service-connected disability benefits. Diseases include: prostate cancer, Hodgkin's disease, multiple myeloma, respiratory cancers (lung, bronchus, larynx, trachea), non-Hodgkin's lymphoma, chloracne, porphyria cutanea tarda, soft-tissue sarcoma and acute/subacute peripheral neuropathy.*

Radiation Exposure: *If your work in the military exposed you extensively to ionizing radiation, you may be eligible for service-connected disability benefits if you have become disabled by most types of leukemia or lymphoma, most types of cancer, brain or central nervous system tumors, thyroid disease and multiple myeloma.*

2. Amount of Benefits

The amount of disability compensation to which you are entitled depends on the seriousness of the disability. When you apply for disability compensation, your medical records are examined and VA personnel will examine you. Your disability is given a rating, based on the extent to which it interferes with the average person's ability to earn a living. This rating is expressed in percent of disability—0% to 100% disabled, in increments of 10%.

Unfortunately, this rating system does not normally take into account the real effect of your disability on the work you do. Rather, it applies arbitrary percentages—20% or 30% for the loss of a finger or toe, for example—to the theoretical average person's ability to earn a living. Obviously, the loss of a finger affects a piano player much more than it affects an insurance agent. But the VA usually applies its fixed schedule of disabilities to common injuries and diseases.

However, if your disability does not match any of the simple descriptions in the VA's rating system, the VA may consider the effect of your condition on the work you are able to do when rating your individual disability.

Benefits range from about $100 per month for a 10% disability to about $2,000 per month for total or 100% disability. If you have at least a 30% disability rating, your dependents are also eligible for some minimal benefits. Eligible dependents include your spouse and your children up to age 18, or age 22 if a full-time student, or of any age if disabled. The total amount received depends on the number of dependents and on the disability rating—the higher the rating, the higher the benefits.

3. Changes to Your Rating

Although most service-connected disabilities show up during or soon after military service, some conditions may not have appeared at all, or appeared but were not disabling, until years after you got out of the service. Regardless of when a condition actually becomes disabling, if it can be traced to injury or illness that occurred while you were in the service, it can be compensated.

Example: Claudio's knee was bashed while serving as a cook at a training camp during World War II. The knee healed well and Claudio had no serious trouble with it during the war or the years immediately following it. However, as he got older, his knee got steadily worse. His doctor diagnosed Claudio with a serious arthritic condition in the knee, a result of the wartime injury.

Because Claudio's knee condition resulted from his wartime service, he was entitled to claim disability benefits when the knee began to interfere with his normal activities, even though he made no such claim when he was discharged from the service.

Sometimes, a disability that rated low when it first appeared will grow progressively worse in later years. In such a case, a veteran can claim disability benefits even if he or she was previously rated by the VA as not disabled. Or the veteran can apply for an upgrading of an already existing disability rating if the condition has worsened over time.

Example: Ernie was an M.P. in Japan during the Korean War. While on leave, Ernie picked up a lung infection. The scarring from it, over the years, occasionally gave him minor respiratory difficulty. A few years after his discharge, Ernie applied for a service-connected disability. Although he picked up his illness while on leave, he was eligible for benefits because he had been on active duty during wartime, and he was given a 10% disability rating for his labored breathing.

As he got older, Ernie experienced more breathing difficulties, to the point that even mild exertion made his breathing painful and dangerously difficult. His doctor said that poorer circulation with age was making Ernie's lung condition worse. Since his doctor verified that his condition had worsened, Ernie could apply for an upgrading of his disability rating. The new disability rating was 40%, which meant not only that Ernie's own benefits would be higher, but that his wife was also eligible for some benefits as a qualifying dependent. (See Section B2.)

C. Pension Benefits for Financially Needy Disabled Veterans

A small monthly cash benefit is available to a financially needy wartime veteran who is 100% disabled from causes that are not service-connected. Unfortunately, the amount is usually extremely low, only enough to bring the veteran's total income from all sources to just above the poverty line.

To qualify for this small cash benefit, the veteran must have had 90 days or more of active duty, with at least one day during a period of war. (See Section B1.) However, there is no requirement of service in or near actual combat.

A totally disabled veteran who meets the service requirements is granted an amount that will bring his or her total annual income—including income from private pensions, Social Security and SSI—up to minimum levels established by Congress. Those minimum levels, however, are extremely low: about $800 per month from all sources for a veteran with no dependents, about $1,000 per month for a veteran with one dependent—a spouse, or a child under age 18 or disabled—and slightly higher for each additional dependent.

Some veterans are entitled to a larger benefit if they live in a nursing home, are unable to leave their houses or are in regular need of aid and attendance. Veterans with out-of-pocket medical expenses are also entitled to a larger benefit.

Limits on Assets

The pension described in this section is not intended for veterans who have savings or other assets that could be used, or be cashed in to use, for living expenses. So, even a disabled veteran with little or no income will not qualify for the pension benefits if he or she has assets over a certain limit. The Veterans Administration usually considers $50,000 in total assets to be the limit, depending on the cost of living in the area in which the veteran lives and the amount of ongoing medical expenses which the veteran must pay out of pocket.

D. Survivors Benefits

Several VA programs provide benefits to a veteran's surviving spouse, and in some instances to surviving children.

The VA's Definition of Eligible Marriage

To collect benefits as the surviving spouse of a veteran, you must have been married to the veteran for at least one year and remain married at the time of his or her death.

If you were divorced from the veteran, you cannot claim survivor benefits. Further, even if you were still married when the veteran died, you cannot claim survivor benefits if you marry someone else.

However, if you remarried after the veteran's death but that later marriage has ended, you may again be eligible for survivor benefits through your first spouse's record.

1. Dependency and Indemnity Compensation

The Dependency and Indemnity Compensation (DIC) benefit is paid to the surviving spouse of an armed forces member who died either while in service or from a service-connected disability after discharge. However, no benefits will be paid to the survivor of a veteran who was dishonorably discharged.

The amount of the DIC benefit is calculated based on the highest rank held by the deceased.

The monthly benefits currently range from about $650 for the survivor of low-ranking enlisted personnel to $1,700 per month for the survivor of a high-ranking officer. There are additional payments if there are surviving children under age 18. DIC benefits are not reduced by any other income the surviving spouse may have, and are not affected by the amount of the survivor's assets.

2. Wartime Service Pension

A monthly pension is available to the surviving spouse of a veteran, regardless of whether death was connected to service, if that veteran would have been eligible for a wartime service pension. (See Section C.) This survivor pension, like the veteran's wartime pension, requires that the survivor have a low income, which includes money from any other pensions or Social Security benefits the surviving spouse receives. A veteran's surviving children may also collect a survivor's wartime pension after the veteran's death. Survivor pension benefits are about $500 per month for a single surviving spouse; a greater amount is available if there are dependent children.

3. Aid and Attendance

The Aid and Attendance (A & A) benefit is a special additional program to assist survivors who are eligible for DIC benefits and who are either living in a nursing facility or are housebound. If a survivor is in a nursing facility, an A & A benefit can add as much as $200 per month to whatever DIC benefit he or she is already receiving; for a housebound survivor, the benefit is usually slightly less. The amount of the benefit depends on whether the survivor has additional sources of income, and on the survivor's medical expenses.

E. Medical Treatment

One of the most important benefits available to veterans is free or low-cost medical care. The VA operates more than 150 hospitals throughout the country. In addition, there are a great number of outpatient clinics providing health care for veterans. Also, specialized care may be available at no charge through a VA hospital, while the same care might be unavailable or beyond the veteran's means in the world of private medicine.

Basically, a veteran is eligible for medical care in a VA facility if he or she is unable to afford the care elsewhere. And dependents and survivors of a veteran who has service-connected disabilities, or who receives a veterans pension, are entitled to care in VA facilities if they are unable to afford private care. The VA can also pay for long-term care of an elderly or disabled veteran in a private nursing facility if there is no space in a VA facility.

Even if you qualify for treatment at a VA medical facility, however, you may not always be able to get the care when you need it, or the treatment may be offered to you only at a VA facility far from your home. The reason for these limits, even for eligible patients, is that while there are close to 100,000 beds in VA hospitals, there are a lot more than 100,000 veterans and dependents who need medical care.

To meet the demand for medical care, and particularly for the limited number of hospital beds, the VA has established a priority system for deciding who gets treatment.

- First priority is for emergencies and for patients who have already begun treatment at a particular facility.
- Second priority goes to the treatment of service-connected conditions.
- The next level of priority is for patients who are receiving, or who are eligible to receive, VA disability benefits and who need treatment for non-service-connected conditions.
- The remaining hospital beds are usually filled by veterans and their dependents and survivors who are age 65, receiving a VA pension and who are unable to afford the care elsewhere.

Medicare and VA Medical Treatment

Many veterans who are eligible for VA medical treatment are also covered by Medicare. The general rule is that for any specific medical treatment, you can choose either of the benefits, but not both. This means that if you are treated at a VA facility but you are charged copayments by the VA, Medicare cannot pay for them. However, if you are treated by a private doctor or facility and the VA pays most but not all of the cost, Medicare may be able to pay some of the unpaid amount. If you are treated by a private doctor or facility and Medicare covers the bills, you cannot submit any unpaid portion to the VA.

There is a significant exception to this rule, which occurs where the VA and Medicare cover different services. For example, if the VA authorizes you to receive treatment at a private facility but does not cover all the services you receive, Medicare can pay for any of those services if Medicare does cover them.

Additional Veterans' Programs Are Available

This chapter explains the major programs for which older veterans are usually eligible. However, the VA administers many more programs which a veteran may find useful. The VA also provides financial support for education and vocational training, life insurance, home loans and other housing assistance and a National Cemetery burial program. Eligibility requirements vary for each of these programs, but either active duty or active duty for training are usual requirements. (See Section A.)

F. Getting Information and Applying for Benefits

The VA maintains large Regional Offices in major cities, and many smaller offices known as Veterans Centers in cities both large and small. Although applications are processed and decisions made at the Regional Offices, the Veterans Centers provide information about benefits and claims. The Veterans Centers can also provide you with application forms for various benefits, assist you in filling them out and help you with any appeal if you are denied a benefit.

To find either the Regional Center or the Veterans Center nearest you, look in the Government Pages at the beginning of the white pages of the telephone directory under United States Government, Veterans Affairs Department. The Veterans Administration also has an extensive Website at http://www.va.gov that can be accessed via computer through the Internet.

When appearing in person at a Veterans Center, the veteran should bring discharge papers, medical records if applying for disability benefits and wage or tax records indicating current income if considering an application for wartime service pension benefits. A survivor should bring the veteran's discharge or other military papers, marriage certificate and recent wage or tax records.

Requests for medical treatment or admission to a VA medical facility, or VA coverage of medical treatment by a private facility, is usually handled at the admitting office of the VA medical facility or clinic itself. A veteran seeking medical attention at a VA hospital should bring discharge papers, documents indicating that the veteran is receiving VA disability benefits and whether or not any medical condition is service connected, and documents indicating if the veteran is receiving a VA pension.

■

Private Pensions and 401(k) Plans

Pension plans—retirement funds for employees paid for or contributed to by some employers as part of a package of compensation for the employees' work—became widespread during the Second World War when there were more jobs than workers. Employers used extra benefits such as pensions to attract and keep workers without violating the wartime wage freeze rules. And although no law requires employers to offer pension plans, pensions have become a crucial part of labor negotiations and individual job decisions.

Since the 1980s, however, the number and scope of pension plans have been steadily shrinking and the number of workers covered by pension plans has diminished greatly. This is part of an overall decrease in job stability. Workers are far more frequently laid off, or fall victim to company "downsizing," and as they lose their jobs they also lose the pension benefits that go with longtime employment for the same company. At the same time, fewer companies offer traditional pension plans to most workers, although most executives and upper management still enjoy retirement packages and profit-sharing. With secure, quality jobs scarce, employers no longer have to offer a pension plan to attract most workers.

At some companies, pension plans have been replaced with 401(k) deferred compensation plans. 401(k) plans are not so much pension plans as controlled savings and investment plans—financial structures into which employees can place a certain amount of their wages and the taxes on them are deferred until retirement. Employers have lower administrative costs for these plans than for traditional pension plans, have no obligation to contribute any set amount per year to the employees' accounts and in many plans, do not contribute at all.

This chapter explains how traditional pension plans operate, so that you can understand the information about any specific plan provided by your employer, and so that you can make good decisions about the form in which to take pension benefits. It also discusses what legal protection you have if your pension plan fails or your employer goes out of business. And it explains the relationship between private pension payments and Social Security retirement benefits. The chapter also briefly explains 401(k) deferred compensation plans, which may also be part of an employee's retirement financial picture. (See Section H.)

A. Types of Pension Plans

A pension is an agreement between you and your employer—or among you, your union and your employer—under which the employer contributes a certain amount of money during the years you work. In most pension plans, the employee must also contribute. These contributions create a fund out of which you are paid a certain amount when you retire, usually at age 65, but which often pay a smaller pension at younger ages.

The amount of your pension will depend, in most plans, on the number of credits you accumulate during your years of work with a particular employer. Once you are participating in a pension plan, you begin to accrue or accumulate these benefit credits, usually counted in terms of years of employment. Upon retirement, pension plan administrators determine whether you have enough credits to qualify for a pension. If you qualify, the amount of your pension is determined either by the number of accrued years of employment or by how much has been contributed to your pension account, depending on the type of plan. (See Sections A1 and A2.)

Pensions come in several shapes and sizes, but most plans can be divided into two basic categories: defined benefit and defined contribution plans.

Beware of Plan Integration

No matter what type of pension plan you have, the benefit you actually receive may be much lower than figures presented by the plan first indicate if the payments are integrated with Social Security benefits. (See Section A3.)

1. Defined Benefit Plans

Under a defined benefit plan, you receive a definite, predetermined amount of money when you retire or become disabled. The amount you receive is based on your years of service with a particular employer. Most often, your monthly benefit is a fixed amount of money for each year of service. For example, a plan may pay $20 per month for each year of service. If you worked 20 years for that company, your pension would be $400 per month.

Payments under a defined benefit plan may also be calculated on a percentage of your salary over the years. In such plans, the benefit is figured by taking your average salary over all the years you worked, multiplying that average by the fixed percentage established by the pension plan, and then multiplying that total by the number of years you worked for the company.

Pension Plans and Individual Retirement Accounts

Many people take advantage of a tax break offered by the Internal Revenue Code by contributing up to $2,000 each year to an Individual Retirement Account (IRA). You pay no income tax on contributions to an IRA, or on the interest it earns, until you withdraw the money at age 59-1/2 or later.

However, most people may contribute to an IRA only if they are not working in jobs for which their employers provide a pension plan. And IRAs are generally not available to both spouses in a married couple even if only one of them participates in an employee-sponsored pension plan.

For lower income workers, there is an exception to this prohibition on combining an IRA with a pension plan. If you, or a spouse, participate in an employer-sponsored pension plan and your annual adjusted gross income is less than $25,000—$40,000 for a couple filing jointly—you can make IRA contributions and take the full tax deduction. If you earn between $25,000 and $35,000 in adjusted gross income—between $40,000 and $50,000 for a couple—the amount of your IRA tax deduction is reduced: for every $1,000 of income over the limit, the $2,000 IRA tax deduction is reduced by $200.

Even if you cannot get the immediate tax deduction for IRA contributions because you participate in a pension plan and earn more than the income limit, the earnings on any contributions you have made remain tax deferred until retirement.

Once you and your spouse retire or move to another job without a pension plan, you can invest in an IRA and take the full tax deduction. And you can continue to contribute to an IRA even after you begin collecting pension benefits.

Example: Bob's average salary over 20 years employment with one employer was $20,000 per year. The company's pension plan used 1% of yearly salary as the pension base. Bob's pension would be calculated by taking 1% of his average salary of $20,000, which is $200. That amount would then be multiplied by Bob's 20 years of service, for a yearly pension of $4,000.

a. No adjustment for inflation

One of the biggest drawbacks of defined benefit plans is that the benefits paid are not adjusted for inflation. The amount you receive in the first year of retirement will be the same as that received in your 20th year of retirement.

Particularly if you retire relatively young and healthy, the defined benefit pension payment that seems sizable to you when you first retire may be woefully inadequate in the later years of your life. If you know that your primary retirement pension will be a defined benefit plan, plus Social Security benefits, you must try to make long-range plans—reduced expenses, increased savings, post-retirement sources of income—which take into account what will be the declining value of your pension over the years.

b. Benefits not affected by private sector pensions

Social Security retirement, dependents and survivors benefits are reduced for people under age 70 who earn more than a certain amount of income each year. However, Social Security counts only income earned from work performed during the year. It does not count income you receive from work you did earlier—and that includes pension benefits, which are based on income from previous years of work. You can receive any amount of private pension benefits without reducing your Social Security benefits in any way. (See Chapters 2 through 4.)

Unfortunately, the reverse is not always true. Some pension plans reduce payments to you if your plan is integrated with Social Security benefits. (See Section A3.)

2. Defined Contribution Plans

Defined contribution plans do not guarantee any particular pension amount upon retirement. They guarantee only that the employer will pay into the pension fund a certain amount every month, or every year, for each employee. The employer usually pays a fixed percentage of an employee's wages or salary, although sometimes the amount is a fraction of the company's profits, with the size of each employee's pension share depending on the amount of wage or salary.

Upon retirement, each employee's pension is determined by how much was contributed to the fund on behalf of that employee over the years, plus whatever earnings that money has accumulated as part of the investments of the entire pension fund.

Example: Earline worked for a company that had a defined contribution pension plan. She had 25 years of accrued benefits when she retired. The plan called for the company to pay into the pension fund 6% a year of an employee's salary. Over the 25 years Earline was covered, her average salary was $15,000 a year. The company had to contribute 6% of $15,000, which is $900, for each of her 25 years—a total of $22,500. If the pension fund money was invested at an average return of 7% a year, Earline's personal pension account would be over $30,000 upon retirement.

3. Integrated Plans

Some pension plans are integrated with Social Security retirement benefits. In such plans, the monthly or yearly pension benefit is reduced by all, or some percentage of, the retiree's Social Security check—although since 1988, the law has required that the plan leave you with at least half of your pension. Social Security benefits can wipe out your entire integrated pension plan earnings for pensions earned before 1988, if those benefits are greater than the pension amount.

These integrated plans work in one of two ways, either establishing a benefit goal for your combined Social Security and pension benefits, or reducing your pension by a set percentage of your Social Security benefits.

a. Benefit goals

Some integrated plans set up what is called a benefit goal for your retirement—the amount of money you should have from a combination of pension and Social Security retirement income. The plan's benefit goal is usually a percentage of your average pre-retirement income. Your pension amount is then only what is needed to make up the difference between your Social Security benefits and this pre-determined benefit goal.

Example: Roberto worked for a company that had an integrated pension plan that set a benefit goal of 40% of the retiree's final salary. Roberto was making $28,000 a year when he retired, so his benefit goal was $11,200 (40% of $28,000) a year, or $933 a month.

Based on his years of service, the company's plan would have owed him $500 a month, without integration. But Roberto also received $650 a month in Social Security retirement benefits, bringing his total Social Security and pension benefits to $1,150 a month. This is $217 more than the benefit goal of $933 a month. So Roberto's pension would therefore be reduced by $217, from $500 a month to only $283 a month from the pension plan.

No Effect for Cost of Living Increases

One small consolation about integrated plans is that once your pension is reduced to fit with your Social Security benefits into the benefit goal, it cannot be reduced further when Social Security benefits rise because of cost of living increases. Although this difference may amount to only a few dollars each year, over all the years of your retirement it could amount to a large increase.

Legal Controls on Pensions

In the past, having a pension plan and collecting on it were not always the same thing. Many people were promised a pension and contributed to the plan for years, only to find that the plan's funds had been stolen or wasted by the company before they could claim their pensions. For other workers, the company went out of business, sometimes under the guise of a buy-out by another company or a convenient bankruptcy, which left the company executives holding stock and positions somewhere else and the employees who expected a pension holding the bag.

Since the passage of the Employee Retirement Income Security Act of 1974, or ERISA, at least some of the worst sorts of these disappearing pension acts have been halted. To protect pension rights, ERISA:

- sets minimum standards for pension plans, guaranteeing that pension rights cannot be unfairly denied or taken from a worker
- provides some protection for workers in the event certain types of pension plans cannot pay the benefits to which workers are entitled, and
- requires that employers provide full and clear information about employees' pension rights, including the way pension benefits accumulate, how the company invests pension funds, and when and how pension benefits can be collected.

b. Benefit offsets

Another common variety of integrated pension is the offset plan, which reduces or offsets pension benefits by a certain percentage of Social Security benefits. For example, an offset plan might reduce your pension benefits by 50% of your Social Security benefits. If you had earned $250 monthly in pension benefits before the offset, but you receive $400 a month from Social Security, your pension would be reduced by $200—50% of the $400 Social Security benefit. In the end, you would only receive $50 a month from the pension fund.

B. Accumulation of Pension Credits

When an employer offers a pension plan, there are basic rules, established by law, for participating in the pension plan. The law also sets a minimum amount of work hours which qualify you for pension credits in any work year.

1. Right to Participate

You must be permitted to participate in a pension plan if you are age 21 or older and have worked for the company for at least one year. One year means a total of 1,000 hours at work in a 12-month period beginning your first day of work; that is an average of 20 hours a week for 50 weeks.

To participate in a plan simply means that your time at the job will be counted toward qualifying for retirement benefits, and the employer must begin making contributions to your pension account if the plan requires ongoing employer contributions. It does not necessarily mean that you will receive a pension, which is a matter that has different rules. (See Section C.)

Although you must be permitted to participate in an employer's pension plan if you meet age and length of employment requirements, it is lawful for an employer to have separate, additional fringe benefits, such as profit sharing, for some categories of employee but not others. Typically, a company will have a pension plan for all employees but additional benefits for executives, or for employees on yearly salary, which exclude employees who work for hourly wages. This distinction is lawful as long as all employees are permitted to participate in the pension plan.

2. Accumulating Pension Credits

The amount of your benefits at retirement depends, in most plans, on the number of pension credits you have accumulated, or accrued, during your years of work with a particular employer. You begin to accrue these benefit credits, generally counted in years of employment, as soon as you are eligible for the plan, usually beginning with the second year of employment.

From the time you begin participating in the plan, you must receive at least 50% pension credit for any year in which you work 1,000 hours or more. The specific amount of hours required to earn full pension credit is up to the individual plan. Upon retirement, the pension plan determines whether you have enough credits under the particular plan's rules to qualify for a pension. The amount of the pension depends on the type of plan and its rules regarding the amount of contributions to your pension fund or the percentage of your salary it will pay. (See Section A.)

C. Vesting of Pension Benefits

Every pension plan establishes a level of accumulated benefits—years of employment—after which you have a legal right to receive a pension at retirement based on those benefits, whether or not you continue to work for that employer up to retirement age. When your accumulated benefits reach this level, they are referred to as vested benefits.

The federal ERISA law does not dictate specific vesting rules each pension plan must follow. However, it has set up mandatory minimum vesting levels protecting workers who have spent several years with the same employer.

It may be important to understand how vesting works in a pension plan for several reasons. Before retiring or changing jobs, you will want to know whether your pension rights have vested. Also, in many pension plans there are different levels of vesting, so you must learn what those levels are to know how much of a pension to count on, and when is the best time to leave the job.

All pension plans are required by law to meet certain minimum vesting schedules. The law regulating pension vesting was changed in 1989, however, and so two sets of rules apply. The first set applies to those who ended their work under a particular pension plan before 1989. A second set of rules applies to those who were still working in 1989 under a pension plan started earlier, and to those who began work in 1989 and later.

The Importance of Vesting When Leaving or Changing Jobs

If you have worked for the same employer for less than ten years, the company's pension plan vesting rules will determine how much of a pension you are entitled to, or whether you are entitled to any pension at all.

If you are considering retiring or leaving for another job and have not yet worked ten years for your current employer, check the company's vesting rules before making a decision about when to leave. You may find that by working an extra year or two, or even just an extra few months, your pension rights will vest, or will reach a higher vesting level, but that if you leave or retire immediately you will have a smaller pension, or no pension at all.

Similarly, if you are considering a new job, you should find out the vesting rules for that employer's pension plan. If you intend to work at the job for only a few years but the vesting rules require a long period of service before you gain pension rights, the job may not be as attractive as a job with a different plan that has partial vesting within a short time.

1. Cliff Vesting

This is one of the most common vesting plans. Under cliff vesting, once you reach a set number of years of employment—that is, the cliff—your pension benefits are 100% vested. This means you have a right to receive the full amount of benefits normally paid at retirement to someone with the number of years you have with that employer. Once you reach 100% vested status, you will receive your full pension at the plan's standard retirement age—usually set at age 65, but plans may set an earlier or later age—even if you leave the company before retirement age.

However, if you leave the company before you reach the cliff age, none of your benefits are protected and you will receive no pension at all from that employer's pension plan.

The amount of your pension will be based on the number of years you worked for that company while participating in the pension plan. Because most plans do not enable you to accumulate benefits until after one year of employment, your benefits years are usually one less than your actual years of work.

Example: Birtukan retired after 23 years with the same company. The company's cliff vesting pension plan paid an average of $10 a month for each year of service after participation began. Birtukan's pension rights vested after ten years with the company. She had 23 years of employment but only 22 years after her pension participation began, so she receives a pension of $10 a month multiplied by 22 years, for a monthly total of $220.

a. Pre-1989 employment

If you were employed at a job with a pension plan and left that job before 1989, your cliff vesting pension must be 100% vested if you had ten years of employment.

b. 1989 and later employment

If you were working for an employer in 1989 or later, regardless of when your employment started, your benefits under a cliff vesting plan become 100% vested after five years employment.

Some Union Plans Continue

Although in general you must be 100% vested after only five years of work if your employment continues in 1989 or after, certain union-negotiated contracts are permitted by law to continue with a ten-year cliff vesting rule. If your pension plan was part of a collective bargaining agreement between your union and a multi-employer industry group, the ten-year rule may continue in effect for the life of the contract. Check with your union pension representative to determine the vesting rules for your plan.

2. Graded Vesting

Graded vesting ensures some benefits to a worker after only a few years of service, with increasing benefits for each year of employment until the worker is 100% vested. The advantage of graded vesting is that a worker gets some pension protection several years before he or she would have gained protection under cliff vesting. The disadvantage is that it takes more years of work for the same employer to become 100% vested.

a. Pre-1989 employment

If you left employment before 1989, graded vesting ensures some benefits after five years of employment, with full vesting after 15 years. After the first five years, you are 25% vested. For each year of service after that, you receive another 5% vested benefits. After ten years of service, your vesting increases 10% per year until you are fully vested after 15 years. Keep in mind that 25% vested, for example, means that at retirement you would be entitled to receive 25% of the full pension to which someone with your same number of years of accrued benefits would be entitled if they were fully vested.

The chart below illustrates a graded vesting plan. In this defined benefit plan, $10 per month is earned for each year of service.

Example: Joachim retired in 1988 after 11 years with a company with a graded vesting pension plan that pays $20 a month for each year of service. After 11 years of service, Joachim would be 60% vested, with ten years of accrued benefits. He would receive 60% of ten years—the first year of employment he accrues no pension benefits—multiplied by $20 a month. That works out to $120 a month. If Joachim waited four more years to retire, he would have 15 years of service which would make him 100% vested. In that case, he would have 14 years of accrued benefits and be 100% vested, for a pension of $280 a month.

b. 1989 and later employment

If you were working for an employer in 1989 or later, regardless of when your employment started, your benefits under a graded vesting plan become 20% vested after only three years of employment. Vested benefits increase 20% a year after that, with 100% vesting reached after seven years.

Pre-1989 Graded Vesting

Years of Service		% Vested		Years of Service		$/Year		Pension/Month
5	=	25%	x	4	x	10	=	10
10	=	50%	x	9	x	10	=	45
15	=	100%	x	14	x	10	=	140
20	=	100%	x	19	x	10	=	190

3. Rule of 45 Vesting

A Rule of 45 vesting plan may not be used for employees who were working in 1989 or later. But if you stopped working for an employer before 1989, your pension rights may be measured by a Rule of 45 plan.

This rule combines the worker's age with years of service to determine when benefits are vested. Under the Rule of 45, your benefits are 50% vested after five years of employment if, adding your age plus your years of employment, the total is 45 years or more. After you reach this 50% vested level, each year of work earns you another 10% vesting. You become fully vested five years after meeting the 45 years test.

You can also meet the vesting limits under the Rule of 45 in another way: no matter what your age, you become 50% vested after ten years of employment. And once you reach the 50% vested level, you get another 10% vesting for each additional year of work.

The chart below illustrates the alternative methods of becoming vested under the Rule of 45.

Example: When he was 30 years old, Phil began working for a company with a Rule of 45 vesting plan. At age 38, Phil became 50% vested because his age (38) plus years of service (8) added up to more than 45 years. If Phil had stopped working for the company at age 38, the company would have to pay him, when he reaches retirement age, a pension worth 50% what a fully vested employee with eight years of employment would get.

If Phil were still with the company at age 43, he would be 100% vested. With the five more years work after reaching 50% vesting at age 38, he gained 50% more vesting—10% for each year. If Phil left his job at age 43, he would receive a full pension based on 12 years of accrued pension benefits—13 years of employment minus the first year, which does not count for pension accrual purposes.

Vesting Under the Rule of 45

Years of Service	and	Age + Service	or	Years of Service	=	Percent Vested
5		45		10		50
6		47		11		60
7		49		12		70
8		51		13		80
9		53		14		90
10		55		15		100

4. Year Vesting

Also called class year vesting, this arrangement was used only with defined-contribution plans, and applied only to employment that ended before 1989. Under year vesting plans, pension fund contributions are vested within five years of the end of the year in which the contributions are made.

For example, contributions made to the pension plan in 1980 would be 100% vested at the end of 1985. When you retire or leave a particular employer, the contributions made to your pension account up to five years before you left work would be vested, and your retirement pension would be based on those amounts, but not on any contributions made during your last five years with the company.

D. How Pension Benefits Are Paid

Pension plans pay retirement benefits in a number of different ways. And often a single plan will offer several options. As you near retirement age—usually 65, but many plans offer early retirement (see Section D5)—it is important to consider how you will receive your pension benefits. The form of payment not only determines when you receive benefits, but also how much in total you receive and whether your spouse or other survivor can continue to get benefits after you die.

The most common kinds of payment plans are discussed below.

Rules Regarding Breaks in Service

Problems may arise for workers who are laid off, become ill or disabled, or who take a lengthy leave of absence before their pension benefits have vested. If your employer terminates your employment and then rehires you as a new employee, you will have lost all the benefits you had accrued before your break in service, as the time off work is called.

The federal ERISA law, however, protects those accrued benefits in some situations.

- You do not lose your accrued benefits because of a break in service if you work over 500 hours for one employer during a year. However, the employer does not have to give you pension credit for that year if you work less than 1,000 hours.
- Even if you work less than 500 hours in a year, you do not lose your previously accrued benefits unless you are off work as many years consecutively as the number of years of accrued benefits you had before the break in service. For example, if you have three years of accrued benefits in your pension plan, you lose those benefits only if you were off work from that employer—worked less than 500 hours in the year—for three consecutive years.

The break in service rule assumes that you eventually return to work for the same employer. If you do not return, you will lose the accrued benefits for good and have no right to any pension unless your benefit rights had vested before you left work.

If you had a break in service before 1974 when ERISA went into effect, the law doesn't protect you. A pension plan may exclude years before a break in service if the break occurred before 1974.

Be Mindful of Tax Consequences

How you receive your pension benefits may depend on your current needs, your life expectancy and your family situation. But part of your decision may be based on the taxes you'll have to pay if you receive your benefits in one form or another. These tax matters are sorted and explained in straightforward language in *IRAs, 401(k)s & Other Retirement Plans: Taking Your Money Out*, by Twila Slesnick and John Suttle (Nolo Press).

1. Lump Sum Payment

Many defined contribution plans offer to pay you the entire amount accumulated in your pension account at retirement. If you need the money immediately to meet living expenses, this is an obvious choice. Also, this entire pension amount can serve as, or add to, a lump sum investment you wish to make in a business, home or other property. Or you may feel that you can invest the money in ways which will give you a greater return than the alternatives offered by your plan.

2. Simple Life Annuity

Annuities pay a fixed amount of benefits every year, although most annuities actually pay monthly, for the life of the person who is entitled to it. In a simple life annuity, when the person receiving the annuity dies, the benefits stop; there is no final lump sum payment and no provision to pay benefits to a spouse or other survivor. If you are relatively healthy when you claim your retirement, a simple life annuity may wind up paying you more over the years than a lump sum pension payment.

3. Continuous Annuity

Some plans offer an annuity that pays monthly installments for the life of the retired worker, and also provide a smaller continuing annuity for the worker's spouse or other survivor after the worker's death. If the worker dies within a specified time after retiring—usually five or ten years—the annuity will be paid to the surviving spouse or other beneficiary for the rest of that period. A retiring worker who chooses this option will receive less in monthly pension benefits—usually around 10% less—than would be paid under a simple life annuity.

4. Joint and Survivor Annuity

A pension plan that pays benefits in any annuity form is required to offer a worker the choice of a joint and survivor annuity in addition to whatever other form of annuity is offered. This form of annuity pays monthly benefits as long as the retired worker is alive, and then continues to pay the worker's spouse for life. Some pension plans also permit a survivor annuity to be paid to a non-spouse beneficiary, but the law does not require that such a benefit be offered.

A worker who chooses the joint and survivor annuity will receive slightly less in pension benefits than under a simple annuity plan; how much less is determined by the age of the worker's spouse or other named beneficiary. The younger the beneficiary—that is, the longer the pension is likely to be paid—the lower the benefits. The amount the survivor receives is usually half of the retired worker's pension amount, although a few plans provide for larger survivor payments.

The rules of many pension plans require a joint and survivor annuity to be the form of pension benefits to any married worker, unless the worker and spouse both sign a written document requesting a different payment form. These rules are intended to prevent a worker from cutting his or her spouse out of pension benefits without the spouse's knowledge.

Choosing the Right Annuity Plan

Before choosing any form of annuity, find out what your pension plan would pay under each alternative it offers. Ask the employer's pension administrator to give you the exact figures, in writing, before you make a decision.

If you need immediate cash, the lump sum payment will be attractive. However, if you or your spouse or partner plan to continue working for some time, an annuity will probably pay you considerably more money over time. If your spouse is likely to outlive you, some form of continuous or other survivor annuity is probably a good idea. If your spouse is likely to outlive you by a long while, then a joint and survivor annuity is probably the best choice.

When you near retirement age, the pension administrator at your company or union will send you a form on which you choose the annuity you want. If you don't receive a form, or you fail to let the pension office know what your choice is, you will automatically receive the joint and survivor annuity. If you want to choose one of the other types of payout, contact the pension office before your retirement date so that you can make your choice in writing.

5. Early Retirement Survivor Annuity

Many pension plans allow you to choose a reduced retirement pension at an age younger than the age at which full retirement benefits are available. Full retirement benefits are usually offered at age 65, although a very few plans still offer full retirement earlier. Early retirement age is usually between 60 and 65.

If your pension plan offers early retirement, it must also offer an early retirement survivor annuity. This kind of annuity gives the spouse, and in some plans another named survivor, a right to collect a pension if the worker dies before normal retirement age. For a survivor to collect such an early retirement survivor annuity, the worker must have reached either the company's early retirement age, or have reached an age ten years younger than the plan's normal retirement age, whichever is later.

In practical terms, this means you must have reached at least age 55. Also, you must have signed a form agreeing to take a reduced early retirement pension in exchange for the protection of your survivor by an early retirement survivor annuity. If your employer has an early retirement provision in its pension plan, you may sign this annuity request form shortly before you reach early retirement age. This choice may be a good one for you if you are planning on claiming early retirement or, because of health reasons, you are concerned that you may not live long enough to retire at your company's normal retirement age.

Working After Retirement

If your benefits have vested when you reach the retirement age established by your pension plan—usually 65—you are free to retire from the employer who pays your pension and work for someone else, or open your own business, while collecting your full pension.

However, if you return to work for the employer who is paying your pension benefits, the employer can suspend payment of your pension for as long as you continue working.

If you are covered by certain multi-employer pension plans negotiated as part of an industry-wide union contract, your pension benefits can be suspended if you return to work for a different employer whose employees are covered by the same contract. See your union representative to find out if your pension agreement is in this category.

E. Getting Additional Information

All employees must be provided with a Summary Plan Description that explains how a pension plan works and explains the benefit choices. An employee must be provided with a Summary Plan Description within 90 days after qualifying as a participant in the plan, usually one year after the first day as a full-time employee. The plan description explains rules regarding participation, benefit accrual, vesting, pay-out options, retirement ages and claim procedures. You are entitled to an updated Summary Plan Description from the personnel or pension plan administrator's office where you work, or at the pension office of your union.

In addition to the general plan description, you are entitled to a statement of your personal benefit account that explains how much in benefits you have accrued and what benefits have vested, or when they will vest. Not all employers provide this statement regularly; you may have to make a written request for it. You are also entitled to a copy of your benefit statement if you leave your job.

Each pension plan must make a yearly report to the federal government about the investments of the money in the plan fund. You should be able to see a copy of the latest annual report or to obtain a copy at minimal expense at the pension plan administrator's office.

And any time you have a question about your pension plan which is not answered by either the Summary Plan Description, your benefit statement or the summary of the annual report, you may make a written request for the information to the plan administrator. If the administrator's office does not give you a satisfactory answer, then direct your questions to the local area office of the federal government's Labor-Management Services Administration. You can find its number in the government listings of the white pages of the telephone book under United States Government, Department of Labor.

F. Procedure for Claiming Your Pension

All pension plans must have an established claim procedure and all participants in the plan must be given a summary of the plan which describes that procedure. If you don't have a plan summary, you can get one from the company's personnel or pension office. (See Section E.)

1. How to File

Pension claims must be filed in writing. Before you file your claim, compare each of the possible payment plans to see which one best fits your needs. (See Section D.) If no written claim is filed requesting a different payment plan, the pension will automatically be paid in the form of a joint and survivor annuity. When you file your claim, you will receive a written notice explaining the basis for determining the amount of your benefits and the method in which it will be paid.

2. Appealing a Pension Decision

If you disagree with either the amount of your benefits or the method in which they are to be paid, you have 60 days from the date you receive a written notice to file a written appeal of that decision. The details for where and how this appeal is filed are explained in the plan summary. If you are considering an appeal, or have filed one, you have the right to examine the pension plan's files and records regarding your pension account, and you can present written materials that correct or contradict information in those files.

Within 60 days of filing your appeal, the pension plan administrators must file a written decision on the appeal. If your claim is still denied, or you do not receive the full amount of the benefits to which you believe you are entitled, you have a right to press your claim in either state or federal court.

G. Protecting Your Pension Rights

Many people work long and hard for a company, expecting that a promised pension will be there when retirement arrives, only to find that the company is sold or goes out of business before a pension claim can be processed. Or the pension fund is mismanaged and goes broke, jeopardizing benefits. If these things occur, you have some protection under ERISA. (See Section A3.)

1. If Your Pension Plan Is Changed

When a company is sold or reorganized, it often changes the rules of its pension plan. However, once your pension benefits have vested under an existing plan, you cannot legally be deprived of any of those benefits by a change in the plan's vesting rules. The law does not protect you, however, if your pension rights had not yet vested when the pension plan is ended.

Under federal law, if the company you work for is taken over by a new company which keeps the existing pension plan, your years of service continue to accumulate and the benefits you receive must at least equal the benefits you would have received under the old plan. The law does not obligate a new company to continue paying into the existing pension plan, however. If the pension plan is discontinued, your benefits will not increase even though you continue to work. If the new company institutes its own pension plan, however, your continued work may accumulate credits under that plan, eventually entitling you to a second pension. These rules do not protect you from changes in a pension plan which occurred before ERISA went into effect in 1974.

2. If the Plan Ends or the Fund Goes Broke

In recent years, a number of pension funds have gone broke, either through mismanagement or outright fraud. Under ERISA, there is some protection against such pension fund collapse. The Pension Benefit Guaranty Corporation (PBGC), a public, nonprofit insurance fund, provides some limited coverage against bankrupt pension funds. Should a pension fund be unable to pay all its obligations to its retirees, the PBGC may pay some of the pension fund's unfulfilled obligations.

The PBGC does not cover all types of pension plans, nor does it guarantee all pension benefits of the plans it does cover. Only defined benefit plans are covered. And only vested benefits are protected by the insurance. Also, the PBGC only covers retirement pension benefits; other benefits, such as disability, health coverage and death benefits, are not usually covered. And once the PBGC steps in to administer a pension plan and make payments to current and future retirees, no additional pension benefits accrue for those still working. No pension benefits will vest if they have not already been vested under the plan's rules.

The PBGC will pay the full value of a retiree's or disabled worker's pension under the rule of the plan, but only up to certain limits. In 1999, those limits were $3,051 per month for a worker retiring at age 65, with lower amounts for those retiring earlier. The maximum amount increases slightly each year. If the pension was supposed to provide for survivor benefits, the maximum amount guaranteed is reduced by .09% for each year the spouse is younger than the deceased worker. If the spouse is the same age as the worker, the amount is decreased by 1%. If the spouse is older, the benefit goes back up by 0.45% for each year difference in age. And the PBGC will pay the full amount of the survivor's annuity.

If you have a question about termination of benefits because of failure of your pension plan or the sale or end of your employer's company, write or call the Pension Benefit Guaranty Corporation, Participant Services, P.O. Box 19153, Washington, DC 20036-9153; 202-326-4100. You may also get information from the PBGC Website at www.pbgc.gov.

You may also get information and assistance regarding your rights under pension plans from the independent, non-government Pension Rights Center, 918 16th Street, NW, Washington, DC 20006; 202-296-3778.

Enforcing Your Pension Rights in Court

You can file a lawsuit in federal court to enforce any rule or provision of the ERISA law, or any of your rights under a pension plan that is covered by ERISA rules. In particular, you can file a federal court lawsuit:

- to recover benefits that have been unfairly denied
- to change a ruling made by the pension plan that would affect your future benefits, such as a determination about eligibility, accrual, vesting, break in service
- to force the plan to provide information required by ERISA
- to correct improper management of the plan or its funds, and
- to protect any other right established by the rules of your particular pension plan or by ERISA.

H. 401(k) Deferred Compensation Plans

Many employers that offer retirement benefits do so through a 401(k) deferred compensation plan—the name taken from the number of an IRS regulation that provides the plan with its tax-deferred status. 401(k) plans are deferred compensation programs in which employees invest part of their wages, sometimes with added employer contributions, to save on taxes; they are not actually pension programs that establish a right to retirement benefits. This section explains the basics of 401(k) plans.

1. Structure of 401(k) Plans

In a 401(k) plan, an employee contributes out of his or her salary to one of several retirement investment accounts set up by the employer and administered by a bank, brokerage or other financial institution. Depending on the rules of the particular plan, the employer often makes some additional contribution in addition to the amount the employee sets aside. However, unlike traditional pension plans, the employer has no obligation to contribute anything and can change the contribution amounts from year to year. These plans are cheaper for the employer than more traditional pension plans because employees make the primary contributions from their salaries, the employer has no fixed obligation to contribute and when the employer does contribute, it does so as a tax-deductible business expense.

2. Investment Choices

401(k) plans do not require either the employee or the employer to contribute any set amount each year. An employee can contribute a limited part of his or her wages each year. That amount is limited to the lower of either 25% of wages, or a set amount established by the IRS each year—in 1999, the amount was $10,000. The maximum permissible contribution amount goes up each year with the rise in the cost of living. There is no legal limit on the amount an employer may contribute, but the amounts are usually a percentage of the amount of the employee's contribution.

A 401(k) plan usually offers the employee a choice among different investments for the deferred income. Some plans offer a selection of pre-approved savings accounts, money market funds, stocks and bonds and mutual funds. Other plans permit employees to select their own investment funds or even to buy individual stock shares on the open market. However, there are usually some limits on the number of investments offered and on the frequency and amount of changes in investments that can be made in a given period of time.

401(k) Plans Raise Tax Questions

A 401(k) plan offers some tax advantages over other types of company pension plans. Income tax on the funds invested in the 401(k) plan is deferred until you withdraw the money after retirement. Since most people's income is lower after retirement, the tax bite from 401(k) withdrawals is usually less than the amount you would have paid at the time you earned the money. Also, taxes on income earned from 401(k) plan investments are deferred until the money is withdrawn.

These potential tax advantages raise questions about when it is best to begin withdrawals and how much to withdraw from the plan. These tax considerations are fully explained in *IRAs, 401(k)s & Other Retirement Plans: Taking Your Money Out*, by Twila Slesnick and John Suttle (Nolo Press).

401(k) Investments May Be Risky
Along with choice of investments for the employee comes the risk of poor returns. Unlike traditional pension plans that sink or swim on the total pension fund's portfolio and are backed up by the government's Pension Benefit Guaranty Corporation, the amount of an employee's 401(k) plan fund at retirement depends entirely on how well the plan's individual investments do over the years. An employee who makes particularly risky investments could wind up with less in 401(k) funds than he or she invested.

3. Withdrawing Money

One of the advantages of most 401(k) plans is that they permit you to withdraw your deferred compensation earlier than pension plans. Most 401(k) plans permit withdrawal without any tax penalty at age 59-1/2, or at age 55 if you have stopped working. Funds may be withdrawn in a lump sum or in monthly allotments. Money that remains in the account, including future earnings, will not be taxed until withdrawal. 401(k) plans also allow your beneficiaries to withdraw the 401(k) funds without tax penalty if you die at any age.

If you withdraw funds before the age permitted by the rules of your plan, you will pay a 10% penalty on the amount withdrawn, plus all income taxes at your current tax rate. And IRS rules require that you begin withdrawing funds by at least age 70-1/2. The amount you must withdraw to avoid a tax penalty is determined by the IRS based on your age and the year you were born. The administrator of your plan can tell you your minimum withdrawal amount.

Some 401(k) plans also permit withdrawing funds without penalty if needed for a family emergency, such as for medical expenses, or for investment in a home. And in some plans, you can take out a loan from your own 401(k) funds, up to 50% of the total in the account or $50,000, whichever is less, if you have sufficient collateral and you repay it within five years. There are strict rules applying to such withdrawals and loans. Check with your 401(k) plan administrator or a financial advisor.

■

Medicare

The horrendous cost of medical care and medical insurance, coupled with the lack of a comprehensive health plan available to all, has rightfully been termed a national disgrace. Yet whenever discussion of this monumental failure makes its way into the political arena, proposals for creating a decent health care system run into dual roadblocks. The first is mounted by heavily bankrolled corporate interests—pharmaceutical, medical technology and hospital companies, the insurance industry and most doctors' groups—who fight any limits on their profit-making. The second is set up by politicians who refuse to take any steps which might be considered against the interests of the moneyed portion of the population who oppose equitable distribution of the nation's wealth.

In 1965, however, over howls of protest by many in corporate boardrooms and government, the Medicare national health insurance system was introduced as a way of providing a certain amount of guaranteed coverage for older citizens. And for over 30 years now, Medicare has been carving an inroad into the mountain of consumer health care costs. Medicare pays for most of the cost of hospitalization and much other medical care for older Americans, amounting to about half of all medical costs for those 65 and over. Medicare now provides this coverage for almost 40 million people, most of them age 65 and over.

Despite its broad reach, Medicare does not pay for many types of medical services, and pays only a portion of the costs of other services. In total, Medicare pays only about half of all medical costs for people over 65. And with attacks on Medicare gaining political momentum, the chunk of medical care costs Medicare will continue to cover is likely to be even smaller.

This chapter discusses the Medicare system, what it covers and how much it pays. Chapter 13 shows you how to apply for Medicare and take full advantage of its benefits. And a number of chapters that follow present detailed information about how to fill the gaps in Medicare coverage. Medigap supplemental insurance is discussed in Chapter 14, while the various Medicare managed care plans are sorted out in Chapter 15. If you have low income and few assets, Chapter 16 explains the government Medicaid program, which provides free coverage in place of buying private insurance or a managed care plan.

A. The Medicare Maze

Until recently, understanding Medicare and filling some gaps in its coverage was fairly simple. Every recipient followed the same procedures and received the same coverage. They went to any doctor, hospital or clinic they chose, the medical providers determined what services were required and, with few exceptions, Medicare paid its share of the bills.

This original form of Medicare is known as fee for service, meaning that Medicare pays the provider a set fee for each specific service. In covering medical costs not paid by Medicare, recipients had three choices. They could:

- pay out of their own pocket
- buy a private supplemental insurance policy—referred to as medigap insurance—that paid much of what Medicare did not, or
- qualify for Medicaid coverage, a federal program that pays almost all health care costs for low income recipients that are not picked up

by Medicare. (This program is called Medi-Cal in California.)

Beginning in the late 1980s, insurance companies broke into the Medicare market in a big way, offering an additional choice. They offered Medicare recipients the option of joining managed care plans that covered Medicare gaps and some services Medicare does not cover at all. These plans—the most common of which are Health Maintenance Organizations (HMOs)—are usually less expensive than medigap supplemental insurance policies.

"Medicare + Choice"—New Name, Same Game

In 1997, Congress gave a name to all Medicare options, called "Medicare + Choice." While the name sounds new and improved, Medicare choices remain just about the same as before. The new name simply refers to all the different Medicare-related insurance plans available to fill the gaps in basic Medicare coverage. The name Medicare + Choice itself does not refer to any particular form of supplemental coverage; it is just an umbrella title for the various insurance alternatives, most of which existed before the 1997 changes.

B. Medicare: The Basics

Medicare is a federal government program that assists older and some disabled people in paying their medical costs. The program is divided into two parts. Part A is called hospital insurance and covers most of the costs of a stay in the hospital, as well as some follow-up costs after time in the hospital. Part B, medical insurance, pays some of the cost of doctors and outpatient medical care.

Medicare is operated by the Health Care Financing Administration, part of the Department of Health and Human Services, in cooperation with the Social Security Administration. The Medicare program's daily business, however, is run by private companies, called carriers or intermediaries, operating under contract with the federal government. Most of a patient's direct contact with Medicare comes with the company—Blue Cross, Blue Shield or other large insurance company—that administers Medicare in each state. One of the outrages of the current Medicare political storm is the failure to address the ways in which giving Medicare administrative monopolies to these bloated, private insurance companies drives up the cost to the public.

The Fearful Cost of Getting Sick

The result of this country's woeful health care coverage is that, regardless of the amount of their savings, almost all Americans fear the financial jaws of a serious medical crisis. And people on fixed incomes fear it the most. Anyone who has been faced with even a brief stay in the hospital or the need for extensive medical care knows that getting sick or injured can be an economic catastrophe.

Since 1950, the cost of a hospital stay has risen more than 1,000%—eight times greater than the rise in the overall cost of living. In 1980, the average hospital stay cost more than $3,000; by 1999, the figure was more than $5,000. In 1980, the average out-of-pocket yearly medical costs for people 65 or over was around $2,000; by 1999, the average was nearly $5,000.

1. Medicare and Medicaid: A Comparison

People are sometimes confused about the differences between Medicare and Medicaid. Medicare was created in an attempt to address the fact that older citizens have medical bills significantly higher than the rest of the population, while it is much more difficult for most seniors to continue to earn enough money to cover those bills. However, eligibility for Medicare is not tied to individual need. Rather, it is an entitlement program; you are entitled to it because you or your spouse paid for it through Social Security taxes.

Medicaid, on the other hand, is a federal program for low-income, financially needy people, set up by the federal government and administered differently in each state.

Although you may qualify and receive coverage from both Medicare and Medicaid, there are separate eligibility requirements for each program; being eligible for one program does not necessarily mean you are eligible for the other. Also, Medicaid pays for some services for which Medicare does not.

Medicaid is explained in full in Chapter 16, but as you read this chapter on Medicare, the chart that follows may help you understand the basic differences between the two programs.

C. Part A Hospital Insurance

Medicare is divided into two parts. Hospital insurance, referred to as Part A, covers most of the cost of care provided when you are admitted to a hospital as an inpatient. (See Section C.) Medicare Part B medical insurance covers part of the cost of medical services provided when you are not a patient in a hospital. (See Section E.)

1. Who Is Eligible

There are two types of eligibility for Medicare Part A hospital insurance. Most people age 65 and over are covered for free, based on their work records or on their spouse's work records. People over 65 who are not eligible for free Medicare Part A coverage can enroll in it and pay a monthly fee for the same coverage.

a. Free coverage

Most people age 65 and over are automatically eligible for Medicare Part A hospital insurance and do not have to pay any monthly premium for it; the coverage is free.

The two largest categories of people automatically eligible are:

- People age 65 or older who are eligible for Social Security retirement benefits, or have civil service retirement work credits equal to an amount that would make them eligible for Social Security retirement. (See Chapters 2 and 9.) You are eligible for automatic Medicare coverage even if you do not actually begin collecting your retirement benefits at 65, as long as you are eligible to collect them. If you wait to claim retirement benefits until after 65, you may still begin Medicare coverage at 65. However, if you begin collecting retirement benefits before age 65, you must wait until age 65 to get Medicare coverage.
- People age 65 or older who are eligible to collect Social Security dependents or survivors benefits. Note that those who are age 65 and eligible for dependents benefits when a spouse turns 62 are entitled to Medicare coverage whether or not the spouse actually claims retirement benefits.

Some additional categories of people may also be eligible for free coverage:

- People who reached age 65 before January 1, 1968, even if not eligible for Social Security benefits, if they are U.S. citizens or lawfully in the United States for five consecutive years immediately before applying for Medicare.
- Women who reached age 65 before 1974, and men who reached 65 before 1975, who have three Social Security work credits from covered employment for each year after 1966 before reaching age 65. (See Chapter 1, Section D.)
- People of any age who have been entitled to Social Security disability benefits for 24 months.
- Anyone who has permanent kidney failure requiring either a kidney transplant or maintenance dialysis, if the person or spouse has worked a certain amount at jobs covered by Social Security. For details of this coverage, check with your local Social Security office. If you have any trouble qualifying for Medicare based on kidney failure, contact the National Kidney Foundation, 30 East 33rd Street, New York, NY 10016; 800-622-9010.

A Comparison of Medicare and Medicaid

MEDICARE	MEDICAID
WHO IS ELIGIBLE	
Medicare is for almost everyone 65 or older, rich or poor, for certain people on Social Security disability, and for some people with permanent kidney failure.	Medicaid is for low-income and financially needy people, including those over 65 who are also on Medicare.
Medicare is an entitlement program; people are entitled to Medicare based on their own or their spouse's Social Security contributions, and on payment of premiums.	Medicaid is an assistance program only for the needy.
WHO ADMINISTERS THE PROGRAM	
Medicare is a federal program. Medicare rules are the same all over the country. Medicare information is available at your Social Security office.	Medicaid rules differ in each state. Medicaid information is available at your local county social services, welfare or Department of Human Services office.
COVERAGE PROVIDED	
Medicare hospital insurance (Part A) provides basic coverage for hospital stays and post-hospital nursing facility and home health care.	In many states, Medicaid covers services and costs Medicare does not cover, including prescription drugs, diagnostic and preventive care and eyeglasses.
Medicare medical insurance (Part B) pays most of basic doctor and laboratory costs, and some of other outpatient medical services, including medical equipment and supplies, home health care and physical therapy. It covers none of the cost of prescription drugs.	
COSTS TO CONSUMER	
You must pay a yearly deductible for both Medicare Part A and Part B. You must also pay hefty copayments for extended hospital stays.	Medicaid can pay Medicare deductibles and the 20% portion of charges not paid by Medicare. Medicaid can also pay the Medicare premium.
And under Part B, you must pay the 20% of doctors' bills it does not pay, and sometimes up to 15% more. Part B also charges a monthly premium.	In some states, Medicaid charges consumers small amounts for certain services.

b. Paid coverage

If you are age 65 or over but not automatically eligible for free Part A hospital insurance coverage (see Section 1a), you can still enroll in the Medicare hospital insurance program if you pay a monthly premium. The amount of your premium depends on the number of Social Security work credits you or your spouse have, and on how long after your 65th birthday you apply for coverage.

If you or your spouse have 30 or more work credits, the monthly premium is lower—$166 per month in 2000. If neither you nor your spouse have 30 work credits, the monthly premium is higher—$301 per month in 2000. Also, if you enroll in Part A coverage more than a year after you turn 65, your premium will be 10% higher than these monthly figures.

If you enroll in paid Part A hospital insurance, you must also enroll in Part B medical insurance, for which you pay an additional monthly premium. (See Section D.) However, you may enroll in Part B without Part A.

Expanded Medicare Part A

Free Medicare Part A hospital insurance has been expanded to cover some participants in state, county and non-profit retirement plans who did not pay into the Social Security system. Beginning in 1988, those retirees who paid out of their own pockets for Part A coverage for seven years are eligible for free coverage.

The U.S. Health Care Financing Administration (part of the Department of Health and Human Services) is supposed to notify everyone who becomes eligible in this way. If you believe you are eligible but have not received any notice, contact your local Social Security office. But until you receive an official notice from the HCFA verifying that your coverage is now free, be sure to continue paying your premiums.

The Importance of Comparing Costs

If you are considering enrolling in and paying for Medicare Part A hospital insurance, it may be cheaper for you to do so through an HMO or a health plan. The cost of such coverage will be part of the broader coverage and cost for full participation in the HMO or health plan, which will vary among different plans. Before purchasing Medicare Part A coverage as an individual, compare premiums and benefits of various group plans.

2. Types of Care Covered

Part A hospital insurance pays much of the cost you incur directly from a hospital as part of inpatient care. Under some circumstances, it also covers some of the cost of inpatient treatment in a skilled nursing facility (see Section C6) and by a home health care agency (see section C7). Doctors' bills are not included in Part A coverage; they are covered under Medicare Part B. (See Section D.)

A few basic rules apply to all claims under Part A hospital insurance coverage, whether for inpatient care at a hospital or nursing facility, or for home health care.

a. Doctor-prescribed care

The care and treatment you receive must be prescribed by a licensed physician.

b. Reasonable and necessary care

The inpatient care you receive must be medically reasonable and necessary. This means that the care you require can only be provided to you if you are admitted to a hospital or nursing facility. If you could receive the particular treatment just as well and safely as a hospital outpatient, at the doctor's office or at your home, Part A will not cover you if you receive that treatment as an inpatient. Also, Part A will not normally cover the cost of hospitalization for elective or cosmetic surgery—except for reconstructive surgery after an accident or disfiguring illness—since they are not considered medically necessary.

No Coverage for Custodial Care

Part A hospital insurance covers only skilled medical treatment of illness or injury. It does not pay for a stay in a hospital or nursing facility, or for care from a home health agency, when the services you receive are primarily to make life more comfortable—to help with dressing, eating, bathing, moving around. In reality, distinctions between medical treatment and custodial care sometimes blur, which can result in disputes between Medicare administration and patients. (See Sections C6 and C7.)

3. Medicare-Approved Facility or Agency

Medicare issues licenses to hospitals, nursing facilities and health care agencies certifying that they meet its standards for quality of care and staffing. Medicare will only cover care provided by facilities it approves.

Find out in advance if the facility to which you plan to be admitted, or the home health care agency you intend to hire, is approved by Medicare and accepts Medicare payment. Check with the facility's admissions services or administrator's office, or with the administrator of the home health care agency.

Nowadays it is rare to find a hospital or skilled nursing facility that is not Medicare-approved. Some home health care agencies, however, are not Medicare-approved. That does not necessarily mean that the agency is not reputable. Under most circumstances, Medicare Part A pays for very little home care, anyway. (See Section C7.) So if Medicare is not going to cover much of your costs, you may want to switch to an agency that is good and less expensive, but not Medicare-approved, as soon as Medicare coverage ends.

4. Facility Review Panel Approval

Each hospital and nursing facility has a panel of doctors and administrators that reviews your doctor's decision to treat you as an inpatient or at a nursing facility. The panel usually agrees with your doctor's initial decision to have you admitted to the facility for specific treatment. And the panel and your doctor usually agree on how long you should remain in the facility. Sometimes, though, the panel decides you do not need to be an inpatient to receive certain treatment. Or it decides that you could be discharged from the facility earlier than your doctor has recommended. The panel and your doctor will then consult with one another, and usually they reach an agreement.

If your doctor and the review panel do not agree that you require inpatient care, or they differ as to your discharge date, the question of whether Medicare Part A will pay for your inpatient care is referred to a Peer Review Organization (PRO). (See Chapter 13, Section F.)

Limitation on Psychiatric Hospitals

Medicare Part A covers inpatient psychiatric hospital care. However, if you receive inpatient care in a psychiatric hospital, the total number of days covered is limited. (See Section D3.)

5. Foreign Hospital Stays

Generally, Medicare does not cover you outside the United States, Puerto Rico, the Virgin Islands, Guam and American Samoa. There are, however, three exceptions to this rule.

- If you are in the United States when an emergency occurs and a Canadian or Mexican hospital is closer than any U.S. hospital with emergency services, Medicare will help pay for your emergency care at that foreign hospital.
- If you live in the United States and a Mexican or Canadian hospital is closer to your home than the nearest U.S. hospital, Medicare can cover your care there even if there is no emergency.
- If you are in Canada while traveling directly to Alaska from one of the other states, or from Alaska to one of the other states, and an emergency arises, you may be covered for your care at a Canadian hospital. However, Medicare will not cover you if you are vacationing in Canada.

Consider Travel Insurance

Since there is no Medicare protection for you while you are traveling outside the United States, and if you have no other medical insurance that would cover you while traveling, it might be wise to look into traveler's insurance. These short-term policies are available for a one-time-only premium and cover you under various terms and conditions while you are abroad. A travel agent should be able to give you information on such coverage. Many medigap supplemental insurance policies and Medicare managed care plans provide coverage for foreign travel emergencies. If you have such coverage, you may not need extra travel insurance.

Inpatient Care Generally Covered by Part A

The following list gives you an idea of what Medicare Part A does, and does not, pay for during your stay in a participating hospital or skilled nursing facility. Remember, though, even when Part A covers a cost, there are significant financial limitations on its coverage. (See Section D.)

Medicare Part A hospital insurance covers:

- a semi-private room (two to four beds per room); a private room if medically necessary
- all meals, including special, medically required diets
- regular nursing services
- special care units, such as intensive care and coronary care
- drugs, medical supplies and appliances furnished by the facility, such as casts, splints, wheelchair; also, outpatient drugs and medical supplies if they permit you to leave the hospital or nursing facility sooner
- hospital lab tests, X-rays and radiation treatment billed by the hospital
- operating and recovery room costs
- blood transfusions; you pay for the first three pints of blood, unless you arrange to have them replaced by an outside donation of blood to the hospital, and
- rehabilitation services, such as physical therapy, occupational therapy and speech pathology provided while you are in the hospital or nursing facility.

Medicare Part A hospital insurance does not cover:

- personal convenience items such as television, radio or telephone
- private duty nurses, or
- private room, unless medically necessary.

6. Skilled Nursing Facilities

A growing number of patients recovering from surgery or a major illness are referred by their doctors to the less expensive alternative to hospitalization provided by skilled nursing facilities. Medicare covers some of the costs of a stay in a skilled nursing facility, but even if you qualify for coverage, there are strict limits on how much it will pay. (See Section D4.)

You must meet two requirements before Medicare will pay for any nursing facility care. You must have a prior stay in a hospital, and your doctor must verify that you require daily skilled nursing care.

a. Prior hospital stay

Your stay in a skilled nursing facility must come after you have spent at least three consecutive days, not counting the day of discharge, in the hospital—and within 30 days of being discharged. If you leave the nursing facility after coverage begins, but are readmitted within 30 days, that second period in the nursing facility will also be covered by Medicare.

Levels of Nursing Facility Care

Most nursing facilities provide what is called custodial care—primarily personal, non-medical care for those who are no longer able to fully care for themselves. For the most part, custodial care amounts to assistance with the tasks of daily life: eating, dressing, bathing, moving around, some recreation. It usually involves some health-related matters—monitoring and assisting with medication, providing some exercise or physical therapy. But it is provided mostly by personnel who are not highly trained health professionals and it does not involve any significant treatment for illness or physical condition. Custodial care often lasts months or years, and is not covered at all by Medicare.

A different, short-term kind of care known as skilled nursing facility care is covered by Medicare, although there are severe limits. (See Section D4.) Skilled nursing facility care, which takes place in a hospital's extended care wing, or in a separate nursing facility, provides high levels of medical and nursing care, 24-hour monitoring and intensive rehabilitation. It is intended to follow acute hospital care due to serious illness, injury or surgery—and usually lasts only a matter of days or weeks.

b. Requiring daily skilled nursing care

Your doctor must certify that you require daily skilled nursing care or skilled rehabilitative services. This care includes rehabilitative services by professional therapists or skilled nursing treatment such as giving injections, changing dressings, monitoring vital signs or administering medicines or treatments, which cannot be performed by untrained personnel. This daily care must be related to the condition for which you were hospitalized.

If you are in a nursing facility only because you are unable to feed, clothe, bathe or move yourself, even though these restrictions are the result of your medical condition, you are not eligible for Part A coverage since you do not require skilled nursing care as defined by Medicare rules. However, if you require occasional part-time nursing care, you may be eligible for home health care coverage. (See Section C7.)

The nursing facility care and services covered by Medicare are similar to what is covered for hospital care. It includes:

- a semi-private room (two to four beds per room); a private room if medically necessary
- all meals, including special, medically required diets
- regular nursing services
- special care units, such as coronary care
- drugs, medical supplies, treatments and appliances provided by the facility, such as casts, splints, wheelchair, and
- rehabilitation services, such as physical therapy, occupational therapy and speech pathology provided while you are in the nursing facility.

Medicare coverage for a skilled nursing facility does not include:

- personal convenience items such as television, radio or telephone
- private duty nurses, or
- a private room, unless medically necessary.

7. Home Health Care

Over the past several years, consumers and progressive health care professionals have increasingly encouraged people to get out of hospitals and nursing facilities and into their own or family members' homes while recovering from injury or illness. From a different perspective, insurance companies have been pressuring hospitals to release patients earlier so that if they continue to receive care, it will be a less costly variety at home.

In response to both these movements, there are many more home health care agencies, available in more areas. Most are able to provide care for patients who no longer need high-level care in a hospital but who still require part-time nursing or physical therapy.

Pros and Cons of Home Health Care

The benefits of properly administered home health care can be enormous. In the first place, the surroundings—your own home, or a friend or relative's—are often more conducive to a speedy recovery than the impersonal and sometimes frightening environment of a hospital. You have familiar things around you, your friends and family can come and go as you and they please, and they can lend a hand with your care. You have greater privacy and are free from dreadful hospital routines which are often more disturbing than helpful. And home health care is far less expensive than a stay in the hospital or in a nursing facility.

On the other hand, home health care is not always the best solution. Hospitals sometimes push people out the door before they are well or strong enough, and as a result they take longer to recover, or suffer more pain and discomfort, than they would if they had remained in the hospital just a few days more. This is particularly true when a patient does not have family or friends available to supplement the care provided by a home care agency.

If you are interested in home health care after a stay in the hospital, or as an alternative to a stay in a hospital or nursing facility, contact a home health care agency recommended by your doctor or the hospital discharge planner. The discharge planner can even contact an agency for you. If home care follows a hospital stay, it may be covered by Medicare, as long as a Medicare-approved agency is used.

You may also get help in locating home health care agencies from a community health organization, visiting nurses association, United Way, Red Cross or neighborhood senior center.

For More Info

For a complete discussion of long-term home health care, particularly for older people, and how to finance it, see *Beat the Nursing Home Trap* by Joseph Matthews (Nolo). See the catalog at the back of this book for ordering information.

a. Coverage provided

Part A home health care coverage requires a prior three-day hospital stay. Home care without a prior hospital stay may be covered by Part B. If you qualify for home care coverage, Medicare pays for the following services provided by a participating home health care agency:

- part-time skilled nursing care—usually two to three visits per week in a plan certified by a physician, and
- physical therapy and speech therapy.

If you are receiving part-time skilled nursing care, physical therapy or speech therapy, Medicare can also pay for:

- occupational therapy
- part-time home health aides
- medical social services, and
- medical supplies and equipment provided by the agency, such as hospital bed, walker, respiratory equipment.

However, Medicare will not pay for a number of services sometimes provided as part of home health care, including:

- full-time nursing care
- drugs and biologicals administered at home
- meals delivered to your home, or
- housekeeping services.

b. Restrictions on coverage

Despite the obvious financial as well as recovery advantages of home health care, Medicare coverage for it is severely restricted.

- The agency providing the care must participate in Medicare—meaning it must be approved by Medicare and must accept Medicare payment. Many agencies do not participate in Medicare, so make sure an agency is Medicare-approved before making arrangements.
- You must be confined to your home by an injury, illness or other medical condition. If you need nursing care or other medical services but you are physically able to leave home to receive it, you might not be eligible for Medicare home health care coverage.
- You must require part-time skilled nursing care or physical or speech therapy. Once home health care coverage begins because you need nursing care or physical therapy, Medicare can continue to pay for care even if you only need occupational therapy—which helps you regain job skills you may have lost because of the illness or injury. Occupational therapy alone, however, cannot justify home health care coverage in the first place.
- Your doctor must determine that you need home health care and must help set up a plan for the care in cooperation with the home health care agency. If your doctor has not

mentioned home care to you but you feel it would be a good idea, make your wishes known. Most doctors will prescribe home care, can give you a referral to a Medicare-approved agency and will cooperate with the home health care agency.

8. Hospice Care

Hospice care is home health care provided to a terminally ill patient who is in the last six months or so of life. Hospice care focuses not on treating the illness or fostering recovery, but on making the patient as comfortable as possible. Good hospice care may combine the efforts of family and a doctor, nurse, social worker, dietitian and clergy, as well as physical therapists and other trained caregivers.

Family members and friends provide daily attention to the patient while health care workers make regular home visits. A physician and nurse are on 24-hour call for telephone consultation, and for home visits whenever necessary. Hospice care can also cover up to five days of inpatient care for the patient to give the family or other primary caregivers a respite from their duties.

a. Coverage provided

Medicare can cover nearly the full cost of hospice care. Hospice care covered by Medicare includes:

- physician services provided by a physician connected with the hospice—Medicare Part B will continue to cover service provided by the patient's personal doctor
- nursing care
- medical supplies and appliances
- drugs for management of pain and other symptoms
- health aide and homemaker services
- physical and speech therapy
- medical social services, counseling and dietary assistance.

Medicare can cover two 90-day periods of hospice care, followed by a 30-day period and, in some circumstances, an indefinite extension period. (See Section D6.)

b. Restrictions on coverage

Care must be provided by a Medicare-approved hospice, under a plan developed by the hospice and the patient's attending physician. The patient's doctor and the hospice's medical director must certify that the patient is terminally ill with a life expectancy of six months or less. And the patient must sign a statement choosing hospice care instead of standard Medicare Part A benefits. However, a patient has a right to cancel hospice care at any time and return to regular Medicare Part A coverage.

D. How Much Medicare Part A Pays

To understand any Medicare decision about how much of your hospital, nursing facility or home care bill it will pay, you have to know the basics of Part A payments. Those basics include benefit periods (see Section D1) and deductible and coinsurance amounts (see Section D2).

1. Benefit Period or Spell of Illness

All rules about how much Medicare Part A pays depend on how many days of inpatient care you have during what is called a benefit period or spell of illness.

A benefit period or spell of illness refers to the time you are treated in a hospital or skilled nursing facility, or some combination of the two, for a particular illness or injury. The benefit period begins the day you enter the hospital or skilled nursing facility as an inpatient—and continues until you have been out for 60 consecutive days. If you are in and out of the hospital or nursing facility several times but have not stayed out completely for 60 consecutive days, all your inpatient bills for that time will be figured as part of the same benefit period.

Two Benefit Spells May Be Better Than One

You can get more total days of full Medicare coverage during two spells of illness than in just one. As a result, it can be in your financial interest to stretch your hospital or nursing facility stays into two benefit periods, if possible. For example, using home health care may help you stay out of the hospital or nursing facility for 60 days before you must return as an inpatient for further treatment. If the timing of your inpatient treatment could be somewhat flexible, discuss that timing and its effect on Medicare coverage with your doctor.

Example: Oscar is in the hospital with circulatory problems, being treated with medication. His doctor recommends surgery, operating on one leg at a time, monitoring the first leg before attending to the second. Oscar and his doctor plan the dates of surgery so that he will be released from the hospital and will convalesce at home, with the help of home health care services, for more than 60 days before he returns to have the second operation.

This way, Medicare will consider the time Oscar spends in the hospital after the second surgery to be part of a new spell of illness, even though it results from the same condition that made the first operation necessary. If there had not been a 60-day break between hospitalizations, Oscar would have been in the hospital a total of more than 60 days and would have had to pay an additional $194 a day in coinsurance for every day after his 60th day in the hospital—up to his 90th day.

2. Hospital Bills

Medicare Part A pays only certain amounts of a hospital bill for any one benefit period.

a. The deductible amount

For each benefit period, you must pay an initial amount before Medicare will pay anything. This is called the hospital insurance deductible. The deductible is increased every January 1. In 2000, the amount was $776.

b. First 60 days hospitalized

For the first 60 days you are an inpatient in a hospital during one benefit period, Part A hospital insurance pays all of the cost of covered services. However, nonessentials, such as televisions and telephones, are not covered. (See Section C2.) You pay only your hospital insurance deductible. If you are in more than one hospital, you still pay only one deductible per benefit period—and Part A covers 100% of all your covered costs for each hospital.

c. 61 through 90 days

After your 60th day in the hospital during one spell of illness, and through your 90th day, each day you must pay what is called a coinsurance amount toward your covered hospital costs. Part A of Medicare pays the rest of covered costs. In 2000, this daily coinsurance amount was $194; it goes up every year.

d. Reserve days

Reserve days are a last resort coverage. They can help pay for your hospital bills if you are in the hospital more than 90 days in one benefit period. But the payment is quite limited. If you are in the hospital for more than 90 days in any one spell of illness, you can use up to 60 additional reserve days of coverage. During those days, you are responsible for a daily coinsurance payment. In 2000, the reserve days coinsurance amount was $388 per day. Medicare pays the rest of covered costs.

You do not have to use your reserve days in one spell of illness; you can split them up and use them over several benefit periods. But you have only a total of 60 reserve days in your lifetime. Whatever reserve days you use during one spell of illness are gone for good. In the next benefit period, you would have available only the number of reserve days you have not used in previous spells of illness.

Saving Reserve Days

Even though you are in the hospital for more than 90 days, you may want to save your reserve days for an even rainier day. For example, you may not want to use your reserve days if you have some private insurance, such as from an employer, that can help cover the costs of those extra days of hospitalization, but you may not have that insurance later in life.

If you want to use your reserve days, you don't have to make a formal request or fill out any form. Medicare will automatically apply them to cover your hospital bills—minus the $388 a day coinsurance you have to pay. But if you do not want to use those reserve days, or want to use some but not all of them, you must notify the hospital administrator or billing office, and you must do it before the reserve days come up.

3. Psychiatric Hospitals

Medicare Part A hospital insurance covers a total of 190 days in a lifetime for inpatient care in a psychiatric hospital or in the psychiatric care unit of a general hospital.

And there is another limit on this coverage. If you are already an inpatient in a psychiatric hospital or in the psychiatric care unit of a general hospital when your Medicare coverage goes into effect, Medicare counts back 150 days from the date your coverage begins and subtracts the days you were an inpatient. All other coverage rules pertaining to hospital coverage apply to coverage for inpatient psychiatric care. (See Sections C6 and D2.)

Example: During the five months before his 65th birthday, Horace spent 60 days in a psychiatric hospital. Those 60 days are subtracted from Horace's lifetime total of 190 days Medicare coverage in a psychiatric hospital. It leaves him with only 130 days more coverage under Part A for psychiatric hospitalization.

4. Skilled Nursing Facilities

Despite the common misconception that nursing homes are covered by Medicare, the truth is that it covers only a limited amount of inpatient skilled nursing care. (See Section C6.)

For each benefit period, Medicare will cover only a total of 100 days of inpatient care in a skilled nursing facility. For the first 20 of 100 days, Medicare will pay for all covered costs, which include all basic services but not television, telephone or private room charges. For the next 80 days, the patient is personally responsible for a daily copayment; Medicare pays the rest of covered costs. In 2000, the copayment amount is $97; the amount goes up each year.

Reserve days, available for hospital coverage, do not apply to a stay in a nursing facility. After 100 days in any benefit period, you are on your own as far as Part A hospital insurance is concerned. However, if you later begin a new benefit period, your first 100 days in a skilled nursing facility will again be covered.

5. Home Health Care

Medicare Part A pays 100% of the cost of your covered home health care provided by a Medicare-approved agency—and there is no limit on the number of visits to your home for which Medicare will pay. Medicare will also pay for the initial evaluation by a home care agency, if prescribed by your physician, to determine whether you are a good candidate for home care. However, if you require durable medical equipment, such as a special bed or wheelchair as part of your home care, Medicare will pay only 80%.

How Part A Payments Are Figured

To get a picture of how the overall Part A payment scheme works, an example of one person's hospital stay may be useful.

Annika was hospitalized for two weeks for a serious intestinal disorder, went home for a week, came back to the hospital for another ten days, was released again and then had to return to the hospital after only a few days at home. After three more weeks in the hospital, surgery became the only option. Annika spent six more weeks in the hospital recovering from the operation. Annika's hospital bill for all this treatment includes the following charges:

Semiprivate room, 80 days at $340/day	$27,200
Operating and recovery room	1,675
Intensive Care, 7 days at $520/day	3,640
Laboratory (including X-rays)	980
Medication	465
Whole blood (6 pints at $32/pint)	192
Telephone	94
Television (12 weeks at $35/week)	420
TOTAL DUE	$34,666

Medicare will pay, for the first 60 days, all covered costs less the $776 deductible:

- Operating and recovery room costs ($1,675)
- Intensive care costs ($3,640)
- The second three pints of blood ($96)
- 53 days in a semiprivate room ($18,020)
- Seven days were in intensive care ($3,640)
- Laboratory work—$900 of the $980 total done in the first 60 days
- Medication—$420 administered during first 60 days

Medicare will not pay for:

- Television or telephone costs; $514 must be paid by Annika.
- The first three pints of blood, because Annika did not replace them; the $96 for blood is Annika's responsibility.
- So Medicare covers all of this $23,941, minus the $776 deductible, for the first 60 days. Annika had to pay only the deductible, plus the first three pints of blood and non-covered telephone and television costs.
- For the last 27 days in the hospital, Annika had to pay her coinsurance amount of $194 per day, for a total of $5,238. Medicare paid the rest.

In all, Annika paid about $6,600 of her nearly $35,000 hospital bill. Remember, though, that Annika will still have to face her doctors' bills, which are covered by Medicare Part B medical insurance. (See Section E.)

Home Care Makes Good Financial Sense

The fact that Medicare will pay for an unlimited number of home health care visits makes home care a very good financial value—in addition to the recuperative benefits of being at home—compared to recovery in a hospital or nursing facility. If you are looking at a long period of convalescence, consider home health care as an alternative to a long siege in the hospital or nursing facility.

6. Hospice Care

Medicare pays 100% of the charges for hospice care, with two exceptions. First, the hospice can charge the patient up to $5 for each prescription of outpatient prescription drugs or biologicals the hospice supplies for pain and symptomatic relief. Also, the hospice can charge the patient up to $5 per day for inpatient care if the patient moves to a nursing facility or hospital for up to five days of respite care.

The amount of hospice care covered by Medicare totals 210 days, broken down into two 90-day benefit periods followed by one 30-day period. These benefit periods can be used together or separately. If you cancel hospice care and return to regular Medicare Part A coverage during any one of the benefit periods, you lose the remaining days of hospice coverage in that benefit period. But additional benefit periods are still available if you again choose hospice care.

E. Part B Medical Insurance

The second half of Medicare coverage, Part B, is medical insurance. It is intended to help pay doctor bills for treatment either in or out of the hospital, as well as many of the other medical expenses you incur when you are not in the hospital.

1. Who Is Eligible

The rules of eligibility for Part B medical insurance are much simpler than for Part A: If you are age 65 or over and a citizen of the United States, or you are a resident of the United States who has been here lawfully for five consecutive years, you are eligible to enroll in Medicare Part B medical insurance. This is true whether or not you are eligible for Part A hospital insurance.

Anyone who wants Part B medical insurance must enroll in the program. Everyone enrolled must pay a monthly premium—$45.50 in 2000. In most years, the premium is raised slightly on January 1.

Medicare Medical Insurance Is Never Enough

Part B Medicare medical insurance is intended to pay for a portion of doctor bills, outpatient hospital and clinic charges, laboratory work, some home health care, physical and speech therapy and a very few drugs and medical supplies. But there are severe restrictions on what is covered and on how much is paid.

Private Medicare supplement insurance—often referred to as medigap insurance—may help you make up the difference. Many people also fill in the gaps in Medicare by joining an HMO or other managed-care health plan that combines basic Medicare coverage with supplemental benefits. (See Chapter 14.) If you cannot afford private supplement insurance, you may be eligible for Medicaid—a public program for people with low income and few assets. (See Chapter 16.)

2. Types of Services Covered

Part B medical insurance is intended to cover basic medical services provided by doctors, clinics and laboratories. However, the lists of services specifically covered and not covered are long, and do not always make a lot of common sense. Making the effort to learn what is and is not covered can be important, since you may get the most benefits by fitting your medical treatments into the covered categories whenever possible.

a. Doctor bills

Part B medical insurance covers medically necessary doctors' services, including surgery, whether the services are provided at the hospital, at a doctor's office or—if you can find such a doctor—at home. Part B also covers outpatient medical services provided by hospital and doctor's office staff who assist in providing care, such as nurses, nurse practitioners, surgical assistants, laboratory or X-ray technicians.

Medicare Pays for Second Opinion Before Surgery

Before undergoing surgery, it is usually medically wise to get a second opinion from another doctor. Second opinions often lead to the decision not to have surgery. Recognizing this, and the savings involved, Medicare will cover your obtaining a second doctor's opinion before undergoing any kind of surgery. And if the second doctor's opinion conflicts with the original doctor's recommendation for surgery, Medicare will pay for an opinion by yet a third doctor.

b. Outpatient care and laboratory testing

Medicare medical insurance covers outpatient hospital treatment, such as emergency room or clinic charges, X-rays, injections which are not self-administered and laboratory work and diagnostic tests, whether done at the hospital lab or at an independent laboratory facility, if that lab is approved by Medicare.

Beware of Outpatient Hospital Charges

Medicare pays only a limited amount of outpatient hospital and clinic bills. And unlike most other kinds of outpatient services, Medicare places no limits on how much the hospital or clinic can charge over and above what Medicare pays. (See Section F6.)

c. Ambulances

Part B medical insurance covers the cost of an ambulance if it is medically necessary—meaning transportation by any other means might endanger your health. Coverage only extends to a trip to or from a hospital or skilled nursing facility. Medicare does not pay for an ambulance trip to a doctor's office.

Medicare does not cover ambulance services used because a patient needs assistance getting out of the house and into a vehicle and no other form of transportation is available. If your doctor requests the ambulance for you, that will raise the likelihood—though not guarantee—

that Medicare will consider it a medical necessity. If your doctor will not order an ambulance, consider free transportation for the elderly offered in your community. Call your local senior center, or the senior information line listed in the white pages of your telephone directory.

d. Administered drugs

Drugs or other medicines administered to you at the hospital or doctor's office are covered by medical insurance. Medicare does not cover drugs you take by yourself at home, including self-administered injections, even if they are prescribed by your doctor. Exceptions to this rule are self-administered oral cancer medication, antigens and immunosuppressive drugs, which are covered by Medicare. Also, flu shots and pneumonia vaccines are covered by Medicare, even though other vaccinations are not; the flu shot you can obtain on your own, but the pneumonia vaccination requires a doctor's prescription.

e. Medical equipment and supplies

Splints, casts, prosthetic devices, body braces, heart pacemakers, corrective lenses after a cataract operation, therapeutic shoes for diabetics and medical equipment such as ventilators, wheelchairs and hospital beds—if prescribed by a doctor—are all covered by Part B medical insurance. This includes glucose monitoring equipment for people who have diabetes.

f. Oral surgery

Some types of surgery on the jaw or facial bones, or on the related nerves or blood vessels, can be covered by Part B medical insurance. However, surgery on teeth or gums, even when related to an injury or a disease that did not originate with the teeth, is usually considered to be dental work and so is not covered by Medicare.

This is one of Medicare's nonsensical bureaucratic distinctions. Although normal dental care is not covered by Medicare, damage to teeth or gums connected to an injury or disease is a medical as much as a dental problem. However, there is one route to coverage: If the work is done by a dentist or oral surgeon, Medicare will cover it if physicians also provide the same kind of care and if Medicare would cover the care if a doctor had provided it. This is usually determined by whether the treatment involves just the teeth and gums (not covered) or also the bones, inside mouth, blood vessels or tongue (covered).

g. Outpatient physical therapy and speech therapy

Part B of Medicare will cover some of the cost of outpatient physical and speech therapy—if it is prescribed and regularly reviewed by a doctor and provided by a Medicare-approved facility or therapist.

But how you receive the therapy will determine how much Medicare will pay.

- If you receive the therapy as part of treatment at your doctor's office, Part B medical insurance will pay the normal 80% of approved charges, less your deductible. (See Section F2.)

- If you receive physical therapy or speech pathology services as an outpatient from a hospital or skilled nursing facility, or from a Medicare-approved home health agency, clinic, rehabilitation agency or public health agency, Medicare will pay 80% of approved charges, less your yearly deductible.
- If you receive therapy while confined to your home, as part of a complete home health care program, Medicare will pay all of the costs with no dollar limit and no deductible. (See Section h.)

h. Home health care

The same home health care coverage is available under Part B medical insurance as is covered by Part A hospital insurance. (See Section C7.) There is no limit on the number of home health care visits that are covered, and you are not responsible for your Part B deductible for home health care. Only skilled nursing care or therapy while you are confined to your home is covered, however, and such care must be ordered by your doctor and provided by a Medicare-approved home health care agency. Part B medical insurance, like Part A coverage, will pay 100% of the approved charges of a participating home health care agency. If you have both Part A and Part B, Part A will cover your home health care following a hospital stay of at least three days; otherwise, Part B will cover it.

i. Chiropractors

Part B may cover some care by a Medicare-certified chiropractor. Generally, Medicare will cover a limited number of visits to a chiropractor for manipulation of neck or back vertebrae that are out of place. Medicare will not, however, cover general health maintenance visits to a chiropractor, nor will it usually cover therapeutic manipulation other than of the vertebrae. And Medicare generally will not cover X-rays or other diagnostic tests done by the chiropractor. Instead, your physician normally must order these tests.

If you go to a chiropractor and hope to have Medicare pay its share of the bill, have the chiropractor's office check with Medicare ahead of time about the treatment being proposed. And even if Medicare initially covers the treatment, it may not do so indefinitely. So, if you continue with the treatments, have the chiropractor's office regularly check with Medicare to find out how long it will pay.

j. Preventive screening exams

Medicare now covers the following examinations to screen for a number of serious illnesses:

- A pap smear and pelvic exam every three years; every year for women at high risk of cervical or pelvic disease. Medicare covers this exam even if you have not yet met your annual Part B deductible.
- Colorectal cancer screening, as your physician deems necessary.

- Bone density tests for women at high risk of developing osteoporosis or any individual who is receiving long-term steroid therapy, who has primary hyperparathyroidism, or who has certain vertebrate abnormalities.
- Blood glucose testing supplies—if prescribed by a physician—for patients with diabetes.
- Beginning Jan. 1, 2000, annual prostate cancer screenings for men over 55.
- Annual flu shot, with no deductible and no coinsurance amount.

k. Mammography

Part B covers a yearly mammogram, even if you have not yet met your annual deductible. The mammogram must be performed by your doctor or by a facility certified for mammography by Medicare.

l. Podiatrists

Medicare covers podiatrist services only when they consist of treatment for injuries or diseases of the foot. However, this does not include routine foot care or treatment of corns or calluses.

m. Optometrists

Medicare covers very limited services by a Medicare-approved optometrist: examination and glasses, contact lenses or intraocular lenses following cataract surgery. Routine eye exams and glasses are not covered.

n. Clinical psychologists or social workers

When a doctor or hospital prescribes it in conjunction with medical treatment, Medicare Part B can cover limited counseling by a clinical psychologist or clinical social worker. The practitioner must be Medicare-approved. If your doctor suggests a clinical psychologist or social worker to help in your recovery from surgery, injury or illness, contact the practitioner in advance to find out whether the services will be approved by Medicare.

o. Daycare mental health treatment

Medicare part B can cover mental health care in the form of day treatment—also called partial hospitalization—at a hospital outpatient department or community mental health center. The facility must be Medicare-approved and the particular day program certified for Part B coverage by Medicare.

3. Services Not Covered by Medicare Part B

When you look at the list of what Medicare medical insurance does not cover, it's easy to understand why people with Medicare still wind up personally responsible for half of their medical bills. It also underlines the need for you to consider additional medical insurance, either through private supplemental plans, an HMO or other managed care plan, or through Medicaid or Qualified Medicare Beneficiary coverage. (See Chapters 14, 15 and 16.)

The categories of medical treatment and services listed below are not covered by Medicare.

However, the non-covered services listed below do not necessarily apply to HMO or other managed care Medicare coverage. Many managed care Medicare plans include some coverage for these medical services even though Medicare itself does not cover them. (See Chapter 15.)

a. Routine physical examinations

Regular or routine examinations are not covered by Medicare. However, laboratory work, diagnostic testing and physical examinations by your doctor are covered if they are part of diagnosis for a particular medical condition or complaint. Understanding the difference between these two types of physical exam—one a routine check-up, undergone simply because time has passed since a previous exam, the other to find the cause of an existing problem—can help you get Medicare coverage for medical care you might otherwise have to pay for yourself.

If something is wrong with you, Medicare will cover examinations to find out what it is, how bad it is, what the treatment should be and how the illness and treatment are progressing. There are no rules that dictate how bad your condition must be before a doctor can examine you. And it is up to the doctor to decide what kind of an examination is necessary to find out what is ailing you—although, to be covered by Medicare, the examination must be reasonably connected to your complaint.

If your doctor decides that a physical examination and testing are necessary to find out what is wrong with you—perhaps you've been tired a lot, or short of breath, or having trouble sleeping, or occasionally having headaches or dizziness—and the examination and testing are medically reasonable given your physical symptoms, then Medicare is likely to cover it. On the other hand, simply complaining of mild, unspecific symptoms and then asking for a broad general physical examination does not guarantee that Medicare will pay for it.

The key is making your doctor aware that Medicare coverage of examinations can be a problem, and getting the doctor to cooperate. If you need to have a check-up or physical or other general testing done, discuss the Medicare coverage question with your doctor ahead of time so he or she can make clear—both on your medical records and on the forms the doctor's office sends to Medicare—that your examination was to find out why you had certain problems or symptoms; it was not merely a routine physical.

The following examples may give you a good idea of how paying attention to this Medicare rule about physical examinations can save quite a bit of money.

Example: Maureen was having trouble sleeping, seemed to get too many colds and was tired a lot. She decided to get a general physical examination since she had not had one for two years. She called her doctor and asked to have a comprehensive physical examination scheduled. The doctor's secretary asked if there was any particular problem, and Maureen said, "No, not really; I just thought it was time to have a check-up." When she came for the examination, she told the doctor that she was just there for a routine exam because it had been two years. She mentioned her trouble sleeping, the colds and the tiredness, but played them down.

The doctor gave Maureen a full physical examination and took blood and urine samples for routine lab testing. Other than slight low blood sugar, nothing out of the ordinary showed up. The doctor suggested changes in Maureen's diet, recommended some vitamins, and sent the $380 bill to Medicare. Medicare refused to pay any of it—the doctor had *reported a routine physical check-up and Medicare reported back that it does not cover routine physical examinations.*

Example: Mavis had the same vague, minor physical problems as Maureen, but Mavis was smarter about handling her doctor's appointment. From her first conversation making the appointment through the examination itself, Mavis said she wanted to be examined for a series of specific problems: sleeplessness, a virus she could not get rid of, headaches and dizziness—the same symptoms Maureen had. The doctor gave Mavis the same examination and lab tests that Maureen had. The results were the same, as was the prescription for vitamins and a change in diet. The doctor submitted Mavis's $380 bill to Medicare, and Medicare paid its share—because the doctor's records indicated not that Mavis had been given a routine physical but that she had been examined and treated for symptoms of which she complained.

b. Treatment that is not medically necessary

Medicare will not pay for medical care which it does not consider medically necessary. This includes some elective and most cosmetic surgery, plus virtually all alternative forms of medical care such as acupuncture, acupressure and homeopathy—with the one exception of limited use of chiropractors. (See Section E2.) This is despite the fact that many people find these therapies more salutary than traditional forms of medical care.

c. Vaccinations and immunizations

Most vaccinations and immunizations—such as those taken before travel abroad—are not covered by Medicare medical insurance. There is one exception for emergencies in which, for example, they are required because of the risk of infection or because of exposure to a communicable disease. Other exceptions are made for the pneumonia vaccination, if prescribed by a doctor, and for a flu shot.

d. Drugs and medicines at home

This is one of the most costly areas of medical care not covered by Medicare. Part A hospital insurance covers drugs administered while you are in the hospital. And Part B medical insurance covers drugs that cannot be self-administered, which you receive while an outpatient being treated at a hospital, clinic or doctor's office. But Medicare does not pay for any drugs, prescription or not, that you can administer or take yourself at home. Insulin for diabetics, for example, is a lifesaving drug, but because it can be self-administered Medicare does not cover it.

A few of the more expensive medigap supplemental insurance policies cover a certain amount of prescription drug purchases each year. (See Chapter 14.) And most HMOs and other managed care plans also cover some prescription medication. (See Chapter 15.) For many people who regularly use expensive medicines, this coverage is the primary reason to choose a particular medigap policy or HMO.

The Bias Against Preventive Medicine

Even though it is unquestioned that preventive medicine, including routine physical check-ups, can significantly reduce the number and severity of illnesses, Medicare reflects the attitude of the traditional medical community which refuses to put money or energy into public health education and disease prevention.

There are several reasons for this.

There is little or no tradition of preventive medicine in the United States, and no national, community-based public health policy or program to encourage it. In addition, since most doctors receive little training in preventive medicine, they don't stress it in their contact with patients. And finally, since medicine is run almost entirely as a business in the United States, the medical community emphasizes high-profit activities such as treatment of disease over low-profit activities such as disease prevention. This is not to say that doctors are evil, but they are part of—and most seem to be dominated by—a large medical business world, and the nature of business is profit.

In recent years, this mindset against preventive medicine has been reversed somewhat by the growth of HMOs and other managed care health plans. These plans are paid a set amount per patient, regardless of how much treatment becomes needed, and so it makes good economic sense for these plans to cut costly treatment by helping people prevent serious illness in the first place. If you have Medicare and also belong to one of these plans, you will be able to get some routine physical examinations and health screenings free, or for minimal payments.

Medicare, too, has finally begun to acknowledge the cost benefits of preventive medicine, now covering flu and pneumonia vaccinations, PAP smears and mammograms. However, Medicare is still woefully backwards when it comes to covering most kinds of preventive medicine, and it remains up to you to find ways to fit examinations into the coverage Medicare does offer.

e. Eyesight and hearing exams

Medicare medical insurance does not cover routine eye or hearing examinations. Neither does it cover hearing aids, eyeglasses or contact lenses, except for lenses required following cataract surgery. However, if your eyes or ears are affected by an illness or injury other than simple loss of strength, examination and treatment by an ophthalmologist—an eye doctor who is an M.D.—or other physician is covered.

f. General dental work

Medicare does not cover work performed by a dentist or oral surgeon, unless the same work would be covered if performed by a physician. In other words, if the treatment is considered medical rather than dental, Medicare may cover it. Generally, Medicare will not cover treatment unless the problem is unrelated to normal tooth decay or gum disease, and involves either the blood vessels, nerves or interior of the mouth, or the bones of the mouth or jaw. (See Section E2.)

You May Be Able to Find Free Drugs

One way some people manage to get around some of the outrageous cost of prescription drugs is to ask the doctor who prescribes them, or your family doctor, for samples of the drugs. Pharmaceutical companies, in an effort to push their particular brand of drugs, send free samples to doctors, and many doctors are willing to dispense those drugs to you free of charge instead of forcing you to buy the drugs on your own.

But many doctors forget what they have in the way of samples, or simply do not offer samples unless asked. It will usually help if you ask your doctor if he or she has samples of the drug you need, explaining that it will be very hard on your pocketbook if you have to purchase them.

F. How Much Medicare Part B Pays

When all your medical bills are added up, you will see that Medicare pays, on average, for only about half the total. Medicare uses a lot of health industry and government doubletalk to explain away its limits on payment, but when all the talk is boiled away, three major reasons remain why Part B medical insurance pays for so little.

First, Medicare does not cover a number of major medical expenses, such as routine physical examinations, medication, glasses, hearing aids, dentures and a number of other costly medical services.

Second, Medicare only pays a portion of what it decides is the proper amount—called the approved charges—for medical services. In addition, when Medicare decides that a particular service is covered and determines the approved charges for it, Part B medical insurance usually pays only 80% of those approved charges; you are responsible for the remaining 20%.

Finally, the approved amount may seem reasonable to Medicare, but it is often considerably less than what the doctor has actually charged you. If your doctor or other medical provider does not accept assignment of the Medicare charges, you are personally responsible for the difference. (See Section F2.)

Now that you know the worst, you can deal with the details of how much Medicare Part B pays. The rules are not hard to understand—just hard to swallow.

1. Deductible Amounts

Before Medicare pays anything under Part B medical insurance, you must pay a deductible amount of your covered medical bills for the year. The deductible amount has been set at $100 for several years, but it is likely to go up in the near future.

Medicare keeps track of how much of the deductible amount you have paid in a given year. It generally does a good job of keeping track, but it is always a good idea for you to keep your own records and double-check the accounting.

2. 80% of Approved Charges

Part B medical insurance pays only 80% of what Medicare decides is the approved charge for a particular service or treatment. You are responsible for paying the other 20% of the approved charge, called your coinsurance amount. And unless your doctor or other medical provider accepts assignment (see Section 5), you are also responsible for the difference between the Medicare-approved charge and the amount the doctor or other provider actually charges.

Help for Low-Income Seniors

Under programs known as Qualified Medicare Beneficiary (QMB), Specified Low-Income Medicare Beneficiary (SLMB) and Qualifying Individual (QI), Medicare recipients who have low incomes and few assets can receive considerable help with their basic Medicare expenses.

If you qualify as a QMB, your state will pay all Medicare premiums, deductibles and coinsurance amounts. If you qualify as an SLMB, your state will pay the monthly Medicare Part B premiums, though not deductibles or coinsurance amounts. If you meet the standards as a QI, your state will pay all or part of your monthly Medicare Part B premium, but not any deductible or coinsurance. (See Chapter 16.)

3. 100% of Approved Charges for Some Services

There are several types of treatments and medical providers for which Medicare Part B pays 100% of the approved charges rather than the usual 80%, and to which the yearly $100 deductible does not apply. In these categories, you are not required to pay the regular 20% coinsurance amount, and in most of them the provider accepts assignment of the approved charges as the full amount, so you actually pay nothing at all. In the case of outpatient mental health care, however, Medicare Part B pays less than the usual 80% of approved charges.

a. Home health care

Whether you receive home health care under Part A or Part B, Medicare pays 100% of the charges and you are not responsible for your yearly deductible. However, if you receive medical equipment—wheelchair, chair lift, special bed—from the home health care agency, you must pay the 20% coinsurance amount.

b. Clinical laboratory services

Medicare pays 100% of the approved amount for such laboratory services as blood tests, urinalyses and biopsies. And the laboratory must accept assignment, except in Maryland where a hospital lab can bill you, as an outpatient, for a 20% coinsurance amount.

c. Flu and pneumonia vaccines

Medicare pays the full 100% of the approved charges for these vaccinations, and the $100 yearly deductible does not apply. However, the provider is not required to accept assignment, so there may be an additional 15% charge on top of the amount Medicare approves.

d. Outpatient mental health treatment

For mental health services provided on an outpatient basis, Part B pays only 50% of approved charges. This is true whether the services are provided by a physician, clinical psychologist or clinical social worker, at a hospital, nursing facility, mental health center or rehabilitation facility. The patient is responsible for the yearly deductible, for the unpaid 50% of the Medicare approved amount, and if the provider does not accept assignment, for the rest of the bill above the Medicare-approved amount, up to an additional 15%.

4. Legal Limit on Amounts Charged

By law, a doctor or other medical provider can bill you no more than what is called the limiting charge, which is set at 15% more than the amount Medicare decides is the approved charge for a treatment or service. That means you may be personally responsible—either out-of-pocket or through supplemental insurance—for the 20% of the approved charges Medicare does not pay, plus any amount the doctor charges up to the 15% limiting charge. Regardless of how much the doctor or other medical provider charges non-Medicare patients for the same service, you can be charged no more than 15% over the amount Medicare approves.

States With Limits on Balance Billing

Several states—Connecticut, Massachusetts, Minnesota, New York, Ohio, Pennsylvania, Rhode Island and Vermont—have passed balance billing or charge-limit laws. These laws forbid a doctor from billing patients for the balance of the bill above the amount Medicare approves. The patient is still responsible for the 20% of the approved charge not paid by Medicare Part B.

The specifics of these patient protection laws vary from state to state: some forbid balance billing to any Medicare patient, others apply the restriction only to patients with limited incomes or assets. To find out the rules in your state, call the following agencies:

- Connecticut Medical Assignment Program: 800-443-9946
- Massachusetts Office of Elder Affairs: 800-882-2003
- Minnesota Board of Aging, Ombudsman: 800-657-3591
- New York State Office for the Aging: 800-342-9871
- Ohio State Department of Health: 800-899-7127
- Pennsylvania State Department of Aging: 717-783-8975
- Rhode Island Department of Elderly Affairs: 800-322-2880
- Vermont Department of Aging & Disabilities: 800-642-5119.

5. Assignment of Medicare-Approved Amount

In most instances, Medicare pays 80% of the approved amount of doctor bills; you or your private insurance pay the remaining 20%. However, you can avoid having to pay anything above the Medicare approved amount if your doctor accepts assignment of that amount as the full amount of your bill.

Most doctors who treat Medicare patients will accept assignment. Some have signed up in advance with Medicare, agreeing to accept assignment on all Medicare patients. They are called Medicare participating doctors, and are paid slightly higher amounts by Medicare than non-participating doctors. Others have not agreed to accept assignment on all patients but will do so on some or most claims.

Unfortunately, many doctors—particularly specialists who have to compete less for patients—still do not accept assignment at all. When you are deciding on a doctor, find out in advance whether the doctor always takes assignment of the Medicare-approved amount, or if he or she is willing to take assignment on your bills.

Mandatory Assignment for Medicaid and QMB Patients

If you receive Medicaid assistance (called Medi-Cal in California) as well as Medicare, or are a Qualified Medicare Beneficiary (QMB), federal law requires that a doctor who agrees to treat you must also accept assignment. (See Chapter 16.)

6. No Limit on Outpatient Hospital Charges

For most outpatient services, Medicare pays 80% of the Medicare-approved amount and you are personally responsible only for the remaining 20% of those approved charges. If you receive outpatient services at a hospital, however, you are responsible not for 20% of the amount Medicare approves but 20% of whatever amount the hospital decides to charge you. And that total amount is not limited in any way by the Medicare-approved amount, as are doctors' fees. (See Section F5.)

Medicare Medical Savings Accounts—An Empty Promise

One of the highly touted options for Medicare coverage created by Congress in 1977 was called the Medicare Medical Savings Account (MSA). This pilot project permits a Medicare enrollee to establish a personal medical savings account, with certain tax advantages, from which money can be drawn to pay medical bills.

The plan will only work, however, if insurance companies offer a special high deductible policy that pays a portion of a recipient's bills when the yearly deductible is met. While insurance companies have issued these policies for non-Medicare consumers, they have not issued them for Medicare recipients. As a result, the Medicare MSA system remains in mothballs.

Beware of Huge Outpatient Hospital Bills

Because there is no limit on how much hospitals can charge Medicare patients for outpatient services, they are now trying to make as much money as possible from outpatients.

They do this in two ways. First, they try to have Medicare patients receive treatment on an outpatient rather than inpatient basis—even if it would be medically good practice and the physician involved would prefer to have the patient treated in a hospital. Second, hospitals jack up to astronomical levels the cost of outpatient services because they know they can bill the patient for 20% of the full amount.

The result of this loophole in the Medicare law is that hospitals have been sticking Medicare patients for almost 40% of total payments for outpatient costs. For outpatient surgery, radiology and other diagnostic services, patients are winding up responsible for about 50% of total payments to hospitals. And over the next few years, hospitals are expected to raise their outpatient charges so high that the patient's portion of the payment is expected to reach a staggering 70%.

There are several ways to try to combat hospital practices of overcharging for outpatient services. First, before you receive an outpatient service, check with the hospital administrator or financial office personnel to see if the hospital will accept the Medicare-approved amount as the total bill—meaning you or your private insurance would be responsible for only 20% of that approved amount.

If not, ask your doctor if the service can be performed either in the doctor's office or at an independent laboratory instead of at the hospital. If the service can only be performed at a hospital, explain the Medicare payment problem to the doctor and ask if there is another hospital where you might receive the services and which would charge only the Medicare-approved amount.

Finally, if you cannot find a way to receive the outpatient services at a Medicare-controlled cost, you might want to consider receiving the service or treatment as an inpatient. Of course, inpatient treatment would have to be medically defensible, and many services simply do not justify an inpatient stay. But other treatments may be performed either as inpatient or outpatient services. And while hospitals are trying to force people to receive these services only as outpatients—a non-radical mastectomy is a recent example—a doctor can usually put pressure on the hospital to permit you to receive the service as an inpatient.

Ask your doctor if the treatment or service you are to receive as an outpatient might instead justify that you go into the hospital for an overnight stay. If so, you would only be responsible for the yearly inpatient deductible, which might be considerably less than what you would owe as an outpatient. And if you have already paid your hospital deductible for the current benefit period, you might not owe anything at all.

Private Fee-for-Service Plans Outside Medicare

Some businesses, unions and other organizations offer general health insurance plans—either during employment or retirement—that accept people eligible for Medicare. A private health insurance plan that accepts Medicare enrollees must offer at least as much coverage as basic Medicare would provide, and most of these plans provide more than that.

If you choose to join or remain with such a health plan once you become eligible for Medicare, the plan—and not Medicare—makes all decisions about coverage for specific services and amount of payment.

You may be responsible for plan premiums and copayments, as well as the difference between what the plan pays the provider and what the provider actually charges. Unlike with regular Medicare, there is no legal limit on the amount a provider may charge you above what the insurance pays.

■

Medicare Procedures: Enrollment, Claims and Appeals

Chapter 12 describes the several ways in which someone can be eligible for Medicare. Most people are eligible for Part A hospital insurance free of charge; if you are not eligible for free Part A coverage, you may enroll in it and pay a monthly premium. Part B medical insurance coverage is available to most people age 65 and older, and everyone covered pays a monthly premium for it.

This chapter explains how to enroll in Medicare Part A and Part B. (See Sections A and B). It also explains how to get Medicare to pay its share of your medical bills once you are enrolled. (See Section C.) It shows what portion of the bill you must pay yourself. (See Section D.) And it includes an explanation of how to read the notice Medicare sends you. (See Section E.) Finally, it explains how to appeal a Medicare decision regarding your claim. (See Section F.)

A. Enrolling in Part A Hospital Insurance

Medicare Part A, also called hospital insurance, covers most of the cost of inpatient care in a hospital or skilled nursing facility, and also the costs of home health care. Most people 65 or older are eligible for Part A coverage, either free of charge along with their eligibility for Social Security benefits, or for a monthly fee. This section explains that some people are automatically eligible and do not have to enroll in Part A, other people have to enroll but receive free coverage and still other people must enroll and pay monthly premiums.

1. Those Who Receive Social Security Benefits

If you are already receiving Social Security retirement, dependents or survivors benefits or Railroad Retirement benefits, before you turn age 65, you don't need to do any paperwork to enroll in Medicare Part A hospital insurance. Social Security will automatically enroll you, and coverage will take effect on your 65th birthday. About three months before your 65th birthday, Medicare will mail you a Medicare card and information sheet.

Likewise, if you receive Social Security disability benefits for two years, regardless of your age, you will be automatically enrolled in Medicare Part A, effective 24 months from the date Social Security declared that your disability began. The Medicare card you receive in the mail will indicate that you are enrolled in both Part A and Part B. If you do not want to be enrolled in, and pay the monthly premium for, Part B, there is a form for you to sign and return to Medicare. If you do want to be enrolled in both Parts A and B, you don't have to do anything. Just sign your card and keep it handy.

If you are receiving Social Security benefits but do not receive your Medicare card in the mail within a month of your 65th birthday, or within a month of your 24th month of disability benefits, contact your local Social Security office or call the Social Security office at: 800-772-1213.

Managed Care Plans Handle Medicare Paperwork

Many people about to qualify for Medicare have HMO or other managed care insurance that they intend to keep when they become eligible for Medicare. Other people decide to join an HMO or other managed care plan when they first become eligible for Medicare.

If you intend to remain with your current insurance plan when you become eligible, it can sign you up for Medicare and switch you to the plan's Medicare coverage. Begin this process two to three months before you become eligible for Medicare.

Similarly, if you decide to join a managed care plan for the first time when you become eligible for Medicare, you can sign up for Medicare at the same time you sign up for the plan. Try to get the paperwork started at least two months before your Medicare eligibility begins.

About Your Medicare Card

When you are enrolled in Medicare, you will be sent a Medicare card that has several pieces of information on it. It includes:

- your name
- whether you have both Part A and Part B coverage or just Part A
- the effective date of your Medicare coverage, and
- your health insurance claim number—also called your Medicare number—which consists of your Social Security number and one or two letters.

Always carry your Medicare card with you. You will be asked to present it when you seek medical treatment at a hospital, doctor's office or other health care provider. And you must include your Medicare number on all payments of Medicare premiums or correspondence about Medicare.

If you lose your Medicare card, you can have it replaced by applying in person at your local Social Security office or by calling Social Security's main office at: 800-772-1213.

2. Those Who Do Not Receive Social Security Benefits

If you are soon to turn 65 but you are not receiving Social Security retirement, dependents or survivors benefits, Railroad Retirement benefits or federal civil service retirement benefits, you must apply at your local Social Security office to receive Medicare Part A benefits. If you are going to apply for retirement or other Social Security benefits to begin on your 65th birthday, you can apply for Medicare at the same time, at your local Social Security office.

a. Who is eligible

If you are eligible for Social Security benefits, you can receive free Medicare Part A coverage at age 65 whether or not you actually claim your Social Security benefits. For example, many people who continue working after reaching age 65 do not claim retirement benefits until later. Still, they can receive free Part A Medicare coverage if they apply for it at their local Social Security office.

Also, if you are not automatically eligible for free Part A coverage, you may be able to purchase it for a monthly premium—the amount of the premium depending on how many work credits your or your spouse has earned. (See Chapter 12, Section C1.)

b. When to apply

Whether you wish to claim Social Security benefits and Medicare, or just Medicare, apply well before you turn 65. You are eligible to apply as early as three months before your 65th birthday.

Signing up early is important for two reasons. First, it will ensure that your coverage begins as soon as you are eligible, on your 65th birthday. Second, if you wait more than three months after your 65th birthday to enroll, you will not be allowed to enroll in Part B until the following January 1, and your eligibility will not begin until July 1 of that year. (See Section B3.)

Avoid Delays in Part B Coverage

If you do not enroll in both Part A and B during your initial enrollment period, your enrollment in Part B will not only be delayed, but you will also have to pay a higher monthly premium for it. (See Section B3.)

c. When benefits begin

If you apply for Part A of Medicare within six months after you turn 65, your coverage will date back to your 65th birthday. But if you apply after that, your coverage can only date back six months from the month in which you apply. If your Medicare eligibility is based on disability, however, your coverage can date back one year from the date on which you apply.

3. Appealing Denial of Coverage

Eligibility for coverage by Part A of Medicare depends solely on your age and on the number of Social Security work credits you or your spouse has acquired. (See Chapter 12, Section C.) You can only be denied coverage by Medicare Part A if there is a dispute about whether you have reached 65, about the number of your or your spouse's work credits or about the validity of your marriage.

Decisions about these matters are handled not by Medicare but by Social Security. And like any other decision of the Social Security Administration, a decision denying eligibility for Medicare Part A hospital insurance coverage can be appealed. The appeal process is the same as for appealing other Social Security decisions. (See Chapter 8.)

B. Enrolling in Part B Medical Insurance

Medicare's Part B, referred to as medical insurance, covers doctors' services plus laboratory, clinic, home therapy and other medical services you receive other than when you are a patient in a hospital or skilled nursing facility. Most people age 65 are eligible for Part B. Everyone must pay a monthly premium to enroll, although some people may pay for Part B fees in the premiums they pay to Health Maintenance Organizations or other managed care plans.

This section explains who is automatically enrolled in Part B, who must take steps to enroll and when to do so.

1. Those Who Receive Social Security Benefits

If you are under age 65 and already receiving Social Security retirement, dependents or survivors benefits, you will be automatically enrolled in both Medicare Part A and Part B within three months before you turn 65. Your coverage will become effective on your 65th birthday. Near that time, you will be sent your Medicare card through the mail, along with an information packet. The monthly premium for Part B coverage will be deducted automatically from your Social Security check, beginning with the first month after your 65th birthday.

If you do not want Medicare Part B coverage—because, for example, you are still working and are covered by an employment-related health plan—notify Social Security of that fact on the form that comes with your Medicare card. If you reject Part B coverage when you are first eligible for it, you can enroll in Part B later on, although only during the first three months of any year. And if you enroll later, your premiums may be higher. (See Section B3.)

2. Those Who Do Not Receive Social Security Benefits

If you are turning 65 but are not eligible for Social Security benefits, or are not yet going to claim benefits to which you are entitled, you may still enroll in Part B medical insurance at your local Social Security office.

You can enroll during an initial period of seven months, which begins three months before the month you turn 65 and ends three months after the end of that month. For example, if you turn 65 in July, your initial enrollment period starts April 1 and ends October 31. However, the earlier you enroll during this initial period, the better. If you enroll during the three months before you turn 65, your coverage will begin on your 65th birthday. If you enroll during the remaining four months of your initial enrollment period, your coverage may be delayed from one to three months after you sign up, depending on how long it takes to process your application.

3. Delayed Enrollment

If you do not enroll in Part B medical insurance during the seven-month period just before and after you turn 65, but later decide you want the coverage, you can sign up during any general enrollment period held January 1 through March 31 every year. If you sign up any time during one of these general enrollment periods, your coverage will begin on July 1 of the year you enroll.

Your monthly premium will be higher if you wait to enroll during one of the general enrollment periods instead of when you turn 65. For each year you were eligible for Part B coverage but did not enroll, your premium will be 10% higher than the basic premium.

C. Medicare's Payment of Your Medical Bills

Medicare does not handle day-to-day paperwork and payments with patients and doctors or other health care providers. It contracts out this work to what are called Medicare carriers or intermediaries. These are huge private corporations such as Blue Cross or other large insurance companies, each of which handles claims for an entire state, and sometimes more than one state.

The Medicare intermediary in your state receives, reviews and pays claims. It sends notices that tell you and the medical provider of the amount of benefits paid, the amount of your medical bill that has not been paid and the amount the health care provider is legally permitted to charge. (See Section E.) And it is with the intermediary that you will initially correspond if you want to appeal a decision about Medicare coverage of health care charges. (See Section F.)

Medicare intermediaries handle billing for inpatient charges covered under Part A differently from outpatient charges covered under Part B. This section explains the differences in the billing process.

Free Late Enrollment If Covered By Current Employment Health Plan

If you are covered by a group health plan based on your own or your spouse's current employment, you can enroll in Part B coverage after your 65th birthday without having to wait for the open enrollment period and without any penalty. This exception only refers to a group health plan based on current employment, not based on retirement benefits from employment.

If you have delayed signing up for Medicare Part B because you have been covered by a health plan based on current employment, you can sign up for Part B coverage at any time while you are still covered, or within seven months of the date you or your spouse ends that employment, or the date the health coverage ends, whichever comes first.

1. Inpatient and Home Care Bills

Medicare Part A covers inpatient care in a hospital and skilled nursing facility, as well as some home health care. (See Chapter 12, Sections D4 and D5.)

a. Medicare billed directly by facility

When you first check into a hospital or skilled nursing facility, you present your Medicare card to the admissions office and it takes care of the rest. Similarly, when you and your doctor make arrangements for a Medicare-approved home care agency to provide your care, you give the agency your Medicare number and it takes care of all the paperwork. The provider—the hospital, skilled nursing facility or home health care agency—sends its bills directly to Medicare. The patient should not have to do a thing to get Medicare to pay its part of the bill.

The hospital, nursing facility or home care agency accepts as payment in full the amount the Medicare intermediary decides is the approved charge for those of your inpatient services that are covered by Medicare. Unlike doctors' bills—in which you may be personally responsible for the difference between Medicare's approved charges and the actual amount of a bill—a hospital, nursing facility or home care agency is not permitted to bill you for any covered inpatient charges over the amounts paid by Medicare. The Medicare carrier will also send you a copy of the bills so that you will know how much has been paid and how much you must cover on your own.

b. Patient billed for some charges

The hospital, nursing facility or home care agency will bill you, and your private Medicare supplement insurance company if you have such insurance, for:

- any unpaid portion of your deductible
- any coinsurance payments—for example, for hospital inpatient stays of more than 60 days, and
- charges not covered at all by Medicare, such as for a private room you requested that was not medically necessary, or for television and telephone charges. (See Chapter 12, Section C.)

The Medicare carrier will send you a form called a Medicare Summary Notice that will show what hospital services were paid for and the portion of your deductible for which you are responsible. (See Section E.) The hospital or other facility will bill you directly for the unpaid portion of your deductible and for those amounts not covered by Medicare or by Medicare supplemental insurance. (See Chapter 14.)

2. Outpatient and Doctor Bills

How much of your covered doctor and outpatient medical bills Medicare Part B will pay depends on whether your doctor or other medical provider accepts assignment of the Medicare-approved amount as the full amount of the bill. (See Chapter 12, Section F.) If assignment is accepted, you—assisted by private medigap insurance or Medicaid—are responsible only for your yearly deductible of $100, plus the 20% of the approved charges Medicare does not pay. If the doctor or other provider does not accept assignment, then you and your additional insurance are also responsible for all amounts of the bill up to 15% more than the Medicare-approved amount.

Catching Overbilling

Medicare has been doing a better job in recent years of cracking down on billing errors and fraud by health care providers. But you must still check your bill carefully to determine whether the hospital or other facility has billed you for services you did not receive, or for services that Medicare has paid, or has charged more than once for the same service.

The Medicare intermediary may look closely at the portion of the bill Medicare is supposed to pay, and if you have medigap supplemental insurance, the insurance company will also check the bill. But neither one will carefully examine the amounts for which you are personally responsible.

Check all medical bills to make sure there are no charges for services you did not receive. Then, place the bill from the facility next to the statement from the Medicare carrier and from your medigap insurance company. Compare them to see whether any amount the facility has billed you directly has been paid by Medicare or by your medigap insurer.

If so, you must contact the billing office at the facility, sending a copy of your statement from the Medicare carrier or medigap insurer which shows that the charges have been paid. If the problem is billing for a service you do not believe you received, ask the facility's billing office to send you a copy of the record of your hospital stay where that service was noted.

HMOs and Managed Care Plans Do Their Own Paperwork

If you belong to an HMO or other managed care health plan, the billing office there handles all the Medicare-related paperwork. In fact, Medicare pays most HMOs and managed care plans a flat amount for each enrolled patient, rather than a separate payment for each treatment. All you have to do is pay your plan's own monthly premiums and copayments, and deal with its paperwork. You don't have to handle directly any Medicare forms.

a. Assignment method of payment

If your doctor or other health care provider accepts assignment of your Medicare claim, you are personally responsible for your yearly medical insurance deductible of $100, and then only the 20% of the Medicare-approved amount of the bill that Medicare does not pay. By accepting assignment, the doctor or other provider agrees not to charge you a higher amount than what Medicare approves for the treatment or other covered service you have received.

After you and the health care provider are informed by a Medicare Summary Notice form from Medicare how much the Medicare-approved charges are, the provider's office will either bill you directly for the remaining 20% of approved charges, or bill your medigap supplemental insurance carrier if you have one. (See Section D.)

Example: Franco was examined for a painful knee by his regular doctor, who then decided to refer him to an orthopedist. Franco asked his doctor to refer him to someone who accepted assignment. The orthopedist examined Franco, took X-rays and prescribed exercises and some medication. Franco's own doctor charged $100 for Franco's original examination. The orthopedist charged $150. Both doctors accepted assignment.

Medicare's approved amount for Franco's regular doctor was $75 and for the orthopedist, $120. Because Franco had already paid his yearly $100 deductible for Part B, Medicare paid 80% of the approved amount of each doctor's bill: $60 to Franco's regular doctor (80% of $75 = $60) and $96 to the orthopedist (80% of $120 = $96). Medicare sent these amounts directly to the doctors. Franco only had to pay the 20% difference between the approved amounts and the 80% Medicare paid.

The following chart shows who paid what amount of Franco's bills if his doctors accepted assignment.

PAYMENT OF DOCTOR BILLS—ASSIGNMENT ACCEPTED

	Doctor charges	Amount approved by Medicare	Amount paid by Medicare (80%)	Amount patient pays (20%)
Initial exam	$100	$75	$60	$15
Orthopedic exam	$150	$120	$96	$24
Total	$250	$195	$156	$39

b. Payment when no assignment

If your doctor or other health care provider does not accept assignment of the Medicare-approved charges as the full amount of the bill, you—or you and your medigap supplemental insurance—will owe the difference between what Medicare pays and the full amount of the doctor's bill, up to 15% more than the Medicare-approved amount.

Example: In the example above, Franco's own doctor charged $100 for an examination and the orthopedist charged $150. If neither doctor accepted assignment, the payment amounts would be as follows.

Medicare's approved amount for Franco's regular doctor was $75 and for the orthopedist, $120. Medicare paid 80% of the approved amount of each doctor's bill: $60 to Franco's regular doctor (80% of $75 = $60) and $96 to the orthopedist (80% of $120 = $96). Medicare sent these amounts directly to the doctors. Because there was no assignment, Franco had to pay not only the 20% difference between the approved amounts and the 80% of those amounts Medicare paid, but also the remainder of the unpaid doctors' bills up to 15% above the Medicare approved amount, for a total of 35% of the Medicare approved amount.

The 35% of the approved amount of Franco's regular doctor's bill was $26.25. And 35% above the approved amount of the orthopedist's bill was $42. These were the amounts Franco had to pay.

The following chart shows who paid what amount of Franco's bills if neither doctor accepted assignment.

PAYMENT OF DOCTOR BILLS—ASSIGNMENT NOT ACCEPTED

	Doctor charges	Amount approved by Medicare	Amount paid by Medicare (80%)	Amount patient pays (35%)
Initial exam	$100	$75	$60	$26.25
Orthopedic exam	$150	$120	$96	$42
Total	$250	$195	$156	$68.25

Medicare Billing Paperwork Is Free

Even a doctor or other health care provider who does not accept assignment must fill in the Medicare paperwork and send it to Medicare for payment. And you cannot be charged for processing this Medicare paperwork.

D. Paying Your Share of the Bill

Doctors and other health care providers must wait to find out how much the Medicare-approved charges are before asking you to pay your share. Until they know what the Medicare-approved amount is, they cannot know the legal limit—15% over those approved charges—on how much they can require you to pay. Following your treatment or other service, the doctor's or other provider's office will submit their bills for payment to Medicare. You do not have to submit the paperwork yourself.

If you have private medigap supplemental insurance that pays your deductible and the 20% coinsurance amount Medicare does not pay, the doctor's office will send its paperwork to the insurance company as well as to Medicare. The doctor will receive payment directly from both Medicare and the supplemental insurance, after Medicare has determined the approved amount for the care you received.

Four to six weeks after you receive a Medicare-covered service, the Medicare intermediary will send you a notice, which will include information on:

- how much of each bill is Medicare-approved
- how much of the amount Medicare will pay the provider
- how much of your deductible has been met, and
- how much must be paid by you or your private medigap insurance.

This form is called a Medicare Summary Notice, or MSN. (See Section E.)

E. How to Read a Medicare Summary Notice

The Medicare Summary Notice (MSN) shows how your claims were settled. The MSN is not a bill. It is a tally of procedures and payments for your information. Every time you get an MSN form, you should check several important pieces of information. (See Section 6 below for examples of MSN forms, along with notes pointing out important information.)

1. Date of the Notice

You have six months from the date printed in the top right corner of the first page to appeal any decision that your Medicare carrier makes. (See Section F.) The deadline for filing an appeal is listed on the second page of the MSN.

2. Medicare Intermediary

The name, address and phone number of your Medicare intermediary is listed in a box in the upper right corner of the MSN. You should contact the intermediary if you have questions about the notice or disagree with the way a payment was made and want to appeal. For medical services, this will be the Medicare intermediary in your state that handles almost all Part B claims. For durable medical equipment, however, this will be a regional intermediary, which may be located in another state.

3. Type of Claim

In the middle of the first page, in large, bold capital letters, is a line that reads Part B Medical Insurance. The box under this heading describes the type of claims included in the notice. For example, an MSN might be for Outpatient Facility Claims, referring to laboratory, diagnostic or surgical procedures you received as an outpatient at a hospital or clinic; another notice might be for Assigned Claims, referring to visits to doctors who accepted assignment of the Medicare-approved amount.

4. Services Provided

The name and address of the doctor or provider of services, the dates of the services you received and a description of the specific services are also listed in the box beneath the heading of "Part B Medical Insurance." The Medicare code for each service will be included in parentheses after the description of the service.

Contact the billing office of the health care provider immediately if you believe that the description of the service is incorrect, or if it is correct and you believe it should be a covered service. Ask workers there to check the description of the service and the code number. If there has been a clerical error, it can be changed in informal contact between the doctor's office or other provider and the Medicare intermediary.

Coverage may have been denied because the medical service you received was wrongly described as something Medicare does not cover—a routine physical exam, for example. Or the description may be correct but the Medicare service code may be wrong. Codes can be jumbled by the doctor's office. In that case, the rejected coverage should have been approved. (See Section F2.)

5. Division of the Bills

The Part B Medical Insurance box contains columns that show the cost of each procedure or service and how those costs are divided.

- Amount Charged—The first figure is the amount the doctor or other provider would bill a non-Medicare patient. This usually means nothing to you; a doctor may charge you this full fee only if Medicare does not cover the service at all.
- Medicare Approved—Next comes the amount Medicare sets as its approved charges for the service provided. This is often considerably less than what the doctor or other provider would charge a non-Medicare patient. If the doctor has accepted assignment, this amount will be the total the doctor may collect from Medicare and you or your supplemental insurance. If the doctor or other provider did not accept assignment, the total may only be as much as 15% more than these Medicare approved charges. (See Chapter 12, Section F.)
- Medicare Paid—The third figure is usually the amount Medicare paid to the provider. In the case of unassigned claims, however, this may be titled "Medicare Paid You" and will list the amount Medicare paid you directly.
- You May Be Billed—The most important figure is the amount you may be billed. This is the amount Medicare approved (plus 15%, if assignment was not accepted) minus the amount Medicare actually paid. If you have medigap supplemental insurance, this is the amount that will be billed to it for payment. If you have no supplemental insurance, this is the amount you will have to pay out of your own pocket.

  The amount you may be billed can include:

- the unpaid portion of your $100 annual deductible
- the 20% coinsurance amount Medicare Part B does not pay for most covered services
- up to 15% over the Medicare-approved amount for doctors who did not accept assignment, and
- any amount for services Medicare does not cover at all.

6. Sample Forms

On the next few pages there are three examples of typical Medicare Summary Notices. The first is for a visit to a doctor who has accepted Medicare assignment. The next is for outpatient tests at a hospital. The third is for durable medical equipment. Along the side of each page are notations indicating key points of information in the notice.

MNS Form Example #1

Medicare Summary Notice

Page 01 of 02

July 1, 2000 — Date of Notice

DAISY MAE
1234 BROADWAY
ORANGE, NY 12345

CUSTOMER SERVICE INFORMATION
Your Medicare Number: 123-45-6789A

If you have questions, write or call:
Medicare Intermediary Co.
P.O. Box 123
Blue, NY 12345

Local: (678) 123-4567
Toll-free: (800) 567-8900

HELP STOP FRAUD: Read your Medicare Summary Notice carefully for accuracy of dates, services, and amounts billed to Medicare.

This is a summary of claims processed June 27, 2000

PART B MEDICAL INSURANCE – ASSIGNED CLAIMS — Doctor Accepted Assignment

Dates of Service	Services Provided	Amount Charged	Medicare Approved	Medicare Paid Provider	You May Be Billed	See Notes Section
Claim Number 12345-67890-12345 ORANGE MEDICAL GROUP 6161 Orange Blvd. Orange, NY 12345						
05/15/00	Office Visit, ES (99214)	$75.00	$60.00	$48.00	$12.00	a
	Claim Total	$75.00	$60.00	$48.00	$12.00	

With assignment, doctor is paid only the amount approved

Medicare pays 80% of approved amount; patient or medigap insurance pays 20%

Deductible Information: You have previously met the Part B deductible for 2000

Because patient had already met yearly deductible, Medicare paid the full 80%

Notes Section:

a. This information is being sent to your private insurer(s).

Paperwork also sent directly to medigap private insurance, to pay the remaining 20% ($12)

General Information:

If you change your address, please contact the Social Security Administration by calling 1-800-772-1213.

THIS IS NOT A BILL – Keep this notice for your records.

MSN Form Example #1, page 2

Page 02 of 02

Date of Notice

Your Medicare Number: 123-45-6789A

General Information:

Get the flu prevention shot, NOT the flu. Medicare Part B covers a flu shot to protect you each flu season. You can also protect yourself from some pneumococcal infections by getting a pneumococcal vaccination. Medicare will also pay for your vaccination. One pneumococcal vaccination may be all you ever need. Ask your doctor.

Appeals Information – Part B

If you disagree with any claims decision on this notice, you can request an appeal by January 1, 2001. Follow the instructions below:

1) Circle the item(s) you disagree with and explain why you disagree.

2) Send this notice, or a copy, to the address in the "Customer Service Information" box on page 1.

3) Sign here ____

Phone number (____) _______________

MSN Form Example #2

Medicare Summary Notice

Page 01 of 02

July 1, 2000 — Date of Notice

DAISY MAE
1234 BROADWAY
ORANGE, NY 12345

CUSTOMER SERVICE INFORMATION
Your Medicare Number: 123-45-6789A

If you have questions, write or call:
Medicare Intermediary Co.
P.O. Box 123
Blue, NY 12345

Local: (678) 123-4567
Toll-free: (800) 567-8900

HELP STOP FRAUD: Read your Medicare Summary Notice carefully for accuracy of dates, services, and amounts billed to Medicare.

This is a summary of claims processed June 25, 2000

PART B MEDICAL INSURANCE – OUTPATIENT FACILITY CLAIMS — Charges for tests at hospital as an outpatient

Dates of Service	Services Provided	Amount Charged	Non-Covered Charges	Deductible and Coinsurance	You May Be Billed	See Notes Section
Claim Number 12345-67890-12345 Orange Community Hospital 1600 Health Way Orange, NY 12345 Referred by: R.C. Owen, M.D.						
06/01/00	Echo exam/heart (93307)	$706.00	$0.00	$141.20	$142.20	
	Doppler exam (93320)	323.00	0.00	64.60	64.60	
Claim total		$1,029.00	$0.00	$205.80	$205.80	

Outpatient services may be charged more than Medicare approved amount, but this hospital did not do so

Patient or patient's medigap insurance resonsible for the 20% Medicare did not pay

Deductible Information: You have met the Part B deductible for 2000

THIS IS NOT A BILL – Keep this notice for your records.

MSN Form Example #3

Medicare Summary Notice

Page 01 of 02

July 1, 2000 — Date of Notice

DAISY MAE
1234 BROADWAY
ORANGE, NY 12345

CUSTOMER SERVICE INFORMATION
Your Medicare Number: 123-45-6789A

If you have questions, write or call:
Info-GBA — Processed by special insurance carrier for durable medical equipment
P.O. Box 123
Atlanta, GA 12345

OR CALL US AT:
(800) 666-6666

HELP STOP FRAUD: Read your Medicare Summary Notice carefully for accuracy of dates, services, and amounts billed to Medicare.

This is a summary of claims processed June 27, 2000

PART B MEDICAL INSURANCE – UNASSIGNED CLAIMS — No assignment for medical equipment

Dates of Service	Services Provided	Amount Charged	Medicare Approved	Medicare Paid You	You May Be Billed	See Notes Section
Claim Number 456789012345 A&P Pharmacy, 111 Broadway Orange, NY 12345						
06/01/00	1 pelvic strap (K0031-NU)	$18.00	$18.00	$14.40	$18.00	

Patient paid the pharmacy directly; Medicare reimburses patient for 80%

Deductible Information: You have previously met the Part B deductible for 2000

General Information:

If you change your address, please contact the Social Security Administration by calling 1-800-772-1213.

Get the flu prevention shot, NOT the flu. Medicare Part B covers a flu shot to protect you each flu season. You can also protect yourself from some pneumococcal infections by getting a pneumococcal vaccination. Medicare will also pay for your vaccination. One pneumococcal vaccination may be all you ever need. Ask your doctor.

THIS IS NOT A BILL – Keep this notice for your records.

Don't Let a Doctor Take More Than the Law Allows

Medicare rules are clear—and every doctor and other health care provider knows them. You can only be charged an extra 15% above what Medicare decides is the approved amount for a specific medical service. And the Medicare Summary Notice form does the arithmetic for you, stating the amount of the maximum charge.

If a doctor or other provider did not accept assignment and bills you more than the allowable amount, send the doctor's office a copy of your Medicare Summary Notice form, underlining the spot where the maximum bill is stated—and keep a copy for yourself. If you already paid the bill, and the amount you paid was more than the allowable Medicare-approved amount plus 15%, you are entitled to a refund.

Again, contact the doctor's or other provider's billing office and request your refund, letting them know the date you paid the bill, the amount you paid and the Medicare-approved amount. If they will not refund the overpayment, contact the Medicare carrier, which will then contact the doctor or other health care provider directly.

F. Appealing the Denial of a Claim

Unfortunately, not every request for Medicare payment runs a smooth course. Occasionally, a Medicare hospital or nursing facility review committee may decide your inpatient stay need not last as long as you and your doctor think, and will recommend ending Medicare Part A coverage. Or more commonly, the Medicare carrier will deny Part B coverage for what you believe is a covered medical service. Or sometimes it will cover only some but not all of a treatment that you believe should be covered. You may appeal any of these decisions. This section explains the procedures you must follow.

1. Decisions About Inpatient Care

Occasionally disputes arise about whether treatment as an inpatient in a hospital or skilled nursing facility continues to be medically necessary. These disputes often pit the patient and doctor on one side, and the facility's Medicare review committee on the other. The review committee may believe that the patient can be moved from the hospital to home or to a nursing facility sooner than the doctor advises, or moved from the skilled nursing facility to a nonskilled facility or to home care. If this happens to you, there are several steps you can take to convince Medicare to pay for your continued inpatient care.

a. Coverage decisions

Initial Medicare approval of whether your treatment must be as an inpatient is made by the facility's Utilization Review Committee (URC), a group of doctors and hospital administrators. The committee makes this determination before you are admitted, or within one day of your emergency admission. The URC also periodically reviews your condition and progress in the facility, and can decide—after checking your medical records and consulting with your doctor—that you no longer require inpatient care at that facility.

Such a decision does not mean that you will be kicked out of the facility, but it may mean that the URC will recommend to Medicare that your inpatient stay at the facility no longer be covered by Part A insurance. If you and your doctor believe you should remain in the hospital, there are procedures to follow which may reverse the URC's decision. And even if the decision is not reversed, the process of appealing can give you a bit more time in the facility without being personally responsible for the huge inpatient bills.

Notice of Noncoverage. If the URC decides that your condition no longer requires inpatient care, it will consult with your doctor. If your doctor agrees, the URC will give you a written Notice of Noncoverage stating that your Medicare hospitalization coverage will end on a certain day. If you do not feel that you should be discharged from the hospital at that point, first express your wishes to your doctor. Ask that the doctor request from the URC that a longer period of inpatient care be approved. If your doctor is unavailable, ask to speak with the hospital ombudsman. Many hospitals have an ombudsman who is an independent volunteer whose job is to help mediate disputes between the patient and the hospital.

If the doctor or ombudsman cannot change or delay the URC's decision, or your doctor will not oppose the decision, but you still feel that you should not be discharged, you will have to file an appeal to protect your right to have Medicare Part A cover your inpatient care. (See Section F1.)

If your doctor disagrees with the URC opinion that you should be discharged, the URC will either back off its decision and not contest your Medicare coverage—in which case you will hear nothing about it—or it will ask for an opinion from the state's Peer Review Organization (PRO). The PRO is a group of doctors who are paid by Medicare to review the medical necessity and appropriateness of inpatient care. This is a bit like the foxes guarding the chickens, but the PROs are also medical professionals who respect the opinions of treating physicians. The PRO will review your medical records, the URC's recommendation and your doctor's position.

If the PRO agrees that your continued stay at the hospital is medically necessary, you will hear nothing more about the matter and Medicare will continue to cover your inpatient care. However, if the PRO decides that your inpatient care is no longer medically necessary, you will receive a Notice of Noncoverage stating that your coverage for hospitalization will end as of a certain day.

Health Insurance Counseling & Advocacy Program (HICAP)

Each state has a program assisting people with Medicare, medigap supplemental insurance and Medicaid, including help with understanding bills and filing Medicare appeals. It is called the Health Insurance Counseling and Advocacy Program (HICAP), although in some states it may have another, similar name. It has professional staff plus trained volunteers, and is connected to legal services agencies that can provide free or low-cost legal advice if the matter involves an interpretation of law or a legal fight. HICAP is funded by a combination of federal, state and nonprofit organizations.

The quality of assistance at HICAP programs is generally very high. The offices are usually staffed by dedicated people who are not only knowledgeable and trained to give helpful advice, but who are also willing to fight for your rights. They sit down with you in person, listen to you, look over your papers and help you handle the paperwork and telephoning necessary to make your appeal work.

In larger states, there are many HICAP offices, and you can reach the office nearest you by calling the state's general toll-free number. In smaller states there may be fewer offices, and you will be referred to a HICAP counseling program at a local senior center or other nonprofit organization.

(See Section G for contact information.)

Your Doctor Can Be Your Best Ally

The most important element in winning an appeal, particularly for coverage of inpatient care, is gaining your doctor's cooperation. The decision on a Medicare appeal often depends on what the doctor notes in your medical records about your condition and the treatment involved—and on how much assistance you can get from the doctor in providing clarification to the people doing your Medicare review.

The problem is that many doctors view their responsibility to the patient as including only the technical treatment of a medical condition: your body and how it works. Many doctors are not particularly concerned with how you pay the bill, as long as you pay it. And if it's someone else's bill—the hospital's, for example—the doctor may not care if it's paid at all.

If you are fortunate, your doctor will give some attention to your Medicare needs, calling the Medicare appeal personnel and writing a letter, if necessary. If so, you'll find the Medicare appeal process fairly simple. But if your doctor won't take the time it takes to listen to your Medicare problem and help you with the appeal, you may have a frustrating time, which cannot help your recovery process. It may also prompt you to consider changing doctors.

b. Immediate review

If you receive a Notice of Noncoverage, it will contain important information, including when the URC intends to end your Medicare coverage and whether your doctor or the state PRO has agreed with the decision. Obtaining immediate review—the first step in appealing the decision—differs slightly depending on whether your doctor has agreed with the URC or the decision has been made by the PRO over your doctor's objection.

Immediate review of joint URC and doctor decision. If the Notice of Noncoverage states that your doctor has agreed with the URC that coverage for your inpatient care should end, you must take some action to get the process moving.

If you are in the hospital, chances are you may have physical difficulty making phone calls and having conversations to get your immediate review started. You may have a friend or relative act on your behalf by making the necessary call requesting review of your case. You may also ask your doctor to initiate the review, even though he or she has initially agreed with the URC's recommendation that Medicare inpatient coverage should end on the specified date. And many hospitals have an independent trained volunteer, called an ombudsman, to assist patients in their dealings with the hospital administration. You can ask to speak with the ombudsman, who can then make your request for immediate review.

Once the PRO has been notified that you are requesting immediate review, they will contact you in order to discuss the matter.

Request an immediate review by the PRO by noon of the first work day after you receive the Notice of Noncoverage. Contact may be made by phone or in writing at the number and address of the PRO given on the Notice.

A representative of the PRO will speak with you directly about why you believe you still require inpatient care—and with the doctor who had you admitted to the hospital, or with the physician overseeing your care.

Try Again With Your Doctor

Help from your doctors is the best hope you have of convincing the PRO to approve your continued coverage. Speak with the doctor again and try to change his or her mind. Sometimes a doctor agrees with the URC decision on care without consulting the patient, or based on an expectation of the patient's improvement that has not occurred. Also, there may be more than one doctor treating you. If so, try to enlist the help of your other doctors. Ask them to speak with your admitting physician to convince him or her that you need more inpatient care.

The PRO will review your case and within a matter of days inform you directly of its decision—either by phone or in writing. If the PRO agrees with the facility that your coverage should end, coverage will continue only until noon of the day after you receive notice of the PRO's decision. After that, the facility will bill you for all inpatient costs.

Continued Coverage During Review

If you have requested an immediate review, Medicare will continue to cover your inpatient care until the PRO makes a decision.

Immediate review of a URC decision your doctor opposes. If your doctor believes that you need to remain in the hospital but the URC disagrees, the URC will have taken your case to the PRO before you receive a Notice of Noncoverage. And the Notice will tell you that the PRO has already agreed with the URC.

You must still ask the PRO for immediate review. But unless you and your doctor can present some strong reasons why the decision should be changed, it will likely remain in effect.

The review process should then proceed as follows.

- Contact the PRO at once by phone or in writing to explain why you believe your continued inpatient care is necessary.
- Ask your doctor—or several doctors if more than one is treating you—to immediately call the PRO to give reasons why your inpatient care continues to be medically necessary. If doctors who are treating you have not previously been in contact with the PRO regarding your case, they can help immensely now by backing up what your admitting physician has said about your continuing need for inpatient care.
- Within three working days of your request for review, the PRO will notify you in writing of its decision.
- Medicare Part A coverage will end the third day after you receive the Notice of Noncoverage, even if the PRO has not yet decided. If the PRO takes the full three days to decide on your coverage and then agrees with the Notice of Noncoverage, you will be personally responsible for the full cost of one full day of hospital costs—the day after coverage stops but on which the PRO has not yet decided.

If the PRO upholds the decision that your inpatient coverage should end, that is not the last word on your Medicare coverage. Similarly, if you did not request immediate review, you can still appeal the decision of noncoverage. Several stages of appeal are open to you. (See Sections 1d, 1e and 1f, below.)

c. Have your bill submitted to Medicare

Whether or not you asked for immediate review, you must ask that the hospital or other facility billing office submit the bill to the Medicare intermediary for payment. If you can get strong backing from your doctors, the intermediary might reverse the decision of the URC. Without such support, however, the intermediary will probably uphold the decision of the URC. Either way, if you want to pursue an appeal of the decision, you must have the hospital submit the bill to Medicare. Only by getting a Medicare carrier's decision can you move your appeal to the next stage.

Unfortunately, while the intermediary is deciding on your claim, the hospital or nursing facility may bill you for the uncovered part of your inpatient stay. If you pay the bill and later win your appeal, Medicare will reimburse you.

d. Reconsideration of carrier's decision

If the Medicare intermediary denies the claim for payment of part of your inpatient bill, you have 60 days from the date you receive the notice denying payment to file a request for reconsideration. The address to send this request will be on the notice denying your claim.

This request for reconsideration can be in the form of a simple letter explaining why your stay in the facility continues to be necessary. Once again, however, it is not so much what you say in your letter as whether you have the support of one or more of your doctors. Ask each of your doctors who supports your position to send a letter to the intermediary stating his or her medical opinion, and also to give you a copy. Attach a copy of each doctor's letter to your request for reconsideration, and keep an extra copy for yourself.

It is sometimes difficult to get a doctor to write a letter on your behalf, even if the doctor supports your position. Sometimes it is simply a matter of the doctor being too busy, or not concerned enough with your financial problem, to speak with you in person before you must send in your request for reconsideration. Other doctors charge a fee for writing any letter that does not involve consultation about treatment—as opposed to payment of bills—and the fee may be too high for you. If you have not obtained a letter from a doctor who supports your position, at least list his or her name and phone number in your request to the carrier, and ask that the carrier contact the doctor before completing its reconsideration.

The intermediary will give you a written decision on its reconsideration. If it still denies coverage, you have 60 days to begin the next step in the appeal process.

Put Everything in Writing and Keep Copies

Keep copies of all correspondence and other papers concerning Medicare claims and appeals. Also, keep notes on all conversations you have with your doctor, representatives from the hospital, the PRO and the intermediary. Write down the date of the conversation, the name of the person with whom you talked and what information was given or taken.

e. Request an administrative hearing

You have 60 days from the date of the intermediary's written notice denying coverage to request a hearing in front of an administrative law judge. You may request the hearing only if the amount you're contesting is $100 or more.

The form for requesting an administrative hearing is available at your local Social Security office. This form, the process for requesting the administrative hearing, and the hearing itself, are exactly the same as for Social Security appeals. (See Chapter 8, Sections A and B.)

As with every other stage of a Medicare appeal, your doctors' cooperation is the single most important element. Your doctor could appear personally at the hearing and testify on your behalf in front of the judge, but most doctors would charge an arm and a leg to do this. Instead, ask your doctor—or several of your doctors, if possible—to write an explanation of why your medical condition required inpatient treatment. You can then present the written explanation to the judge. Be aware that many doctors charge for writing such a letter, and Medicare laws permit them to do so.

f. Appeals Council and federal lawsuit

If the decision of the administrative law judge goes against you, you can file an appeal to the Social Security Appeals Council. (See Chapter 8, Section C.) And if that appeal goes against you, you can file an action in federal court challenging the Medicare decision. (See Chapter 8, Section D.) You can only file a lawsuit if the amount you are contesting is $1,000 or more, and because of the time and expense involved, it is likely you would file such a lawsuit only if the amount is quite a bit higher than that. If you are considering such a lawsuit at this stage, consult with an experienced attorney. (See Chapter 8, Section E.) You may be able to get a referral to such an attorney from a HICAP office. (See Section G, below.)

2. Payment of Doctor and Other Medical Bills

During the course of one or more of your Medicare Part B medical insurance claims, you may disagree with the carrier's decision about whether a particular treatment or service is covered by Medicare. If you find that the Medicare carrier has denied coverage for a certain bill, you have a right to appeal. However, the Medicare Part B appeal process is quite limited, and most people have more success informally contacting the carrier than they do with formal appeals.

a. Read the Medicare Summary Notice

The place to start with a question or complaint about your Medicare Part B coverage of a particular treatment or service is the Medicare Summary Notice (MSN) you receive from the carrier. (See Section E.) It not only shows whether a health care service is covered but it also gives a description of the service, a Medicare code number—called a procedure code—for the service and an explanation of why a particular service was not covered.

Certain services are covered if they are described one way by your doctor's office in the Medicare forms they submit, but not covered if described differently. These problems are sometimes caused simply by the wrongly placed checkmark—for example, indicating a routine physical exam (not covered) instead of indicating physical examination for a particular patient complaint (covered). Such a mistake could be made by any number of people involved in handling your claim: your doctor, by someone in your doctor's office or by someone in the Medicare carrier's vast paperwork machinery.

The MSN may also indicate that you were denied coverage for a particular service because you had the service performed too frequently during a given time. For example, you may have had two mammograms in one year when Medicare normally only covers one per year. However, if the treatment was determined to be medically necessary by your doctor—because, for example, you have a family history of breast cancer, or prior exams have disclosed potential problems—Medicare can and should cover the second mammogram.

In either situation, the next step is to contact your doctor's office to get a letter supporting the medical necessity for the treatment provided.

b. Check with your doctor's office

If you believe that the MSN incorrectly describes the service or treatment you had, call your doctor's office and ask if the claim form sent to Medicare had the same information as shown on your MSN. If either the claim form or the MSN had incorrect information, ask that the doctor's office contact the carrier with the correct information.

If coverage was denied because Medicare claims the treatment was not medically necessary, or that you received the treatment too often, ask the doctor to write a letter explaining why the treatment was medically necessary. Also, ask that doctor to make a copy of any of your medical records that support this conclusion—and to send the letter and records to you so that you can then deal with the Medicare carrier.

c. Contact the Medicare carrier

Most mistakes in billing and coverage are corrected informally, by phone and letter. The Medicare carriers know that mistakes are often made and they would rather correct them quickly and inexpensively than go through a lengthy and more costly appeal process.

The number to call to reach your carrier is printed in the "Customer Service Information" box in the upper right-hand corner of the first page of your MSN. When you reach your Medicare carrier, give your name, Medicare number and the date of the MSN, explaining that you want to discuss coverage of a particular item. Then explain why you believe a mistake was made and describe your doctor's response to the problem. If you have a letter or any medical records from the doctor that explain matters, tell the Medicare carrier what you have. The carrier will either contact your doctor's office or ask you to send in a copy of your doctor's letter, or both.

If this informal contact results in a change in decision by the Medicare carrier, it will send you a revised MSN explaining what the new Medicare payments are and how much you owe. If it does not change the coverage decision based on this informal contact, your next step would be to push on to a more formal written appeal.

d. Written request for review

If you have not been able to resolve the coverage question informally, you have six months from the date of the MSN within which to file a written request for reconsideration of the carrier's decision—also called a request for review. Make a copy of the MSN, circle the items you want to challenge, sign the back of the copy and send it to the carrier listed on the front of the form. Although the MSN says you may write your appeal on the form itself, it is better to send along a separate, signed letter with the MSN, stating your reasons for appealing. There is very little space allowed for your statement on the appeal form, usually not enough to explain your reasoning adequately.

The letter should include your full name as it appears on the MSN, your Medicare number, the date of the MSN, the date of the disputed medical service and a brief explanation of why you believe the treatment or other service should be covered. Include any letter or other records from your doctor that support your position.

Hold on to the Documents

Keep copies of all letters and documents you send or receive from the Medicare carrier and from your doctor. Also, keep notes of every conversation you have with anyone at the Medicare carrier, including the date of conversation, name of person with whom you spoke and any action decided upon in the phone call—such as, you will send them a letter, they will contact your doctor, they will call you back within a week.

Time to Seek Assistance

If you are considering a request for a review of your medical bills, or you have completed the written review and are considering a request for a hearing, it may be time for you to get some assistance from a local Health Insurance Counseling and Advocacy Program (HICAP) office. (See Section G.) This is particularly true if the amount you are contesting would put a sizable hole in your budget.

If you are considering an appeal to an administrative law judge for hearing, you may want to consider not only help from HICAP but also the assistance of an experienced Medicare lawyer. (See Chapter 8, Section E.) HICAP can also help refer you to such lawyers.

On the following pages are samples of request for review letters to a Medicare carrier. There are no magic words you must include in such a letter, but these examples demonstrate the kind of simple information required. A letter should include several key points, each of which should be described as briefly and clearly as possible. Keep in mind that the letter is meant merely to point out how and where the error was made and where proof of the error can be found, not to serve as proof itself. Only your medical records and opinion of doctors can actually prove anything.

First, you should briefly describe the treatment you received.

Second, you should point out the specific reasons why the intermediary's decision not to cover the treatment was incorrect—for example, you did not have merely a routine physical exam but an exam to determine the cause of a specific problem, or, you did not have a dental exam but an examination of the nerves in your jaw made by an oral surgeon.

Third, refer to the doctor's letter or other medical records that support your claim.

Notice that at the bottom left of each letter is the notation "cc:" and next to it the name of the doctor. This indicates to the Medicare carrier that you have sent a copy of this letter to your doctor—an action you should take so that the letter goes into your medical file. Sending a copy of the letter to the doctor will help prepare the doctor if the Medicare carrier contacts him or her, and it may remind the doctor to do a better job of explaining the medical necessity of your care the next time you have treatment.

When the carrier reconsiders your claim, it will review your file, check the documents on which the original decision was made and investigate any new information you have presented or the carrier has obtained by contacting your doctor. You do not have an opportunity at this stage to appear in person and explain things. If a mistake was made because incorrect or incomplete information had originally been provided to the carrier, or someone made a simple clerical error, the carrier is likely to reverse its decision and provide you with coverage. You will then receive a written notice of its review determination and a new MSN. If there is a dispute about whether a certain treatment truly was medically necessary, the carrier may well reverse itself at this stage, but it does so less often than in cases of simple clerical errors or missing documentation from the doctor.

Sample Request for Review Letter

Betty Patient
222 Public Street
Consumer, USA 12345
telephone: (111) 111-1111

March 1, 200_

Transprofit Insurance Company
P.O. Box 123
Moneyville, USA 12345
Re: Request for Review and Reconsideration
Medicare Part B
Medicare Number xx-xxx-xxxxA
MSN Notice dated January 2, 200_

To Whom It Concerns:

This letter is a request for review and reconsideration of a decision made by Transprofit denying coverage of a medical treatment I received on November 1, 200_. A copy of the MSN notice of January 2, 200_, denying coverage, is enclosed.

I believe that Transprofit denied coverage of the mammogram I received on November 1, 200_, from Dr. Alice Well because I had previously had a mammogram in January, 200_, which Medicare covered, and Medicare does not normally cover more than one mammogram per year. However, this second mammogram was medically necessary because I have a family history of breast cancer and because my previous mammogram in January showed some spots of potentially cancerous tissue.

Apparently the original Medicare claim from my doctor's office did not include this background information. However, I am enclosing a copy of a letter from Dr. Well and a copy of the medical records from my January mammogram to indicate why the second mammogram was medically necessary.

Based on this information, please reconsider the original decision denying Medicare coverage of the November 1 treatment.

Yours truly,

Betty Patient
cc: Dr. Alice Well

Sample Request for Review Letter

Andy Q. Everyone
18B Main St.
Anytown, USA 12345
telephone: (222) 222-2222

June 1, 200_

Ourworld Insurance Inc.
P.O. Box 567
Big Money, USA 12345
Re: Request for Review and Reconsideration
Medicare Part B
Medicare Number xx-xxx-xxxxB
MSN Notice dated March 1, 200_

To Whom It Concerns:

This letter is a request for review and reconsideration of a decision made by Ourworld Insurance denying coverage of a medical treatment I received on January 10, 200_. A copy of the MSN notice of March 1, 200_, denying coverage is enclosed.

I believe that Ourworld Insurance denied coverage of the eye exam I received on January 10, 200_, from Dr. Barry Eyesore because Dr. Eyesore's office mistakenly noted on the Medicare claim form that I underwent a routine eye examination refraction on that date, marking on the form procedure code 92015.

This was a mistake. In fact, I had a specific examination and treatment for blurred vision and eye pain that I had been suffering. Dr. Eyesore's records indicate that this was a medically necessary examination for a medical condition, for which he prescribed medication, rather than a routine eye examination. Enclosed is a copy of my medical record from Dr. Eyesore indicating the nature of the exam on that date.

Based on this additional information, please reconsider the original decision denying Medicare coverage of the January 10, 200_ examination and treatment of my eyes.

Yours truly,

Andy Q. Everyone
cc: Dr. Barry Eyesore

e. Request hearing

If the carrier reviews your file and still refuses to cover your treatment, and the amount of the disputed bill is $100 or more, you can continue your appeal by requesting a hearing. To reach the $100 minimum, you can combine different claims as long as each individual claim has gone through the review and reconsideration process. You have six months from the date of the written notice of determination to request a hearing. The address to which to send the request for a hearing is printed on the carrier's written notice of determination following reconsideration.

The letter requesting a hearing is similar to the letter requesting review and consideration, except that you should refer to the date of the carrier's written determination following review in addition to the original MSN.

In separate paragraphs, make the following points.

- Describe the treatment you received and the dates on which you received it. This description should be brief, since the carrier will get its full explanation from your medical records.
- State the specific reasons why the intermediary's initial decision to cover the treatment was incorrect.
- Refer, by name and date, to your doctor's letter and to the specific medical records that support your claim.

Attach to your request for a hearing copies of letters from your doctors and of your medical records, if you have them. Also, call your doctors' offices to request that they send copies of your records to the hearing office at the address you have been given on the notice.

A week before the hearing, call the hearing office and ask whether it has received your letter and any documents you included, plus any medical records you asked your doctor to send. If medical records have not yet arrived and you cannot be sure that your doctor will get them to the hearing in time, ask that the hearing be rescheduled to a later date.

If you want to appear personally at the hearing, make that request in your letter. You will be notified where and when the hearing is to take place. If you later change your mind about appearing, or cannot manage to get to the hearing, you can always call the hearing office to ask that the hearing be rescheduled.

Letter Requesting Carrier's Hearing

Rosa Albertez
3456 Broadway
Anytown, USA 45678
telephone: (333) 333-3333

June 1, 200_

Your Money Insurance Co.
P.O. Box 1234
Greentown, USA 12345
Re: Request for Hearing, Medicare Part B
Medicare Number xx-xxx-xxxxC
Notice of Determination after Review dated May 1, 200_

To Whom It Concerns:

This letter is a request for a hearing by the carrier following a determination made on May 1, 200_. That determination upheld a decision made by Your Money denying coverage of a medical service I received on February 1, 200_, and laboratory work performed on February 5, 200_. A copy of the MSN notice of March 15, 200_, denying coverage is enclosed. Also enclosed is a copy of the written determination after review, dated May 1, 200_.

I believe that Your Money denied coverage of the physical examination I received from Dr. Walter Thorough and of laboratory work ordered by Dr. Thorough because Dr. Thorough failed to include certain information to the carrier. The physical and the laboratory tests were not routine examinations but were a response to severe muscle fasciculation and cramping that I had been suffering over the previous several weeks. Dr. Thorough's records indicate that the examination and laboratory tests were medically necessary to diagnose and treat my condition.

I have enclosed a copy of my medical records from Dr. Thorough, as well as a letter from Dr. Thorough, both of which make clear that the examination and laboratory tests were medically necessary and should be covered by Medicare.

I want to appear personally at the hearing scheduled for this matter.

Yours truly,

Rosa Albertez
cc: Dr. Walter Thorough

f. Hearing before hearing carrier officer

The carrier's hearing is held before a hearing officer who has expertise in medical matters. The hearing officer is not an employee of the carrier, and therefore may be willing to change the carrier's original decision even though the carrier did not do so during its own review.

The hearing is an informal affair in which the hearing officer will ask you to explain why you think the medical services you received should be covered. Your personal explanation probably won't add much to your doctor's letter and your medical records, but it will usually give you an advantage over simply presenting your claim in writing. If you appear at the hearing, you can answer questions the hearing officer might have, and you can check to see that the hearing officer's file contains your medical records and letter from your doctor. If the file is incomplete, you can give copies to the hearing officer right then and there; make sure to bring extra copies of everything to the hearing.

Also, hearing officers are more likely to be sympathetic to a real person than to a file of papers. Of course, this means that you must be honest and polite with the hearing officer; it won't do you any good to rant and rave, or to appear to demand anything unreasonable.

You will receive a written notice of the hearing officer's decision in the mail—usually in two to six weeks. If the hearing officer reverses the carrier's decision, you will receive a new MSN from the carrier explaining the new payment amounts.

g. Hearing before administrative law judge

If your claim for coverage is once again denied after the carrier's hearing, you can request a hearing before an administrative law judge if the amount you are contesting is $500 or more. If the amount in dispute is less than $500, the hearing before the carrier's hearing officer is the end of the line.

You must request a hearing before an administrative law judge within 60 days of the date you receive written notice of the decision by the carrier's hearing officer. (See Chapter 8, Section B.)

h. Appeals Council review

If you do not receive a favorable ruling from the administrative law judge, you may appeal the decision to the Social Security Appeals Council. (See Chapter 8, Section C.) In Medicare Part B claims, the written appeal must be filed within 60 days of the date of the administrative law judge's written decision.

i. Federal court case

It is highly unlikely that a Medicare Part B decision will involve enough money that it would be economically sensible for you, and a lawyer representing you, to file a lawsuit in federal court to challenge a negative decision by the Appeals Council. However, if your claim is for $1,000 or more, you do have such a right. You must file the lawsuit within 60 days of the written decision by the appeals council. (See Chapter 8, Section D.)

G. Health Insurance Counseling and Advocacy Offices (HICAP)

These are the numbers for the central state offices. They can direct you to a local HICAP office near you.

Alabama	800-243-5463
Alaska	800-478-6065
Arizona	800-432-4040
Arkansas	800-852-5494
California	800-434-0222
Colorado	800-544-9181
Connecticut	800-994-9422
Delaware	800-336-9500
District of Columbia	202-676-3900
Florida	800-963-5337
Georgia	800-669-8387
Hawaii	808-586-7299
Idaho	800-247-4422
Illinois	800-548-9034
Indiana	800-452-4800
Iowa	800-351-4664
Kansas	800-860-5260
Kentucky	502-564-7372
Louisiana	800-259-5301
Maine	800-750-5353
Maryland	800-243-3425
Massachusetts	800-882-2003
Michigan	800-803-7174
Minnesota	800-333-2433
Mississippi	800-948-3090
Missouri	800-390-3330
Montana	800-332-2272
Nebraska	402-471-2201
Nevada	800-307-4444
New Hampshire	800-852-3388
New Jersey	800-792-8820
New Mexico	800-432-2080
New York	800-333-4114
North Carolina	800-443-9354
North Dakota	800-247-0560
Ohio	800-686-1578
Oklahoma	800-763-2828
Oregon	800-722-4134
Pennsylvania	800-783-7067
Puerto Rico	800-981-4355
Rhode Island	800-322-2880
South Carolina	800-868-9095
South Dakota	800-822-8804
Tennessee	800-525-2816
Texas	800-252-9240
Utah	800-439-3805
Vermont	800-642-5119
Virginia	800-552-3402
Virgin Islands	809-778-6311
Washington	800-397-4422
West Virginia	800-642-9004
Wisconsin	800-242-1060
Wyoming	800-856-4398

H. Medicare Part B Carriers

ALABAMA

Blue Cross-Blue Shield of Alabama
800-292-8855
205-988-2244

ALASKA

Blue Cross/Blue Shield of North Dakota
800-444-4604

ARIZONA

Blue Cross/Blue Shield of North Dakota
800-444-4604

ARKANSAS

Arkansas Blue Cross/Blue Shield
800-482-5525
501-378-2320

CALIFORNIA

Counties of: Los Angeles, Orange, San Diego, Ventura, Imperial, San Luis Obispo, Santa Barbara: Transamerica Occidental Life Insurance Co.
800-675-2266
213-748-2311
Rest of state: National Heritage Insurance Co.
800-952-8627
530-743-1583

COLORADO

Blue Cross/Blue Shield of North Dakota
800-332-6681
303-831-2661

CONNECTICUT

United Healthcare
800-982-6819
203-237-8592

DELAWARE

Medicare Customer Service Center
800-444-4606

DISTRICT OF COLUMBIA

Medicare Customer Service Center
800-444-4606

FLORIDA

Blue Cross/Blue Shield of Florida
800-333-7586

GEORGIA

Cahaba
800-727-0827
912-927-0934

HAWAII

Blue Cross/Blue Shield of North Dakota
800-444-4606

IDAHO

CIGNA Medicare
800-627-2782
615-244-5650

ILLINOIS

Wisconsin Physicians Services (WPS)
800-642-6930
312-938-8000
TDD 800-535-6152

INDIANA

AdminaStar Federal
800-622-4792
317-842-4151

IOWA

Blue Cross/Blue Shield of North Dakota)
800-532-1285
515-245-4785

KANSAS
Blue Cross/Blue Shield of Kansas
(In state) 800-432-3531
(Out of state) 800-432-0216
(In Topeka) 785-291-4000

KENTUCKY
AdminaStar Federal
800-999-7608
502-425-6759

LOUISIANA
Arkansas Blue Cross/Blue Shield, Inc.
800-462-9666
(In Baton Rouge) 504-927-3490

MAINE
National Heritage Insurance Co.
800-492-0919
781-741-5256

MARYLAND
Medicare Customer Service Center
800-444-4606

MASSACHUSETTS
National Heritage Insurance Co.
800-882-1228
781-741-5256

MICHIGAN
Wisconsin Physicians Service (WPS)
800-482-4045

MINNESOTA
United Healthcare Insurance Co.
800-352-2762
612-884-7171

MISSISSIPPI
United Healthcare Insurance Co.
800-682-5417
601-956-0372

MISSOURI
Blue Cross/Blue Shield of Kansas
800-892-5900
(Kansas City area) 816-561-0900
Rest of state:
Arkansas Blue Cross/Blue Shield
800-392-3070
314-843-8880

MONTANA
Blue Cross and Blue Shield of Montana
800-332-6146
406-444-8350

NEBRASKA
Blue Cross/Blue Shield of Kansas
800-633-1113

NEVADA
Blue Cross/Blue Shield of North Dakota
800-444-4606

NEW HAMPSHIRE
National Heritage Insurance Co.
800-447-1142
781-741-5256

NEW JERSEY
Xact Medicare Services
800-462-9306

NEW MEXICO
Arkansas Blue Cross/Blue Shield
800-423-2925
505-872-2551

NEW YORK

Counties of: Bronx, Columbia, Delaware, Dutchess, Greene, Kings, Nassau, New York, Orange, Putnam, Richmond, Rockland, Suffolk, Sullivan, Ulster, Westchester:
Empire Blue Cross and Blue Shield
800-442-8430
County of: Queens
Group Health Inc.
212-721-1770
Rest of state:
BC/BS of Western New York
800-252-6550

NORTH CAROLINA

CIGNA
800-672-3071
919-665-0348

NORTH DAKOTA

Blue Shield of North Dakota
800-247-2267
701-277-2363

OHIO

Nationwide Mutual Ins. Co.
800-282-0530
614-249-7157

OKLAHOMA

Arkansas Blue Cross/Blue Shield
800-522-9079
405-848-7711

OREGON

Blue Cross/Blue Shield of North Dakota
800-444-4606

PENNSYLVANIA

Xact Medicare Services
800-382-1274

RHODE ISLAND

Blue Cross and Blue Shield of Rhode Island
800-662-5170
401-861-2273

SOUTH CAROLINA

Blue Cross/Blue Shield of South Carolina
800-868-2522
803-788-3882

SOUTH DAKOTA

Blue Cross/Blue Shield of North Dakota
800-437-4762

TENNESSEE

CIGNA Medicare
800-342-8900
615-244-5650

TEXAS

Blue Cross/Blue Shield of Texas
800-442-2620

UTAH

Blue Cross/Blue Shield of Utah
800-426-3477
801-333-2430

VERMONT

National Heritage Insurance Co.
800-447-1142
781-741-5256

VIRGINIA

Fairfax and Arlington Counties:
Medicare Customer Service Center
800-444-4606
Rest of state:
United Healthcare
800-552-3423
540-985-3931

WASHINGTON

Blue Cross/Blue Shield of North Dakota
800-444-4606

WEST VIRGINIA

Nationwide Mutual Insurance Co.
800-848-0106
614-249-7157

WISCONSIN

Medicare/WPS
800-944-0051
608-221-3330
TDD 800-828-2837

WYOMING

Blue Cross and Blue Shield of North Dakota
800-442-2371
307-632-9381

AMERICAN SAMOA

Blue Cross/Blue Shield of North Dakota
800-444-4606

GUAM

Blue Cross/Blue Shield of North Dakota
800-444-4606

NORTHERN MARIANA ISLANDS

Blue Cross/Blue Shield of North Dakota
800-444-4606

PUERTO RICO

Medicare/Triple-S, Inc.
In Puerto Rico: 800-981-7015
In metro area: 787-749-4900

VIRGIN ISLANDS

Triple-S, Inc.
800-474-7448

■

Medigap Insurance

Even for people who have coverage from both Medicare Part A and Part B, a serious illness or injury can cause financial havoc because of the bills Medicare leaves unpaid. Well over half of all Medicare recipients age 65 and over respond to this risk by buying a private supplemental health insurance policy known as medigap or med-sup insurance.

The term medigap comes from the fact that these insurance policies are designed to cover the gaps in Medicare payments. Unfortunately, most medigap coverage is not nearly as complete as its advertising would lead you to believe. The alternatives, HMOs and other managed care plans, typically provide broader coverage at slightly lower cost than most medigap insurance policies. However, HMOs and managed care restrict the doctors and facilities available to you in ways that most medigap policies do not.

Before choosing one type of coverage or another, compare benefits and approaches and measure your preferences against the price you would have to pay for each. This chapter gives you guidance about the gaps in Medicare that need to be filled, and the types of medigap insurance policies that partially fill them. Chapter 15 covers the various types of managed care plans available as alternatives to medigap supplements. Before selecting either a medigap policy or a managed care plan, review the advantages and disadvantages discussed in Chapter 15, and use charts at the end of that chapter to compare the costs and coverage of individual policies and plans.

Insurance From Continuing or Former Employment

Many people who are eligible for Medicare continue to work and have health insurance through their own or their spouse's employer. The law requires employment group health plans to offer the same coverage to people ages 65 and over as they do to younger people.

And many other people keep their job-related health insurance after they retire, as part of their retirement benefits package, although they usually have to pay much more than a current employee.

Employment-based health plans require you to sign up for Medicare when you turn 65, but will cover you in conjunction with Medicare. The health benefits or human resources office at your work or union can explain the details of coordinating coverage.

Just because you are eligible for a work-related health plan, however, does not mean that you have to continue with it. Work-related health insurance has become more expensive and less comprehensive for employees—particularly retired employees. You may find that Medicare plus a medigap policy, or Medicare through an HMO, provides you with better coverage at a better price than does your work's medical insurance combined with Medicare.

Even if you decide not to participate in the regular health plan offered in your workplace, your employer's insurance company may offer you a different policy with limited coverage for some services Medicare does not cover at all, such as prescription drugs, dental care or hearing aids. Compare such a policy with the medigap policies and managed care plans discussed in this chapter to see which one offers you the best coverage for your money.

A. Gaps in Medicare

When considering the kinds of supplemental coverage available, keep in mind the specific gaps in Medicare payments that you are trying to fill. Medicare coverage is explained in detail in Chapter 12, but some of the most significant things it does not cover, or covers but only partially pays, are listed below.

1. Gaps in Part A Hospital Insurance

Medicare Part A covers almost all the cost of most hospital stays. Its most common gap is the deductible, which everyone must pay before Medicare pays any part of a hospital bill. A much less frequent but much more frightening gap is the daily coinsurance amount for hospital stays of more than 60 days. All of the gaps are listed below.

a. Hospital bills

Medicare Part A hospital insurance does not pay the following costs during a hospital stay:

- a deductible for each benefit period—$776 in 2000
- a daily coinsurance amount ($194 in 2000) for each day you are hospitalized more than 60 days and up to 90 days for any one benefit period
- a daily coinsurance amount ($388 in 2000) for each day you are hospitalized more than 90 days and up to 150 days for any one benefit period
- anything past a hospitalization of 150 days
- first three pints of blood, unless replaced, and
- anything during foreign travel.

b. Skilled nursing facility bills

Medicare Part A does not pay the following costs during a stay in a skilled nursing facility:

- a coinsurance amount of $97 per day for each day you are in the facility more than 20 days and up to 100 days for any one benefit period, and
- anything for a stay of more than 100 days.

c. Home health care

Medicare Part A does not pay the following costs for home health care:

- 20% of the approved cost of durable medical equipment or approved non-skilled care, and
- anything for non-medical personal care services.

2. Gaps in Part B Medical Insurance

Medicare Part B can have some very large gaps in the amounts it pays doctors, depending on whether the doctors accept assignment. Everyone faces the 20% of the Medicare-approved amount that Medicare does not pay. And if your doctor does not accept assignment, you are also responsible for up to 15% more than the amount Medicare approves. The other largest uncovered expense, particularly for older people, is for prescription medication.

Medicare Part B does not pay the following costs for doctors, clinics, laboratories, therapies, medical supplies or equipment:

- $100 yearly deductible
- 20% of the Medicare-approved amount
- 15% above the Medicare-approved amount if provider does not accept assignment
- 20% of the total charges for outpatient hospital services
- preventive or routine examinations and testing
- prescription medication
- dental care, or
- routine eye and hearing exams, or glasses or hearing aids.

B. Standard Medigap Benefit Plans

In the first 20 years of Medicare's existence, insurance companies produced a dizzying array of insurance policies intended to supplement Medicare coverage. At best, they were confusing to consumers. At worst, they offered unnecessary or duplicate coverage and contained numerous escape clauses by which the insurance companies avoided payment. Finally the federal government stepped in to regulate medigap policies. Now, insurance companies can only offer ten standardized benefit plans, referred to by all insurance companies as Medicare supplement benefit plans A through J.

Beware of Private Coverage Agreements

A few doctors who regularly treat Medicare patients try to pad the amounts Medicare and medigap insurers will pay them by inducing patients into private side agreements. In these side deals—sometimes called retainer agreements or prepayment contracts—the doctor agrees to accept assignment of Medicare amounts and sometimes to waive the yearly Medicare deductible and copayment amounts. In exchange, the patient agrees to undergo and pay for, sometimes in advance, certain services Medicare does not cover at all, such as routine physical exams and testing. Other agreements require that the patient pay a set amount out of pocket for a service that Medicare would normally cover.

These agreements can result in Medicare patients paying hundreds, even thousands, of dollars for services that should be covered by Medicare, or which they may not need. Some of these doctors claim that these agreements preserve the freedom of the patient to have the doctor they want. In truth, they blackmail the patient into paying, or finding another doctor. They bilk unnecessary expenditures from the patient and set up an unhealthy forced relationship between doctor and patient. Under Medicare rules, virtually all these contracts are illegal.

If you are offered any such contract, turn it down. And report the matter to the United States Department of Health and Human Services at: 800-638-6833. Or contact your state's department of insurance, which you can find under the State listings in the Government section at the front of the white pages of your telephone directory.

Delay May Limit Your Choices

As with all insurance, the people who need medigap coverage the most often have the hardest time getting it. If you might conceivably need coverage some day, an insurance company will sell you a policy. But if your medical condition indicates that you are quite likely to need the coverage soon, the insurance company will reject your application. The federal government has set rules which limit this practice somewhat. An insurance company must accept your medigap application—at the normal price—during the first six months of your Medicare coverage. If you wish to purchase a medigap policy after that initial six-month period—because you want to switch from another policy or from a managed care plan—the insurance company may review your medical record and reject you if it considers you to be a bad profit risk. (See Section C.)

Not every company offers every plan. And only the benefits included in the plans are standardized. Other important aspects—initial eligibility, premium increases and pre-existing illness exclusions—vary from policy to policy and require careful comparison shopping. (See Section C.)

When you consider medigap policies, your task is to see how many of the gaps in Medicare payments you can fill within the constraints of your budget. The broader the coverage in a medigap policy, the higher the cost. And although the benefits are standardized, the cost of a standard policy varies widely from company to company. So you must determine not only which benefit plan best suits your needs, but which company offers which plan at the best price. Then examine the other elements of each policy, such as premium increases and preexisting illness exclusions, before making your choice. (See Section C.)

Medigap Does Not Cover Long-Term Care

Many older people fear the possibility of living out the final years of life in a nursing home. The prospect of nursing home life itself provokes distress for many, as does the financial ruin that can be brought about by the cost of long-term care. Unfortunately, neither Medicare nor medigap supplemental insurance nor managed care health plans protect against this potentially enormous cost. Medicare covers only a limited period of skilled nursing facility care and covers nothing of long-term custodial, or non-medical, care in a nursing home. Medigap policies and HMOs similarly fail to cover long-term nursing home care.

Long-term care at home is increasingly an option for people who in years past would have been forced to enter a nursing home. More services are available at home, and more agencies and providers offer home care. However, neither Medicare nor medigap policies cover long-term home health care.

There is a type of private insurance that can cover some of the cost of long-term nursing home or at-home care. Referred to as long-term care insurance, it is available in a variety of benefit packages, but comes with numerous restrictions and exclusions. The cost of these policies varies greatly, depending on the extent of coverage and the age of the person covered.

For a complete discussion of these policies and the kinds of care they cover, see *Beat the Nursing Home Trap* by Joseph Matthews (Nolo Press). See the catalog at the back of this book for ordering information.

I. Basic Benefits Included in All Medigap Plans

The benefits included in the ten standard medigap plans and a chart comparing their coverage follow.

All ten standardized medigap policies begin with the same basic benefits, which pay for the most common and expensive costs that Medicare does not pay. However, if a particular medical service is not covered by Medicare, the medigap basic benefits will not help pay for it.

All medigap policies pay at least the following basic benefits.

Medigap: It Pays to Shop Around

The federal government decides what benefits must be included in standard medigap policies. But it does not control prices, which vary widely. Prices vary for different ages. They also change from state to state, reflecting regional health care costs and level of competition for customers.

But the price for the same policy may vary tremendously even within the same state. A study in late 1997 found that even the most basic Plan A policy varied in cost as much as $1,300 per year in some states. Other standard policies also had wide price disparities.

Most of the time there is no basis for the price disparities other than "name" recognition. Don't fall for the first policy that comes along. Even when you've decided what standard policy you want, comparison shop for the best price from several different insurance companies.

a. Inpatient hospital costs

For every benefit period, every plan pays all your Medicare Part A coinsurance amounts through your first 90 days as an inpatient, plus your coinsurance amount for any reserve days. After your reserve days are used up, every plan pays for the entire Medicare approved amount of hospital charges for an additional 365 days. The basic plan also pays for the first three pints of blood you receive. However, it does not pay your Part A deductible.

b. Medical expenses

Every plan pays the 20% coinsurance amount Medicare Part B does not pay. It also pays the 20% of Medicare-approved home health care amounts not paid by Medicare. The basic medigap benefits do not, however, include your Part B deductible or the 15% above the Medicare-approved amount that a doctor is allowed to charge if he or she does not accept assignment. (See Chapter 12, Section F.)

Check Premium Raises

It is always important to check the terms under which an insurance company may raise the amount of your premium. But it is particularly important when the initial premium already stretches your budget. Pay particular heed to the rules regarding hikes in medigap insurance premiums. (See Section C.)

2. Standard Medigap Plans

There are currently ten standard Medigap policies available—summarized in the chart below and discussed more fully in the sections that follow.

The Ten Standard Medigap Insurance Policies

All plans include these basic benefits:

Hospitalization: Medicare Part A coinsurance plus 365 days of coverage after Medicare ends

Medical costs for outpatients: Medicare Part B coinsurance (20% of Medicare-approved costs)

	Plan A	Plan B	Plan C	Plan D	Plan E	Plan F	Plan G	Plan H	Plan I	Plan J
Medicare Part A Deductible		X	X	X	X	X	X	X	X	X
Medicare Part B Deductible			X		X					X
Skilled Nursing Coinsurance			X	X	X	X	X	X	X	X
Foreign Travel			X	X	X	X	X	X	X	X
At-Home Recovery				X			X		X	X
Preventative Care					X					X
Doctors' Excess Charges						(100%) X	(80%) X		(100%) X	(100%) X
Prescription Medicine								($1,250) X	($1,250) X	($3,000) X

a. Plan A

Includes: basic benefits only

Plan A medigap policies include only the basic benefits discussed earlier. (See Section B1.) Because of their limited benefits, Plan A policies are the least expensive.

Plan A policies are most useful if the doctors who regularly treat you accept assignment of Medicare-approved amounts, and you can afford to pay for the uncovered costs of doctors who do not accept assignment but by whom you might have to be treated. (See Chapter 12, Section F.) Also, you must be able to afford the Part A hospital insurance deductible, bearing in mind that because there is a separate deductible for each separate hospital stay, you may have to pay it more than once in a year. (See Chapter 12, Section D.)

If these potential expenses plus the cost of a Plan A policy would put a severe strain on your finances, consider the alternative of an HMO, which may provide broader coverage for less money. (See Chapter 15.)

b. Plan B

Includes: basic benefits, Medicare hospital deductible

In addition to the basic benefits, a Plan B policy also pays your Medicare Part A deductible.

If your doctors all accept assignment but your budget would be severely strained if forced to meet more than one hospital deductible in a year, Plan B may be marginally better for you than Plan A. However, if you have to pay more than a few dollars a month more for Plan B than for Plan A, it may be a bad bargain.

Measure the yearly cost of a Plan B against the cost of a Plan A policy. If you are reasonably healthy—meaning you do not expect frequent hospitalizations—and the difference in premiums is more than 25% of the Part A Medicare deductible ($776 in 2000), it is probably not worth the extra premium and you should stick to a Plan A policy.

c. Plan C

Includes: basic benefits, Medicare hospital & medical deductibles, skilled nursing coinsurance, foreign travel

Plan C adds three benefits beyond those offered in Plan B. First, it pays your yearly Medicare Part B deductible of $100. But since this policy will probably cost you more than $100 per year over Plan A or B, that isn't a good reason to purchase it.

Second, Plan C policies cover the Medicare coinsurance amount for skilled nursing care. Remember that under Medicare skilled nursing coverage, you are personally responsible for a coinsurance amount ($97 per day in 2000) for stays of 21 to 90 days in a skilled nursing facility. This can add up to a considerable amount of money, but it applies only if you are covered by Medicare for short-term skilled nursing care in a nursing facility. (See Chapter 12, Section C6.) If you have a medical condition that puts you in and out of the hospital, this can be a valuable addition to your policy. But the odds are low that most people will be in a skilled nursing facility for more than 20 days more than once or twice in a lifetime.

Finally, Plan C offers some coverage for medical care while traveling outside the United States. For people who travel abroad frequently, this can be a valuable benefit. After you pay a $250 deductible, Plan C pays for 80% of emergency medical costs you incur abroad. For purposes of these policies, emergency means any unplanned medical costs; it is not restricted to what in the U.S. would be called "emergency room" treatment. However, there are some restrictions on the coverage. Your emergency medical care must begin within the first 60 days of each trip abroad; if you take long trips, this policy will not protect you after the first two months. And there is a $50,000 lifetime maximum on these foreign travel medical benefits. If you spend a good portion of each year abroad, you may need a separate—that is, non-medigap—health insurance policy to cover you fully for treatment received outside the United States.

Remember that your overseas medical care must be emergency care; if you regularly spend time abroad and simply want to be able to see a doctor for ongoing medical problems, this policy will not cover such visits.

The cost for Plan C policies is considerably higher than for Plan A or B, but runs about the same as for Plans D and E.

d. Plan D

Includes: basic benefits, Medicare hospital deductible, skilled nursing coinsurance, foreign travel, at-home recovery

Plan D is the same as Plan C except it does not pay the $100 yearly Medicare medical insurance deductible. It does, however, pay for a certain amount of at-home recovery following an injury, surgery or illness.

There are significant restrictions on this coverage. First, it pays only for unskilled personal care—and pays for that only when it has been ordered by your doctor while you are also receiving skilled home health care covered by Medicare. (See Chapter 12, Section C7.) The Plan D policy pays for up to $40 per visit, up to seven visits per week, but for no more than the number of Medicare-covered home health visits you receive. And there is a yearly maximum of $1,600.

With all these restrictions plus the relatively low odds that you will use Medicare-covered skilled at-home care, this coverage is of limited value. A Plan D policy is preferable to a Plan C only if it is available for about the same money and other terms, such as preexisting illness exclusions. (See Section C.).

e. Plan E

Includes: basic benefits, Medicare hospital deductible, skilled nursing coinsurance, foreign travel, preventive care

Plan E adds minimal coverage of some preventive care but eliminates Plan D's coverage of at-home recovery. Plan E only pays for $120 per year of such preventive health care and screening, so it's not much of a benefit.

If you are deciding between the $1,600 per year of at-home coverage included in Plan C and the $120 per year covered by Plan D, offered at virtually the same price, Plan C is a better bet.

f. Plan F

Includes: basic benefits, Medicare hospital and medical deductibles, skilled nursing coinsurance, foreign travel, at-home recovery, 100% of Medicare medical insurance excess physician charges

Plan F offers the most significant added benefit beyond Plans B, C, D and E—payment of 100% of what a doctor actually charges you above the Medicare-approved amount. Doctors who do not accept assignment are permitted to charge a patient up to 15% more than the Medicare-approved amount for any covered service. (See Chapter 12, Section F.) If you receive extensive medical care from doctors who do not accept assignment, that extra 15% mounts up quickly.

Because the extra 15% of medical bills can amount to a lot of money, insurance companies charge higher premiums for Plan F than for the plans discussed previously. If you are in generally good health and the few doctors you see all accept assignment, this higher premium may not be worth the extra coverage. If, on the other hand, you require frequent or extensive medical care and you receive it from doctors who do not all accept assignment, Plan F may be worth the higher premiums.

g. Plan G

Includes: basic benefits, Medicare hospital deductible, skilled nursing coinsurance, foreign travel, at-home recovery, 80% of Medicare medical insurance excess physician charges

Plan G is similar to Plan F, with three significant differences. Plan G does not cover the $100 per year Medicare medical insurance deductible Plan F covers, but it does cover at-home recovery as in Plan D. Another difference between Plan G and F is that Plan G only covers 80% of the 15% excess doctor's charges, while Plan F covers 100% of those charges.

If you are likely to require frequent or extensive treatment by different doctors and you cannot be sure whether they will accept assignment, the extra coverage of Plan F may be worth its higher cost. On the other hand, if your medical bills are not very high, even though you see a doctor who does not accept assignment, the lower premiums for reduced coverage under Plan G may be a better bargain for you.

h. Plan H

Includes: basic benefits, Medicare hospital deductible, skilled nursing coinsurance, foreign travel, prescription drugs

Plan H, along with Plans I and J, provides coverage for something many older people spend a lot of money on but Medicare does not cover: prescription medication. After you pay a yearly deductible of $250, Plan H pays up to 50% of the cost of your prescription medication, to a maximum yearly amount of $1,250. To get the full $1,250 in benefits, the total cost of your prescription drugs for the year would have to reach $2,750.

However, Plan H does not cover any of the 15% excess charges a doctor may bill you above what Medicare approves.

This plan is a good one if your doctors accept assignment and you regularly take expensive prescription medication.

i. Plan I

Includes: basic benefits, Medicare hospital deductible, skilled nursing coinsurance, foreign travel, 100% of Medicare medical insurance excess physician charges, at-home recovery, prescription drugs

Plan I is the second most expensive policy because it includes two of the most significant benefits: coverage of charges by doctors who do not accept assignment and prescription medication. It also includes at-home recovery. This policy is a very good one if you can afford the premiums.

However, even if you can afford it, an insurance company that has the policy might not offer it to you. If you have a history of high medical bills or medication costs, an insurance company might not be willing to sell you a Plan I policy. There is one way around this resistance: if you sign up for the policy during your open enrollment period in the six months immediately following your first enrollment in Medicare Part B, an insurance company that offers Plan I in your state must sell it to you. (See Section C.)

j. Plan J

Includes: basic benefits, Medicare hospital and medical deductible, skilled nursing coinsurance, foreign travel, 100% of Medicare medical insurance excess physician charges, at-home recovery, preventive care, extended prescription drugs

Plan J is the luxury model of medigap policies. It is also the most expensive. And because its coverage is the most extensive, insurance companies tend not to sell it to people who have had extensive recent medical treatment or prescription drug costs, unless they sign up in the mandatory open enrollment period in the six months immediately following first enrollment in Medicare Part B.

In addition to what Plan I covers, Plan J pays the yearly Medicare medical insurance deductible ($100) and provides a limited amount ($120) of preventive care. Most significantly, it more than doubles the total amount of benefits Plan I pays for prescription medication—up to $3,000 per year. It still only pays 50% of the cost of medication and there is still a $250 deductible you must first pay for prescription medication. So you can only reach the full $3,000 in coverage if your total bill for prescription drugs is $6,250.

Medicare SELECT Medigap Policies

In addition to regular fee-for-service medigap policies, there is a category of supplemental insurance that is partly fee-for-service and partly managed care. It is called Medicare SELECT. A SELECT policy must provide the same benefits as any of the standard A through J medigap policies, but it has a two-tiered payment system.

If you use hospitals—and under some policies, doctors—who are members of the policy's network, the policy pays full benefits. If you use a provider outside the network, the policy pays reduced benefits. In this way, a Medicare SELECT medigap policy works like a Preferred Provider Organization or HMO with Point-of-Service option, except that those managed care plans usually cover more services than most medigap policies. Because of these restrictions, Medicare SELECT policies are somewhat less expensive than regular medigap policies.

C. Terms and Conditions of Medigap Policies

In addition to the services covered, the amount of benefits and the monthly cost of a medigap insurance policy, there are several other things to consider before making a final decision. Most important are terms affecting how much in premiums you will be required to pay in the years to come—and therefore whether you will still be able to afford the policy when you may need it most. Also important are terms that determine whether you are covered for a particular illness during a certain time period after you purchase the policy.

1. Premium Increases

It is one thing to find insurance coverage you can afford today. It may be quite another to find a policy that you can continue to afford in the future when your income and assets have decreased and the policy premium has increased. In choosing a medigap policy, consider how much policy premiums will rise over time. If the current premium will already be a significant strain on your financial resources, consider a less expensive policy, because any policy is sure to get more expensive in the future. For example, in 1996 and 1997, the cost of premiums from most medigap insurers rose a startling 25% to 40%.

There are several ways insurance companies set up premium increases in medigap policies. Choosing the best premium increase terms is something for you to consider along with other terms of the policy.

a. Level premiums

The best method for the consumer is what's called level premiums. This means that premiums do not go up on your policy as you reach a certain age, but only when the insurance company raises premiums on all medigap policies of the type you have. Of course, the premiums will go up regularly, but the amount they go up will be at least partially controlled by market forces and by your state's insurance commission.

b. Attained age

These policies base the premium upon your age, increasing it each time you attain a certain age plateau, such as 70, 75, 80. These policies look attractive if they offer relatively low prices at age 65. Once you have signed up, though, these policies stick you with large premium rises at the next attained age. And the older you get, the more difficult and expensive it is to drop one policy and get a new one.

When considering a policy with attained age premium rises, ask to see not only how much it would cost you at your present age, but also the current premium costs at each of the next age levels. That will give you a sense of how high the rates jump for that policy. Figure that your premiums will rise by at least the same percentages, and calculate how much your policy is likely to cost at your next two age levels. Only then will you have a realistic picture of how much this policy will truly cost.

c. Issue age

The initial premium for an issue age policy is determined by your age when you first purchase it. From then on, as long as you keep the same policy, you pay the same premium as someone else who buys the policy at the same age at which you bought it. For example, if you buy an issue age medigap policy at age 65, in five years you will pay the same as a person who first buys the policy at that time at age 65. Your premium will steadily rise, but the increases may tend to be controlled by the insurance company's need to keep the premium competitive to continue signing up new policyholders.

d. No age rating

Very few insurance companies sell policies that charge the same amount regardless of age. These policies tend to be a bit more expensive for people ages 65 to 75 and a bit less expensive for people 75 and over.

2. Open Enrollment

The federal government has passed a law providing what is called open enrollment. This law forbids insurance companies from denying a medigap policy to anyone who buys it within the first six months after first enrolling in Medicare Part B. For most people, this means the first six months following their 65th birthday. If you did not enroll in Medicare Part B when you turned 65 but later sign up for it during one of the yearly general enrollment periods (January to March), you will have a six-month open enrollment period for medigap policies beginning July 1 of the year you sign up for Part B coverage.

If you did not sign up for Part B at age 65 because you were covered by an employment-related health insurance plan, you will have a six-month open enrollment period for medigap policies beginning the date your Part B coverage begins regardless of when you sign up for it.

Going Back to Medigap

There might be circumstances where, through no fault of your own, you lose your existing supplemental coverage. For example, your medigap insurance company may go out of business, your Medicare managed care plan may drop coverage in your area or you may move to a state where the insurance company does not do business. In any of these situations, you will have a short time—63 days—to purchase one of four standard medigap policies (A, B, C or F) offered in your area.

If you chose a managed care plan when you first became eligible for Medicare at age 65, you have a special 12-month period where you may drop that coverage and buy a medigap policy instead. During those 12 months, you may enroll in a medigap policy—A, B, C or F—and your medical history will not be examined first.

3. Initial Eligibility

If you find a policy you like but you try to buy it after your open enrollment period has ended, the insurance company may decide not to sell it to you. Insurance companies try to identify in advance people who are likely to collect a lot of benefits, then refuse to sell them a policy. They do this by asking to examine your medical records over the previous few years and refusing to sell you a policy if you have had a significant amount of medical treatment or you have a condition that is likely to require extensive medical treatment in the near future. Almost all insurance companies require such initial eligibility reviews—sometimes called medical underwriting—for medigap plans H, I and J, which provide the most extensive benefits. Many insurance companies do not bother with such review for medigap plans A through G.

4. Preexisting Illness Exclusion

Most policies contain a provision excluding coverage, for a set time immediately after you purchase a policy, of any illness or medical conditions for which you received treatment within a given period before your coverage began. Six months is a typical exclusion period. Many policies provide no coverage for six months after you buy the policy for illnesses you were treated for within six months before the policy starts. Usually, the shorter the exclusion period, the higher the premium.

If you have a serious medical condition that may require costly medical treatment at any time, and you have been treated for that condition within the recent past, consider a policy with a short exclusion period or none at all.

D. Finding the Best Medicare Supplement

Shopping for a medigap policy can be difficult, not only because of the differences in policy terms among the ten standard policies, but because of the wide spectrum of prices among insurance companies. At the end of Chapter 15 is a chart to help you do a side-by-side comparison among different medigap and managed care plans.

1. Using an Insurance Agent

If you use an insurance agent to present you with a choice of Medigap policies, make sure he or she is experienced with the provisions of several different policies. The benefits may have been standardized into ten policy plans, but other terms of the policy are also important and price varies widely. (See Section C.) Insurance agents tend to work with policies from certain companies and may not know of less expensive or less restrictive policies from other companies. So you may want to consult more than one agent.

Even if you arrange to get your insurance through an agent, keep your own ears and eyes open for policies that might fit your needs. Friends, relatives and organizations to which you belong may all be resources to find out about available plans. And senior organizations can be a good source of information. (See Section D2.) A good insurance agent should be willing to find out the details of a policy you have located yourself. If the agent cannot or will not check on such a policy, it is probably time to find a new agent. Likewise, if an insurance agent is unwilling to sit down with you and compare the coverage and costs of different policies, then you ought to comparison shop for a new insurance agent.

Finally, remember that insurance agents normally do not sell HMO memberships, although some do handle enrollment in managed care plans. And if they do not handle HMO membership or enrollment in a managed care plan, they cannot make money signing you up for one. Therefore, be cautious about an insurance agent who tries to convince you that a medigap policy is better for you than an HMO or managed care plan. That is a decision you have to make yourself after comparing the cost, benefits and other factors of each plan. (See Chapter 15.)

2. Senior Associations

A number of organizations of seniors or retired people advertise or offer medigap insurance policies. Some offer excellent policies, with a good range of terms and premiums. Organizations may be able to provide good prices if insurance companies compete for the large business they provide.

But some senior organizations act almost as fronts for insurance companies. These organizations may appear to exist for the benefit of older people, offering a number of programs or services for seniors. But many of these alleged benefits are nearly worthless, and in truth these organizations exist to sell themselves through membership dues and products, including overpriced insurance, under the umbrella of protecting senior citizens.

The best way to tell whether the policies offered by a particular organization are good or bad is to compare their specific terms and prices with those of other policies offered by different insurance companies or health plans. In the final analysis, it is the terms of the policy, not an organization's good intentions or friendly advertising, that determine the quality of your coverage. The insurance company, not the senior organization, determines your coverage and pays your claims.

Help With Decisions About Medigap and Managed Care

Each state has a program to assist people with Medicare, medigap supplemental insurance and HMOs and other managed care plans. It is called the Health Insurance Counseling and Advocacy Program (HICAP), although in some states it may have another, similar name.

HICAP has professional staff and volunteers who are not only knowledgeable about the rules pertaining to Medicare and medigap insurance but also about what policies are available in your state and what HMOs and other managed care plans are available in your local area. HICAP staff can look over particular insurance policies and managed care plans and help you see the strengths and weaknesses of each.

In larger states there are many HICAP offices, and you can reach the office nearest you by calling the state's general toll-free number. In smaller states there may be fewer offices, and you will be referred to a HICAP counseling program at a local senior center or other nonprofit organization.

(See Chapter 13, Section G, for contact information.)

Beware of Mail-Order and Limited-Offer Policies

Beware of policies you receive unsolicited in the mails. Their flashy promises often far outstrip their coverage. If you do become aware of a policy through the mails, and its provisions seem good to you after comparing it with other policies, check the reputation of the company offering the policy with your state's insurance department or commission, or consult with your state or local consumer protection agency.

Also be wary of policies that are offered with short-time enrollment periods. You have likely heard or seen advertisements for insurance that holler: "Limited offer! One month only! Buy now, the greatest offer in years! Once the offer is over, you'll never get another chance at an opportunity like this again! Once-in-a-lifetime offer!"

This is nonsense.

If it's a reputable company with a legitimate policy to offer you, the same or similar terms will be available any time—although you must keep in mind your own six-month open enrollment period after you sign up for Medicare Part B. (See Section C2.) These advertising slogans are just another way insurance companies have of pressuring you into buying a policy without first carefully considering and comparing its terms.

Most companies permit you to look over your policy and carefully examine its terms for ten days before you are obligated to keep it. If you decide you don't want the policy for any reason, you can return it within ten days to the company or to the insurance agent you bought it from and get a refund of all the money you have paid up to that point. And if you are buying a new medigap policy to replace one you already have, you are legally entitled to 30 days to review the new policy to decide whether you want to keep it. You can cancel it without penalty at any time during those 30 days.

3. Only One Medigap Policy Required

You need only one policy to supplement your Medicare coverage—and it is illegal for an insurance company to sell you a health insurance policy that duplicates coverage you already have with a medigap policy. When you apply for a medigap policy, you will be asked to provide information concerning any health insurance policies you have. This gives written notice to the seller of your policy—insurance agent, broker or company representative—about your existing insurance so that you will not be held responsible for paying for duplicate coverage if the insurer mistakenly sells it to you.

If you already have medigap insurance but want to replace it with a new policy, some rules help protect you while you make the change. (See Section D4.)

4. Replacement Policies

If you are considering replacing your existing policy with a new one, there are a number of things to keep in mind.

First, even if your new policy would ultimately provide better coverage, it may have a preexisting condition exclusion that would deny you coverage for up to six months after you switched policies. If you have been treated in the previous six months for any serious medical condition that might require further treatment in the near future, don't cancel a basically good policy for one that is only slightly better.

Second, unless you are signing up within the first six months following your enrollment in Medicare Part B, the new insurance company from which you applied for coverage might reject you if you have had serious medical problems in the recent past. Don't cancel your old policy until you have been given written notice from the insurance company—not just from the agent or broker who sold you the policy—that your new policy is in effect.

When you apply for a replacement policy, you must sign a statement agreeing that you will drop your old policy when the new one takes effect. The law gives you a review period within which to decide between the old and new policies. Once you have received written notice of your acceptance in the new insurance plan, and you have been given a written copy of the new policy, you have 30 days to cancel either the new policy or the old one.

Dread Disease Policies: A Dreadful Idea

A few insurance companies offer policies that do not provide medigap supplemental coverage, but provide particularized health coverage that may overlap some with medigap policies and even Medicare coverage itself. Most of these policies cover treatment for a specific disease and are known as indemnity or "dread disease" policies. They are often solicited over the phone or by direct mail and are offered at low monthly premiums.

One of these policies may initially sound promising if it covers a particular disease—for example, a specific type of cancer—for which you have a high risk. However, close examination of these policies usually shows them to be a waste of money. They pay only a small, set amount of money for each day you are hospitalized or for each medical treatment for the specific disease, usually far less than the Medicare deductible or coinsurance that a medigap policy would pay.

And because they only pay when you are treated for the specific disease, you wind up needing to carry a medigap policy anyway to cover all medical bills not related to this particular disease. Or if you don't carry a medigap policy, you will be responsible for paying out of pocket for all medical bills not covered by this specific-disease policy. Either way, these policies are a bad investment.

■

Medicare Managed Care Plans

Medicare managed care plans fill the gaps in basic Medicare, as do medigap policies. But the two systems operate in different ways. As explained in Chapter 14, medigap policies work alongside Medicare: medical bills are sent both to Medicare and to a medigap insurer, and each pays a portion of the approved charges. Medicare managed care, on the other hand, provides all the coverage itself, including all basic Medicare coverage and other coverage to fill the gaps in Medicare coverage. The extent of coverage beyond Medicare, the size of premiums and copayments and decisions about paying for treatment are all controlled by the managed care plan itself, not by Medicare. (See the charts in Section C below to help compare specific policies.)

There are two widely divergent views of managed care. To some, it is an economical way to provide health care. To others, it is an insurance industry attack on access to quality health care. And both views are correct. In return for coverage beyond basic Medicare, managed care plans charge a low monthly premium—or none at all—and small copayments. But they also restrict in several ways the patient's choices about health care services. And they pressure doctors to limit treatments and the length of hospital stays for their managed care patients. If you are considering a Medicare managed care plan, you must decide whether any of the plans available in your area offers adequate care at an affordable cost.

Joining Managed Care Means Leaving Medicare

If you join a Medicare managed care plan, you leave the Medicare program altogether. The insurance company that runs the managed care plan gets a monthly payment from Medicare on your behalf. The plan then approves or denies all of your medical coverage. If it denies coverage, it also decides any appeals.

If you leave a managed care plan, you are always permitted to rejoin traditional Medicare. But if you return to Medicare after the first year following your initial Medicare eligibility, you may find that not all medigap supplemental insurance policies will accept you. And you may be able to join another managed care plan only during open enrollment.

A. The Structure of Managed Care

The basic premise of managed care is that the member-patient agrees to receive care only from specific doctors, hospitals and others—called a network—in exchange for reduced overall health care costs. There are several varieties of Medicare managed care plans. Some have severe restrictions on consulting with specialists or seeing providers from outside the network. Others give members more freedom to choose when they see doctors and which doctors they may consult for treatment. Generally, more choice translates into higher cost.

1. Health Maintenance Organization (HMO)

The HMO is the least expensive and most restrictive Medicare managed care plan. There are four main restrictions.

a. Care within the network only

Each HMO maintains a list—called a network—of doctors and other health care providers. The HMO member must receive care only from a provider in the network, except in emergencies. If the plan member uses a provider from outside the network, the plan pays nothing toward the bill. And because a plan member has technically withdrawn from traditional Medicare by joining managed care, Medicare pays none of the bill, either. The plan member must pay the entire bill out of pocket.

Because of this restriction, it is very important to find out whether the doctors and other providers you use are included in the HMO's network. This is particularly true for your primary care physician who not only will handle routine medical problems but also decide if you should be referred for treatment or to a specialist. It is also important to make sure that the hospital in your vicinity, or a hospital you and your doctor prefer to use, is in the network. If all of your doctors and your preferred hospital are in the HMO's network, the restriction may not be as important to you.

However, HMOs and other managed care plans do add and drop doctors and hospitals when they refer too many patients to specialists or spend more of the HMOs resources on patient care than other doctors and hospitals in their area. And doctors groups and hospitals leave HMOs that become stingy in reimbursing for medical care or authorizing services for their patients. If the plan or your providers decide to cut their ties, you won't be able to continue seeing your regular doctors. So, even if you begin a managed care plan with all the right doctors and hospital, you may later find yourself traveling long distances to get to a new hospital and searching for new doctors, or searching for a new managed care plan or medigap policy.

This unpredictability with managed care plans makes it important for you to discuss with your doctors any particular HMO you are considering. Ask whether your doctor has experienced problems with the plan, particularly with approval of treatments, referrals to specialists or early release from inpatient hospital care. It may be useful to talk with the billing office staff at your doctor's office, since they there have daily contact with the insurance company bureaucracy.

Some doctors are uncomfortable speaking with patients about insurance companies. But responsible physicians will at least tell you if their offices are considering dropping a particular plan altogether.

Emergency and Urgent Care Anywhere

Federal law requires that all plans cover emergency services nationwide, regardless of restrictions they place on the use of doctors and hospitals for routine care. The law also requires that plans pay for covered services you receive from a non-plan provider if the treatment was urgently needed while you were temporarily outside the plan's geographic service area. (See Section B.5, below.) Urgently needed care is for an unforeseen illness or injury for which a reasonable person would not wait until they could return home to seek medical help.

This required emergency coverage does not apply to most foreign travel. However, some plans offer such coverage on their own. If you travel or live any part of the year outside the United States, but are not covered while abroad, it may be a good idea to buy a temporary policy covering you for the time you are out of the country.

b. All care through primary care physician

An HMO member must select a primary care physician from the plan's network. This is the doctor all members must see first for all medical needs. An HMO member may not see other doctors or providers—even from within the plan's network—or obtain other medical services without a referral by their primary care physician. Even if you regularly see a variety of specialists, your primary care physician must refer you to those doctors. You may not simply make an appointment to see them on your own.

This system encourages the primary care physician—who is paid less than a specialist by the plan—to take care of medical problems that don't absolutely require a specialist. Because of the hassle of the extra step, it also discourages the plan member from seeking specialist care. This restriction is a significant reason that managed care is cheaper for insurance companies than traditional fee for service policies. Since many seniors require specialist care, this restriction is also a reason that many of them reject HMO coverage in favor of medigap insurance or less restrictive types of managed care.

c. Prior HMO approval of some services

HMOs require that your primary care physician or other network physician obtain prior approval from the plan for certain medical services the doctor may want to prescribe. If plan administrators do not believe a service is medically necessary, or believe service from a non-specialist or other less expensive treatment would do just as well, they may deny coverage for that prescribed service.

d. Limited appeal rights

Within every HMO plan, a member has a limited right to appeal the plan's decisions. But for the vast majority of HMOs, reviewers who work for the HMO hear the appeal. There is no review by outside experts, and no appeal to Medicare; only a few HMOs have outside review panels that consider appeals in serious cases. (See Section B.4, below.)

2. HMO with Point-of-Service (POS) Option

A few HMOs have a significant wrinkle that makes them more attractive—and more expensive—than standard HMO plans. These plans offer what is called a point-of-service option. This option allows a member to see physicians and other providers who are not in the HMO's network, and to receive services from specialists without first going through a primary care physician. However, if a member does go outside the network or sees a specialist directly, the plan pays a smaller part of the bill than if the member had followed regular HMO procedures. The member pays a higher premium for this option than for a standard HMO plan, and a higher copayment each time the option is used.

3. Preferred Provider Organization (PPO)

Although it has a different name, the PPO works the same as an HMO with a point-of-service option. If a member receives a service from the PPO's network of providers, the cost to the member is lower than if the member sees a provider outside the network. PPOs tend to be more expensive than standard HMOs, charging both a monthly premium and a higher copayment for non-network services. However, many people find that the extra flexibility in choosing doctors is an important comfort to them, and therefore worth the extra money.

4. Provider Sponsored Organization (PSO)

The PSO is a group of medical providers—doctors, clinics and a hospital—that skips the insurance company middleman and contracts directly with patients. As with an HMO, the member pays a premium, as well as a copayment each time a service is used.

Some PSOs in urban areas are large conglomerations of doctors and hospitals that offer considerable choice in providers. But many PSOs are small networks of providers that contract through a particular employer or other large organization, or that serve a rural area that has no HMO.

Joining and Leaving a Plan

Within the first six months of signing up for both Part A and Part B of Medicare, a managed care plan must accept you without reviewing your medical condition or history. Every Medicare managed care plan must also have at least one month of open enrollment—no checking of medical history—per year. And many plans have continuous open enrollment, which mean they will accept anyone eligible for Medicare at any time.

Leaving a Medicare managed care plan can sometimes be more difficult than joining one. Through the end of the year 2001, a member of a Medicare managed care plan may leave and join another managed care plan or return to traditional Medicare at any time (with 30 days notice to the plan). Beginning January 1, 2002, however, a managed care member may leave only during the plan's open enrollment period.

B. Choosing a Medicare Managed Care Plan

To evaluate a managed care plan, get a complete written explanation of its coverage, costs and procedures. These are usually contained in a printed brochure called a Summary of Benefits. Also, get a chart showing premiums and copayments. Compare that written information with each important category discussed in this chapter.

If you do not understand exactly what the coverage, costs and procedures are, ask a plan representative to point out where they are explained in the written information. If you can't get an important piece of information in writing, don't join the plan.

More Info On Medicare

In the second half of 1999, the Health Care Financing Administration mailed a handbook entitled "Medicare & You 2000" to everyone enrolled in Medicare. In addition to basic Medicare information, the handbook offers some comparative statistics about Medicare HMOs available in your area. Unfortunately, this comparative data is extremely sketchy. And it is likely to go quickly out of date.

You can get more current information by calling 1-800-MEDICARE (1-800-633-4227) for automated answers to frequently asked questions or to talk to a Medicare representative. You can also find information by looking at the "Medicare Compare" link on Medicare's website at www.medicare.gov. Both of these services provide information on costs and benefits for each plan available in your area, as well as information on the quality of care and patient satisfaction. You may also obtain an address and phone number for the plan's representative in your area for further details.

The best way to analyze your managed care coverage is to compare the costs and benefits side by side with Medigap and any other plan you are considering using the charts found at the end of this chapter.

1. Choice of Doctors and Other Providers

For many people, the most important factor in choosing a Medicare HMO or PSO is whether the doctors, hospital and other providers they already use and trust are in the plan's network of providers. If the people and places you prefer for care are in the network, the tight restrictions of HMOs and PSOs may not have much effect on you, at least for the foreseeable future. But if not, you would be faced with finding new doctors, which is never an easy or comfortable process. And you might have to use a hospital that is more distant from your home, leaving you a little less secure.

The problem is not quite as great with PPOs, or HMOs with a point-of-service option. These plans permit you to use providers who are not in the plan's network. So, if you want to continue with a particular doctor or provider who is not in the network, you may do so, but with a higher copayment each time you use the non-network provider. If you are treated by non-network doctors very often, the extra payments may wind up canceling out the cost advantage of managed care.

2. Access to Specialists and Preventive Care

The requirement that you must visit your primary care physician to obtain specialist referrals is one of the main objections to managed care. Try to learn how difficult it is to get a referral to a specialist with any plan you are considering.

a. Covering referrals

Your primary care physician refers you for testing, laboratory work and treatment by specialists. Speak with your primary care doctor and other physicians you see regularly about their experiences with a particular plan. Does the plan often overrule the doctor's recommendation? Has the plan set guidelines for the doctors that might affect their ability to send you for treatment?

b. Access to specialists

Medicare rules require managed care plans to develop a specific treatment plan for patients with a complex or serious condition, such as heart disease, cancer and kidney failure. The plan must outline what specialists you require and it must allow you to see them without a referral from your primary care doctor. If you have a condition that requires care by specialists, find out from the plan whether your condition is considered sufficiently serious or complex to permit direct access to your specialists.

c. Preventive care options

Under Medicare rules, a managed care plan must permit members to obtain routine preventive women's health care screening from a gynecologist without first seeing a primary care physician. It must also permit a member to obtain Medicare-mandated mammograms without a referral. Find out from a managed care plan what other preventive care services—such as annual physical exam, prostate screening for men, cholesterol testing or hearing exams—the plan permits members to schedule on their own.

Now You Get It, Now You Don't

Unlike medigap insurance policies, the government does not regulate managed care plan coverage except to insist that the plans offer at least basic Medicare benefits. Nor is there any regulation of premiums and copayments. What this means is that managed care plans are free to change coverage and charges at any time.

To compete with other insurance, your plan might expand coverage. In recent years, for example, short-term custodial care and overseas travel coverage have been added to many plans, although most charge an added premium for these "extras."

But plans will just as often cut back on coverage. In some plans, benefits are shifted from no-premium plans to deluxe plans with a premium. Raising copayments for specific services—particularly prescription drugs—is also common, as is restricting access to certain medications.

3. Total Cost

Many managed care plans charge no premium to members. Other plans charge a relatively small premium—especially PPOs, and HMOs with point-of-service option or "deluxe" coverage, such as unlimited prescription drugs. Usually, these premiums are lower than for medigap policies. But premiums don't tell the whole story. You must add up other costs to see if a managed care plan is a better financial deal for you than medigap.

a. Copayments

A copayment is the amount a plan member must pay out of pocket for each visit, service or drug prescription. There is usually no copayment for hospital stays, surgery, laboratory work and skilled nursing care and home health care that would be covered by basic Medicare. But there is a copayment for most doctor visits, usually $5 to $15. Many older people consult with several doctors fairly frequently. If you do, then the copayments can mount up quickly.

b. Prescription drug copayments

The most expensive out of pocket medical cost for many seniors is for prescription drugs. Managed care plans all cover some amount of prescription medication. But they require patient copayments and impose restrictions that vary considerably depending on the category of drugs you use.

Managed care plans separate drug coverage and copayments into several categories—each of which carries different cost restrictions.

- *Generic versus brand name*—Managed care plans encourage use of generic drugs, usually by offering much lower copayments, such as $5 per generic prescription compared to $15 to $25 for brand name drugs. Other plans place a yearly limit on the amount they will spend for brand name medication. If you frequently use and strongly prefer a particular brand name drug, this price difference can be important.
- *Formularies*—Most managed care plans maintain a preferred list of drugs, called a formulary. With some managed care plans you may use drugs not on the formulary, but for a

higher copayment. With other plans, if you use a drug that is not on the formulary, the plan pays nothing at all.

It is best to pick a plan that pays something for non-formulary drugs, because managed care plans often change the drugs in their formulary. If a brand name drug you use is dropped from the list in favor of a cheaper generic the plan will still pay something for the brand name drug if you choose to continue using it.

- *Mail order drugs*—Many people who take regular medication have found that they can get it cheaper by ordering large quantities through a mail order drug company instead of using a local pharmacy. Mail order drugs are cheaper for managed care plans, too. Some plans offer lower copayments for medicines ordered this way.

Tracking Membership Satisfaction

You will not learn about member complaints from a managed care plan. But it pays to see if many members complain about crucial services. Most complaints focus on:

- rejecting referrals to specialists
- ordering early discharge for hospital inpatients
- dropping coverage in certain geographic areas
- dropping doctors and hospitals from the network
- raising copayments
- switching drugs on the plan's formulary, or
- dropping extra coverage.

Your state Department of Insurance or Department of Corporations are charged with monitoring managed care plans, but their efforts are spotty. Some keep good track of complaints and make them public. But many keep poor track of complaints or refuse to release information about them.

An excellent and free source of information about managed care plans is the Health Insurance Counseling and Advocacy Program. You can find your local office by calling the central HICAP office in your state, listed in Chapter 13, Section G.

4. Review Process

About 30% of Medicare managed care patients report having been denied coverage for treatments their plans deemed to be medically unnecessary or experimental. And if you are denied coverage for a treatment or service, Medicare will not help you. The appeals procedure is run by the plan. The prospect of having your wishes and those of your doctor overruled by the insurance company is always enraging. When the treatment is for a serious illness, the plan's rejection can be devastating.

Before joining any managed care plan, explore its appeal or review process. The procedures should be explained in the Summary of Benefits booklet the plan gives to potential members. If the review process is not fully explained, request written information from a plan representative.

a. What the law requires

All Medicare managed care plans are legally required to put a denial of coverage in writing within 14 days of a request for coverage—and within 72 hours of a request if the treatment involves urgent care. If you appeal the denial, the plan must decide the appeal within 30 days of the time the appeal is filed, or within 72 hours if the condition is urgent. If the denial is based on a determination that the treatment or referral is not medically necessary, the law requires that any review of the decision be made by a physician with expertise in the area of medicine involved.

b. Who makes the decisions

Beyond these few legal controls, however, the process by which decisions are reviewed is completely up to the plan. And the most important element of that process may be who does the reviewing. There are three types of review:

- *Internal review only*—Panels of managed care plan doctors and health care managers—medical accountants, basically—decide appeals. These panels are less likely than an external reviewer to reverse a denial of treatment. Unfortunately, most managed care plans use only internal review boards.
- *External review chosen by plan*—In cases where care has been denied as not medically necessary or as experimental, some plans permit external review. However, most plans choose and pay the outside reviewer, which raises concerns about the impartiality of the review process.
- *Independent external review*—Independent review boards are best for plan members. Although consumer groups are pushing the managed care industry hard in this direction, truly independent reviews are still rare.

5. Extent of Service Area

Consider the extent of a plan's service area, particularly if you live in a rural or spread-out suburban area. If the service area is not broad enough to include a good selection of specialists, you may find your future care choices limited.

Also, see if the plan has what are called extended service areas. Some plans permit you to arrange medical care far from your home if you travel frequently or spend a regular part of the year away from its primary service area. This allows you to take care of non-urgent medical needs, even if you are not at your primary residence.

6. Other Plan Features

In addition to the key features of managed care plans, many plans offer a variety of other features beyond basic Medicare coverage. The following extra benefits are either minor services provided by some plans or major medical expenses for which some plans pay a small portion. If you are likely to use any of these benefits, the plan that offers them may be more attractive to you.

a. Short-term custodial care

Following an injury, surgery or serious illness, you may not be strong enough to take care of yourself, but may not require skilled nursing care. Instead, you might need custodial care—help with dressing, bathing, eating and other regular activities of daily living.

Custodial care is not covered at all by Medicare, unless you are already receiving skilled nursing care or therapy. But some managed care plans do offer coverage for short-term custodial care, either at home from a certified home health care agency, or in a certified nursing facility. The number of home care visits or days in a nursing facility is limited, there may be copayments and plans usually charge a premium for the coverage. Despite these limitations, this can be valuable added coverage, because almost every senior can use this kind of care at some point.

b. Medical equipment

Medicare pays 80% of the amount it approves for doctor-prescribed medical equipment, such as wheelchairs, hospital beds, ventilators and prosthetic devices. But the recipient is responsible for 20% of the approved amount, plus anything above that amount if the equipment company does not accept Medicare assignment. (See Chapter 12, Section E.) Some managed care plans pay the full cost of prescribed medical equipment, although it must be purchased or rented from a provider in the plan's network.

c. Chiropractic care, acupuncture and acupressure

Medicare pays for a very limited amount of chiropractic care, and pays nothing at all for acupuncture or acupressure treatment. Some managed care plans cover a greater amount of chiropractic care. And a few recognize the value of acupuncture and acupressure and pay for some of the cost. Treatments must be received from providers in the plan's network, and there is almost always a copayment for each visit. However, if you regularly use one of these treatments and your practitioner happens to be in the plan's network, this coverage can be a good money-saver.

d. Routine physical exams

Unlike Medicare, virtually all managed care plans pay completely for at least one routine physical exam per year. Managed care plans have figured out that it is cheaper for them—not to mention healthier for members—if illnesses are detected early during routine physical exams.

e. Foreign travel immunizations and emergency coverage

Many people travel abroad to visit family; others hope to do some foreign traveling during retirement. Medicare provides no coverage for medical costs incurred outside the United States, nor do most managed care plans. But a few plans offer coverage for emergency care while abroad. And some also offer free or low-cost immunizations for foreign travel. If you plan on traveling abroad frequently or for long stays, this coverage can be valuable.

f. Eye examinations and glasses

Medicare covers only eye examinations and optometry services connected to eye disease or other medical conditions. It does not pay for any part of regular vision testing or for eyeglasses or contact lenses, except after cataract surgery. A number of managed care plans offer some kind of bonus vision coverage, although none of them pays the full cost of glasses. Some plans cover one eye examination every two years from a network optometrist and offer a set annual amount—usually $50 to $100—toward prescription lenses. Instead of a set amount, other plans offer discount examinations, lenses, frames and contacts. These plans, too, include only network optometrists; they often simply hook you up to an existing chain of optometry clinics and provide you with a discount.

g. Hearing tests and hearing aids

Some managed care plans offer a free regular hearing exam, plus discounts on hearing aids. As with other managed care coverage, the care must be obtained from a hearing center that is connected to the plan's network.

h. Dental work

Some managed care plans offer discounts on dental work. The discounts usually include a low copayment for cleaning and examination and up to a 35% reduction in the cost of other services. The networks of dentists are usually quite limited, however. Finding a network dentist with whom you are comfortable is the key to whether this extra coverage is worthwhile.

i. After-hours advice and treatment

People don't always become ill during regular office hours. But visiting an emergency room can be a miserable—and often unnecessary—experience. Some managed care plans maintain 24-hour phone lines staffed by experienced nurses offering medical advice that can help you stay out of an emergency room. Other plans—usually Provider Sponsored Organizations or individual groups of doctors within a larger HMO—even maintain evening and weekend clinics. There, you can consult with one of the plan's doctors, usually for a lower copayment and less stress than a visit to an emergency room.

j. Chronic disease management and wellness programs

The present insurance-run managed care industry recognizes how much money it saves by monitoring and managing chronic conditions and offering programs to improve general health. As a result, many managed care plans offer free or low-cost educational and monitoring programs to help people with chronic illness keep their conditions under control. Some programs include blood pressure and cholesterol education for heart patients; diabetic classes to control blood sugar levels; and classes for Parkinson's patients to reduce their risk of falls. Some plans offer programs to help people lead healthier lives, such as nutrition and exercise programs to improve flexibility and cardiac health, to help lose weight and to quit smoking.

C. Comparing Medigap and Managed Care Plans

After you have located several medigap and managed care plans that seem to fit your needs and budget, the best way to compare them is to see their costs and coverage side by side. Refer to the chart below for a side-by-side comparison of the major benefits of medigap and managed care plans. Then, use the next chart to help you compare the actual plans you are considering.

Comparing Medigap to Managed Care

	Medigap	Managed Care
Choice of Doctor and Providers	As long as doctor or other provider accepts Medicare, a medigap policy will cover whatever Medicare does.	Restricted to doctors and providers in the network. PPO and some HMO options allow non-network providers at higher cost.
Access to Specialists	As long as specialist accepts Medicare, a medigap policy will cover whatever Medicare does.	Must get referral from primary care doctor. Limited direct access available for some serious conditions.
Premiums	Varies, with higher cost for plans with more services. Policy A: $40–$100/month. Policies B-G: $60–$170/month. Policies H-J: $100–$250/month.	No premium for basic HMO. Member must pay Medicare Part B. Broader coverage or more provider choices may cost between $25–$100/month.
Copayments	No copayments for services.	Require copayment for most services, currently $5–$25 per visit.
Prescription Drugs	No payment for self-administered medication in most plans. Policies H, I and J pay 50% with annual limit of $1,250 for H and I plans. J plan has $3,000 limit after $250/year deductible.	Copayment of $5–$25 per drug prescription. Generally less expensive than under medigap policies. Amount depends on use of generic or brand name and specific plan formulary list.
Treatment Approval	Automatic if service is covered by Medicare.	Coverage denied if treatment is considered medically unnecessary or experimental.
Geographic Mobility	Most policies may be used wherever you obtain Medicare-covered services in the United States.	Non-emergency coverage limited to specific geographical area. Some plans offer care away from home. All plans must cover emergency care anywhere.
Emergency Care Overseas	Covered by plans C–J.	Some plans cover for higher premium.
At-Home Recovery	Covered by plans D, G, I and J, but only if also receiving skilled nursing care at home.	Some plans cover for higher premium and copayment.
Preventive Health Screenings	Limited coverage in plans E and J.	Most plans offer physical exams and free or low-cost screenings, although premiums and copayments may be higher.
Eye Exams and Glasses	No, unless connected to illness or injury.	Most offer limited discounts on exams and lenses.
Hearing Exams and Aids	No, unless connected to illness or injury.	Most offer limited discounts on exams and hearing aids.
Dental Discounts	No.	Some offer limited discounts.
Wellness Programs	No.	Many offer a variety of low-cost or free wellness programs, including heart healthy education, weight loss, quitting smoking and cholesterol management.
Chiropractic Care	Only if covered by Medicare.	Some offer broader coverage than Medicare.

Comparing Medigap Policies and Managed Care Plans

		Plan Name	Plan Name	Plan Name	Plan Name	Plan Name
Cost (monthly premium)						
Copayments (amount I must pay per visit) Medicare gaps left unfilled						
Is there coverage outside the plan?	Yes					
	No					
Cost of care outside the plan						
Prescription drug coverage	Copayment					
	Annual limit					
Dental care covered	Yes					
	No					
Choice of dentists	Yes					
	No					
Short-term custodial care	Yes					
	No					
Eyeglasses	Copayments					
	Visits per year					
Other services:						
Hearing exam	Yes					
	No					
Chiropractic	Yes					
	No					
Foreign travel	Yes					
	No					
Exercise program	Yes					
	No					
Other	Yes					
	No					

Medicaid and State Supplements to Medicare

When all types of medical expenses for older Americans are added up, Medicare pays for only about half of them. This leaves most people with considerable worry about how they will cover the rest. One approach is to buy private Medicare supplement insurance; another is to enroll in a managed care health plan. (See Chapters 14 and 15.) But many people cannot afford such insurance or health plans. For a number of low-income people, fortunately, there are some alternatives.

If you have a low income and few assets other than your home, you may qualify for assistance from your state's Medicaid program. Medicaid pays not only Medicare premiums, deductibles and copayments, it also covers some services Medicare does not. (See Sections A, B and C.)

If you have too much income or too many assets to be eligible for Medicaid, you may still qualify for several Medicaid-administered programs to help you meet medical costs: Qualified Medicare Beneficiary (QMB), Specified Low-Income Medicare Beneficiary (SLMB) or Qualifying Individual (QI). (See Section F.)

A. Medicaid Defined

Medicaid is a program established by the federal government and administered by the individual states, which helps pay medical costs for financially needy people. Medicaid operates in addition to Medicare to pay for some of the medical costs Medicare doesn't cover.

The basic difference between the two programs is simple: Medicare is available to most everyone age 65 or over, regardless of income or assets, while Medicaid is available only to those of any age who are financially needy. Need is defined by the Medicaid program in the state in which a person lives and varies somewhat from state to state. There are currently more than 30 million people who receive some form of Medicaid assistance; about one-fourth of them are also on Medicare. (See Chapter 12, Section A, for a comparison of the programs.)

There are federal guidelines for Medicaid, but they are fairly broad and each state is permitted to make its own rules regarding eligibility, coverage and benefits. This chapter explains the basic eligibility and coverage rules of Medicaid, and indicates where eligibility standards are higher or lower than the basic levels.

B. Who Is Eligible

Generally, states use one of two ways to determine who is eligible for Medicaid. One bases eligibility on income and assets alone (Categorically Needy), the other on income and assets plus medical costs (Medically Needy).

1. Categorically Needy

To qualify for Medicaid as Categorically Needy, your income and assets must be at or below specific, predetermined dollar amounts. Most states use the same eligibility rules that are used for the federal Supplemental Security Income, or SSI, program to determine Medicaid eligibility. Other states establish their own Medicaid standards, which are more difficult to meet than SSI standards.

a. SSI rules

In most states, you can automatically receive Medicaid if you are eligible for SSI assistance. This means you can be eligible for Medicaid even if you own your own home, regardless of its value, and own a car worth up to $4,500. To qualify, your monthly income must be no more than $300 to $500—$500 to $700 for a couple—depending on the state in which you live. You may also have cash and other assets worth up to $2,000 for an individual; $3,000 for a couple. You are also allowed to have a few other miscellaneous assets—engagement and wedding rings, household goods, a burial plot and fund, life insurance. (See Chapter 6, Section A3.)

The following states use SSI standards to determine Medicaid eligibility:

Alabama	New Mexico
Alaska	Oregon
Colorado	Rhode Island
Delaware	South Carolina
Idaho	South Dakota
Mississippi	Tennessee
Nevada	Wyoming

b. More difficult to qualify than for SSI

A number of states require that to qualify for Medicaid, you must have even lower income and assets than SSI standards, including a dollar limit on the value of your home and lower value of your automobile and personal property.

States with these tougher standards are:

Connecticut	New Hampshire
Hawaii	North Carolina
Illinois	North Dakota
Indiana	Ohio
Minnesota	Oklahoma
Missouri	Virginia

2. Medically Needy

Some states provide Medicaid coverage for certain people who would not be eligible for it under rules which look only at their income and assets. These states provide Medicaid coverage to people—referred to as Medically Needy—

whose income and assets are over the eligibility levels for that state but whose medical expenses will reduce their income or assets to eligible levels. This process of subtracting actual medical bills from income and assets is called spending down, in Medicaid slang. This is because medical bills would force you to spend your extra money down to the point that you would meet eligibility levels.

The following states offer Medicaid coverage to those who are found to be Medically Needy based on their income and assets plus their current or expected medical bills:

Arizona
Arkansas
California
Connecticut
District of Columbia
Florida
Georgia
Illinois
Iowa
Kansas
Kentucky
Louisiana
Maine
Maryland
Massachusetts
Michigan
Minnesota
Montana
Nebraska
New Hampshire
New Jersey
New York
North Carolina
North Dakota
Oklahoma
Pennsylvania
Texas
Utah
Vermont
Virginia
Washington
West Virginia
Wisconsin

Example: Roberta's savings are $2,000 more than what is allowed to qualify for Medicaid as Categorically Needy by the rules in her state. However, surgery, home nursing care, physical therapy and medication left Roberta with medical bills of almost $3,000 that were not paid for by Medicare. Roberta's state offers Medicaid coverage to the Medically Needy. If she paid her $3,000 medical bills, she would be spending her savings down to a level that would meet the Medicaid standards. Instead of forcing her to spend that money and be reduced to Medicaid savings levels, Roberta qualifies immediately for Medicaid, which will pay the bills.

Some Protection Even If Not Eligible for Medicaid

If your income and assets are low but slightly too high for you to be eligible for Medicaid in your state, you may still be eligible for Qualified Medicare Beneficiary (QMB), Specified Low-Income Medicare Beneficiary (SLMB), or Qualifying Individual (QI) benefits that help meet medical costs not paid for by Medicare. (See Section F.)

Medicaid Through Managed Care

In a few areas around the country—it varies from county to county—a state's Medicaid program offers coverage through a local HMO or other managed care plan. These Medicaid programs require that medical services be received from participating doctors, hospitals, clinics and other medical providers. These programs deliver medical care much like non-Medicaid managed care plans do, except for how they handle fees and copayments. (See Chapter 15.) Each participating managed care plan operates differently. To find out if you live in an area with managed care Medicaid—and to learn about its advantages and disadvantages over standard Medicaid—contact a HICAP office near you. (See Chapter 13, Section G.)

3. Determining Income and Assets

Generally, in determining eligibility Medicaid considers your income and assets plus those of your spouse, if you live together. If you are divorced or separated and living apart, your spouse's income and assets are not counted, except to the extent that your spouse is actually contributing to your support.

This rule of considering a spouse's income in determining Medicaid eligibility has had the unfortunate effect of keeping many older couples from marrying. They fear that if they marry, a serious illness could bankrupt both of them before they would become eligible for Medicaid assistance. The couple also suffers because if they do not marry, neither can take advantage of Social Security or private pension benefits payable to a spouse.

The income or assets of your children, other relatives or friends, even if you live with them, are not considered in deciding your Medicaid eligibility. However, if you receive regular financial support from a relative or friend—cash or help with rent—Medicaid can consider that assistance as part of your income. Also, if you are living with children or other relatives and they provide all of your food and clothing while permitting you to keep all of your income and assets, Medicaid could figure out a dollar amount for that support and count it as part of your income. This does not happen frequently. But it is possible that during the application process, the person reviewing your eligibility could visit your home and determine whether you are receiving substantial, regular income in the form of non-cash support.

Medicaid Rules When One Spouse Is in a Nursing Home

Medicaid has developed a series of complicated rules—different from the regular Medicaid rules—to determine whether a person in a nursing home is eligible for Medicaid coverage if the other spouse remains at home. Most states look only at income in the nursing home resident's name, but some states consider the joint income of both. A monthly allowance is permitted for at-home spouses, who are also allowed to keep their homes and to retain between $12,000 and $60,000 in other assets, depending on the state.

However, these rules also allow Medicaid to place a lien on the home or on other assets in an amount equal to the entire amount Medicaid spends on nursing home care for the spouse. When the at-home spouse dies or sells the house, Medicaid will enforce the lien, taking money that the at-home spouse would otherwise be able to spend or leave to survivors.

To take best advantage of Medicaid coverage for long-term care, it is important to understand these rules and also the alternatives to nursing homes that can best serve your needs while preserving as much of your savings as possible.

Long-term care and how it is paid for, including a comprehensive discussion of Medicaid nursing home rules, is covered fully in *Beat the Nursing Home Trap* by Joseph Matthews (Nolo Press). See the catalog at the back of this book for ordering details.

C. Medical Costs Covered by Medicaid

Medicaid covers the same kinds of services that Medicare covers and, in most states, also covers a number of medical services Medicare does not. One of its best features is that it covers most long-term care, both at home and in nursing facilities. It covers not only long-term skilled nursing care, but also non-medical personal care—the need for which forces many people into nursing homes and keeps them there for years.

Medicaid also pays many of the amounts Medicare does not pay in hospital and doctor bills. Specifically, this means Medicaid pays:

- the inpatient hospital insurance deductible and coinsurance amounts that Medicare does not pay
- the Medicare medical insurance deductible
- the 20% of the Medicare-approved doctors' fees that Medicare medical insurance does not pay, and
- the monthly premium charged for Medicare Part B medical insurance.

1. Services Covered in Every State

In every state, Medicaid covers a number of medical services, paying whatever Medicare does not. Because these services are required by federal law to be provided all Medicaid recipients, the state cannot charge you anything for these services.

Services covered by Medicaid for all patients in all states include:

- inpatient hospital or skilled nursing facility care
- nursing home care in approved facilities
- outpatient hospital or clinic treatment
- laboratory and X-ray services
- physicians' services
- home health care, and
- transportation—by ambulance, if necessary—to and from the place you receive medical services.

2. Optional Services

In all states, Medicaid also covers many of over 30 other types of medical services. However, state Medicaid programs are not required to cover these optional services, and in some states they may charge a nominal fee for them. (See Section E2.)

The optional medical services most used by older people and the states that provide coverage for them include:

- prescription drugs—all states
- eye care—the cost of eye exams are covered in all states except Mississippi; the cost of eyeglasses themselves are covered in all states except Delaware, Kentucky, Louisiana and Tennessee
- dental care and dentures—dental care is covered in all states except Colorado, Delaware, Louisiana and Texas; dentures are covered in all states except Alabama, Alaska, Colorado, Delaware, Kentucky, Mississippi, New Hampshire, Oklahoma, South Carolina, Tennessee, Texas, Vermont, Virginia and Wyoming
- non-emergency transportation services to and from medical care—all states except Maryland
- physical therapy—all states except Colorado, Delaware, Louisiana, Missouri, North Carolina, Oklahoma, Pennsylvania, Rhode Island and Tennessee
- prosthetic devices—all states except North Carolina.

The types and amount of coverage for other optional services vary widely from state to state. However, these other optional services often include chiropractic care, podiatry, prosthetics, speech and occupational therapy, private-duty nursing, personal care services, personal care and case management services as part of home care, adult day care, hospice care, various preventive, screening and rehabilitative services and inpatient psychiatric care for those 65 and over.

Coverage Changes Frequently

Medicaid coverage for optional services changes frequently, with states adding some services and dropping others. Check with your local social services or social welfare office to find out what specific medical services are covered by Medicaid in your state. You must also find out the terms on which such optional services are offered. Sometimes you can obtain such services only if the care is provided by county or other local health clinics rather than from a private doctor or clinic of your choice.

D. Requirements for Coverage

The fact that a particular medical service or treatment is generally covered by Medicaid does not necessarily mean it will be covered in every instance. Some general requirements must be satisfied before any covered medical service will be paid for in any case.

Most importantly, the care must be prescribed by a doctor, administered by a provider who participates in Medicaid and determined to be medically necessary.

1. Care Must Be Prescribed by Doctor

The medical service you receive must be prescribed by a doctor. For example, Medicaid will not pay for chiropractic services or physical therapy you seek on your own. And it will pay only for prescription drugs, even if you could get the same or equivalent medicine cheaper over the counter.

For services in which a doctor is generally not involved—regular eye exams, dental care—Medicaid may place restrictions on how often you can obtain a service and who can authorize it. And Medicaid will cover some services for those who qualify as Medically Needy only if care is provided by certain public health hospitals, clinics or agencies.

2. Provider Must Participate in Medicaid

The treatment or other care you receive must be from a doctor, facility or other medical provider participating in Medicaid. The provider must accept Medicaid payment—or Medicare plus Medicaid—as full payment. And if the service is provided by a non-physician such as a physical therapist or chiropractor, or by a home care agency, that provider must be approved by Medicaid.

The number of doctors and clinics in an area that accept Medicaid patients may be limited. You can get referrals from your local social welfare office to providers that accept Medicaid. If you find doctors or other providers on your own, inform them that you are covered by Medicaid and ask whether they accept Medicaid payment before you obtain any services.

3. Treatment Must Be Medically Necessary

All care must be approved by Medicaid as medically necessary. For inpatient care, this process is similar to the one used for Medicare coverage. By requesting your admission to a hospital or other facility, your doctor sets this process in motion. You won't need to be involved and won't even hear about it unless the facility decides you should be discharged before your doctor thinks you should. (See Chapter 13, Section F.)

You must get prior approval by a Medicaid consultant before you obtain certain medical services. The rules vary from state to state, requiring prior approval for such services as elective surgery, some major dental care, leasing of medical equipment, and, in some states, any non-emergency inpatient hospital or nursing facility care.

If a particular medical service requires prior Medicaid approval, your doctor or the facility will contact Medicaid directly. You may be asked to get an examination by another doctor before Medicaid will approve the care, but this does not happen often. If you have questions about the process of prior approval for a medical treatment, discuss it with both your doctor and with a Medicaid worker at your local social service or welfare office. Ask what Medicaid considers most important in making the decision about the medical care you are seeking. By finding out what it is they are most concerned about, you may be able to help your doctor provide the necessary information to Medicaid.

E. Cost of Medicaid Coverage

Almost all Medicaid-covered care is free. And Medicaid also pays your Medicare premium, deductibles and copayments. However, there are a few circumstances in which you might have to pay small amounts for Medicaid-covered care.

1. No Payments to Medical Providers

Hospitals, doctors and other medical care providers who accept Medicaid patients must accept Medicare's approved charges—or the amount approved directly by Medicaid if it is not covered by Medicare—as the total allowable charges. They must accept as payment in full the combination of payments from Medicare and Medicaid, or Medicaid alone; they cannot bill you for the 15% more than the Medicare-approved amount, which they could do if you were not on Medicaid.

2. Fees to States for Medicaid Services

Federal law permits states to charge some small fees to people who qualify for Medicaid as Medically Needy. (See Section B.) If you qualify as Categorically Needy, however, states can charge you a fee only for optional covered services. (See Section C2.) State Medicaid charges will take one of three forms: an enrollment fee, monthly premium or copayments.

a. Enrollment fee

Some states charge a small, one-time-only fee when you first enroll in Medicaid. This fee can only be charged to people who qualify as Medically Needy, not to people who qualify as Categorically Needy.

b. Monthly premium

States are permitted to charge a small monthly fee to people who qualify for Medicaid as Medically Needy. The premium may be charged whether or not Medicaid services are actually used that month. The amounts vary with income and assets, but usually come to no more than a few dollars.

c. Copayments

State Medicaid programs are permitted to charge a copayment, which is a fixed amount for each Medicaid-covered service you receive. If you don't use a Medicaid service, you have no copayment to pay. A copayment can be charged to the Medically Needy for any service, and to the Categorically Needy for optional services only. (See Section C2.)

Medicaid and Private Health Insurance

Insurance companies are not permitted to sell you a medigap insurance policy if you are on Medicaid. However, you are permitted to have other private health insurance—such as that provided by a retirement program or that you purchase to protect against a specific illness—and still qualify for Medicaid.

Medicaid will deduct the amount of your private health insurance premiums from the calculation of your income when determining whether you are under the allowable income levels to qualify for Medicaid in your state.

However, if you do have private health insurance, and a medical service is covered by both your insurance and by Medicaid, Medicaid will pay only the amount your insurance has not paid. If you receive a payment directly from your insurance company after Medicaid has paid that bill, you must return that insurance money to Medicaid.

F. Other State Assistance

Many people with low income and assets have trouble paying the portion of medical bills left unpaid by Medicare, and cannot afford private medigap insurance, but do not qualify for Medicaid. If you have low income and assets but have slightly too much of either to qualify for Medicaid, you may still qualify for help paying Medicare premiums and portions of Medicare-covered costs that Medicare does not pay.

Three cost-reduction programs—called Qualified Medicare Beneficiary (QMB), Specified Low-Income Medicare Beneficiary (SLMB) and Qualifying Individual (QI)—are administered by each state's Medicaid program to help people who fall into this category. They do not offer the extensive coverage beyond Medicare that Medicaid does, but the savings to you in Medicare-related medical costs can be substantial.

1. Qualified Medicare Beneficiary (QMB)

If you are eligible for Medicare and meet the income and asset eligibility requirements for the QMB program, your state will pay all of your Medicare Part A and Part B premiums, deductibles and coinsurance. Depending on how much you use Medicare-covered services in a year, this could mean a savings of up to several thousand dollars.

a. Income limits

To be eligible as a QMB, your income must be no more than slightly above the national poverty level. This figure is established each year by the federal government; in 2000, the income level was about $8,480 per year or $707 per month for an individual; $11,300 per year or $942 per month for a couple. These figures are slightly higher in Alaska and Hawaii. These amounts will go up slightly as the yearly cost-of-living figures are calculated.

As with the calculation of income for SSI eligibility purposes, certain amounts of income are not counted in determining QMB eligibility. Particularly if you are still working and most of your income comes from your earnings, you may be able to qualify as a QMB even if your total income is more than twice these levels. (See Chapter 6, Section A3.) If, after applying these rules, you are anywhere close to the QMB limits, it is worth applying for it.

b. Asset limits

There is a limit on the value of the assets you can own and still qualify as a QMB—generally, no more than $4,000 for an individual, $6,000 for a couple. However, many assets, such as your house, car and certain personal and household goods, are not part of the resources that are counted. (See Chapter 6, Section A3.)

2. Specified Low-Income Medicare Beneficiary (SLMB) and Qualifying Individual

If your income is slightly too high for you to qualify for QMB benefits, you may still be eligible for one of two other state medical assistance programs, Specified Low-Income Medicare Beneficiary (SLMB) and Qualifying Individual. The resource limits for eligibility are the same as for a QMB, but the income limits are 20%-80% higher, depending on the program. If your counted income—after the same adjustments made in calculating income for SSI purposes (see Chapter 6, Sections A1 and A2)—is under $1,200 for an individual, or $1,600 for a couple, you may qualify for SLMB or QI support. (These figures go up slightly each year.)

Because the SLMB and QI programs are for people with higher incomes, they have fewer benefits than the QMB program. The SLMB and QI programs pay all or part of the Medicare Part B monthly premium, but do not pay any Medicare deductibles or coinsurance amounts. Nonetheless, this means savings of more than $500 per year.

G. Applying for Medicaid, QMB, SLMB or QI

Before you can get coverage by the Medicaid, QMB, SLMB or QI programs, you must file a written application separate from the Medicare application process. An application for Medicaid is also an application for QMB, SLMB or QI, so that if you are not eligible for one program, you may still be eligible for one of the others.

This section explains some of the things you will need to do and documents you will need to gather to file a Medicaid, QMB, SLMB or QI application.

1. Where to File

To qualify for Medicaid or the QMB, SLMB or QI programs, you must file a written application with the agency which handles Medicaid in your state—usually your county's Department of Social Services or Social Welfare Department. In many states, if you are applying for SSI benefits at your local Social Security office, that application will also serve as a Medicaid application, and you will be notified of Medicaid eligibility at the same time as you receive notice regarding SSI. (See Chapter 6.)

If you or your spouse is hospitalized when you apply for Medicaid, ask to see a medical social worker in the hospital. He or she will help you fill out the application.

2. Required Documents and Other Information

Since eligibility for Medicaid and the QMB, SLMB or QI programs depends on your financial situation, many of the documents you must bring to the Medicaid office are those which can verify your income and assets.

Although a Medicaid eligibility worker might require additional specific information from you, you will at least be able to get the application process started if you bring with you:

- pay stubs, income tax returns, Social Security benefits information and other evidence of your current income
- papers showing all your savings and other financial assets, such as bankbooks, insurance policies and stock certificates
- automobile registration papers if you own a car
- your Social Security card or number
- information about your spouse's income and separate assets, if the two of you live together, and
- medical bills from the previous three months, as well as medical records or reports to confirm any medical condition that will require treatment in the near future. If you don't have copies of these bills, records or reports, bring the names and addresses of the doctors, hospitals or other medical providers who are treating you.

Even if you don't have all these papers, go to your local social services or social welfare department office and file your application for Medicaid as soon as you think you may qualify. The Medicaid eligibility workers will tell you what other documents you need—and sometimes can explain how you can get necessary papers you don't have or help get them for you.

3. Application Procedure

A Medicaid eligibility worker—or an SSI eligibility worker if you apply for SSI at a local Social Security office—will interview you and assist you in filling out your application. There may be lots of forms to fill out and you may have to return to the office for several different interviews. Do not get discouraged. Delays, repeated forms and interviews do not mean you will not be eligible. The state has institutionalized procedures that make it difficult for people to get through the qualification process, driving some people to give up and fail to claim benefits to which they are entitled. In applying for Medicaid, patience is not only a virtue, it is an absolute necessity.

Normally, you will receive a decision on your Medicaid eligibility within a couple of weeks after you complete the forms and provide the necessary information. The law requires that a decision be made within 45 days. If you don't hear from Medicaid within a month of your application, call the eligibility worker who interviewed you. Sometimes it takes a little polite pushing to get a decision out of an overworked social services agency.

4. Retroactive Benefits

If you are found to be eligible and have already incurred medical bills, Medicaid may cover some of them. This retroactive eligibility can go back to the beginning of the third month before the date you filed your application. Make sure to show your Medicaid eligibility worker any medical bills you have from the three-month period just before you applied.

If you are denied eligibility for Medicaid, QMB, SLMB or QI, you have a right to appeal. (See Section H.)

5. Review of Eligibility

How long Medicaid coverage lasts depends on your finances and your medical costs. Medicaid eligibility is reviewed periodically, usually every six months and at least once a year. If your financial situation has changed to put you over the eligibility limits for your state's Medicaid program, your coverage may be discontinued when the review is completed. Until then, you will be continued on Medicaid or QMB, SLMB or QI coverage, even if your income or assets put you over the limits some months before.

Likewise, if you became eligible for Medicaid as Medically Needy because of high medical costs, but those medical costs have now ended, you may be dropped from Medicaid when the review is completed. Until the review, however, you will remain on Medicaid even if the medical costs stopped several months before. And if new medical costs arise after your coverage has been ended, you may apply again for Medicaid coverage.

H. What to Do If You Are Denied Coverage

If you are denied Medicaid, QMB, SLMB or QI coverage for which you believe you are eligible, go immediately to the office where you applied and ask about the procedure in your state for getting a hearing to appeal that decision. In some states, if you request a hearing in writing within ten days after a notice that existing coverage is going to end, your coverage can stay in effect until after the hearing officer makes a decision.

At an appeal hearing, you will be able to present any documents or other papers—proof of income, assets, medical bills—that you think support your claim. You will also be allowed to explain why you believe you are eligible and why the Medicaid decision was wrong. If expected medical bills, which you claim will qualify you as Medically Needy, is the main question concerning your eligibility, then a letter from your doctor explaining your condition and the expected cost of treatment, would be important.

The hearing itself is usually held at or near the welfare or social service office. You should be notified of the decision on your appeal within 90 days after the hearing. You are permitted to have a friend, relative, social worker, lawyer or other representative appear with you to help at the hearing.

Although the exact procedure for obtaining this hearing, and the hearing itself, may be slightly different from state to state, they all resemble very closely the hearings given to applicants for Social Security benefits. (See Chapter 8.)

Getting Assistance With Your Appeal

If you are denied Medicaid, QMB, SLMB or QI eligibility, you may want to consult with someone experienced in the subject to help you prepare your appeal. The best place to find good quality free assistance with matters pertaining to Medicare, Medicaid, QMB, SLMB and QI programs is the nearest office of the Health Insurance Counseling and Advocacy Program (HICAP). (See Chapter 13, Section G.)

If there is no HICAP office near you, you may be able to find other assistance through your local senior center or by calling the Senior Information line listed in the white pages of your telephone directory.

■

APPENDIX

State Offices on Aging

The offices listed below provide referrals to local agencies that can give information and provide advice on problems with Social Security, SSI and Medicare claims.

Alabama

Commission on Aging
770 Washington, Suite 470
Montgomery, AL 36130
334-242-5743
FAX: 334-242-5594

Alaska

Division of Senior Services
Department of Administration
Juneau, AK 99811-0209
907-465-3250
FAX: 907-465-4716

Arizona

Aging and Community Services Division
Economic Security Department
1789 W. Jefferson St. #950 A
Phoenix, AZ 85005
602-542-4446
FAX: 602-542-6575

Arkansas

Aging and Adult Services
P.O. Box 1437 – Slot 1412
Little Rock, AR 72201
501-682-2441
FAX: 501-682-8155

California

Department of Aging
1600 K Street, 4th Floor
Sacramento, CA 95814
916-322-5290
FAX: 916-324-1903

Colorado

Aging and Adult Services Division
110 16th St., Suite 200
Denver, CO 80202
303-620-4147
FAX: 303-620-4189

Connecticut

Elderly Services Division
25 Sigourney Street, 10th Floor
Hartford, CT 06106-5033
860-424-5277
FAX: 860-424-4966

Delaware

Aging Division
1901 North Dupont Highway
New Castle, DE 19720
302-577-4791
FAX: 302-577-4793

District of Columbia

Aging Office
441 4th Street, NW; Suite 900
Washington, DC 20001
202-724-5622
FAX: 202-724-4979

Florida

Department of Elder Affairs
Building B–Suite 152
4040 Esplanade Way
Tallahassee, FL 32399-7000
904-414-2000
FAX: 904-414-2002

Georgia

Aging Services Office
2 Peachtree Street, NE, 18th Floor
Atlanta, GA 30303
404-657-5258
FAX: 404-657-5285

Guam

Division of Senior Citizens
Dept. of Public Health and Social Services
P.O. Box 2816
Agana, Guam, 96932
011-671-475-0263
FAX: 011-671-477-2930

Hawaii

Hawaii Executive Office on Aging
250 S. Hotel St. #107
Honolulu, HI 96813
808-586-0100
FAX: 808-586-0185

Idaho

Idaho Commission on Aging
3380 Americana Ter. #120
Boise, ID 83706
208-334-3833
FAX: 208-334-3033

Illinois

Aging Department
421 East Capitol Avenue, Suite 100
Springfield, IL 62701-1789
217-785-2870
Chicago Office: 312-814-2630
FAX: 217-785-4477

Indiana

Aging and Rehabilitative Services Divison
Family and Social Services
402 West Washington Street, Room W454
P.O. Box 7083
Indianapolis, IN 46204
317-232-7020
FAX: 317-232-7867

Iowa

Elder Affairs Department
Clemens Building, 3rd Floor
200 10th Street
Des Moines, IA 50309-3609
515-281-5187
FAX: 515-281-4036

Kansas

Department on Aging
New England Building
503 S. Kansas Ave.
Topeka, KS 66603-3404
785-296-4986
FAX: 785-296-0256

Kentucky

Aging Services Division
Social Services Department
275 East Main Street, 6 West
Frankfort, KY 40621
502-564-6930
FAX: 502-564-4595

Louisiana

Elderly Affiars Office
P.O. Box 80374
412 N. 4th St., 3F
Baton Rouge, LA 70802
504-342-7100
FAX: 504-342-7133

Maine

Elder and Adult Services Bureau
35 Anthony Ave.
State House, Station 11
Augusta, ME 04333
207-624-5335
FAX: 207-624-5361

Maryland

Aging Office
State Office Building, Room 1007
301 West Preston Street, Room 1007
Baltimore, MD 21201-2374
410-767-1100
FAX: 410-333-7943

Massachusetts

Executive Office of Elder Affairs
1 Ashburton Place, 5th Floor
Boston, MA 02108
617-727-7750
FAX: 617-727-9368

Michigan

Aging Office
P.O. Box 30026
Lansing, MI 48909-8176
517-373-8230
FAX: 517-373-4092

Minnesota

Minnesota Board on Aging
444 Lafayette Road
St. Paul, MN 55155
612-296-2770
FAX: 612-297-7855

Mississippi

Aging and Adult Services Division
750 State Street
Jackson, MS 39202
601-359-4925
FAX: 601-359-4370

Missouri

Aging Division
Social Services Department
P.O. Box 1337
615 Howerton Court
Jefferson City, MO 65109
573-751-3083
FAX: 573-751-8493

Montana

Senior and Longterm Care Division
Department of Public Health and Human Services
P.O. Box 4210
111 Sanders, Room 211
Helena, MT 59604
406-444-7788
FAX: 406-444-7743

Nebraska

Department of Health and Human Services
Division on Aging
P.O. Box 95044
301 Centennial Mall South
Lincoln, NE 68509
402-471-2307
FAX: 402-471-4619

Nevada

Aging Services Division
Human Resources Department
State Mail Room Complex
340 N. 11th Street #203
Las Vegas, NV 89101
702-486-3545
FAX: 702-486-3572

New Hampshire

Elderly and Adult Services Division
115 Pleasant Street
Annex Building 1
Concord, NH 03301-3843
603-271-4680
FAX: 603-271-4643

New Jersey

Department of Health and Senior Services
Division of Senior Affairs
P.O. Box 807
Trenton, NJ 08625-0807
800-792-8820
FAX: 609-588-3601

New Mexico

State Agency on Aging
La Villa Rivera Building, 4th Floor
224 E. Palace Ave.
Santa Fe, NM 87501
505-827-7640
FAX: 505-827-7649

New York

Aging Office
Empire State Plaza, Building 2
Albany, NY 12223-1251
800-342-9871
FAX: 518-474-0608

North Carolina

Aging Office
CB 29531
693 Palmer Dr.
Raleigh NC 27626-0531
919-733-3983
FAX: 919-733-0443

North Dakota

Aging Services
600 South 2nd Street #1C
Bismarck, ND 58540
701-328-8910
FAX: 701-328-8989

Ohio

Aging Department
50 West Broad Street, 9th Floor
Columbus, OH 43215-5928
614-466-5500
FAX: 614-466-5741

Oklahoma

Aging Services
P.O. Box 25352
312 NE 28th Street
Oklahoma City, OK 73125
405-521-2327 or 521-2281
FAX: 405-521-2086

Oregon

Senior and Disabled Services Division
500 Summer Street, NE
Salem, OR 97310-1015
503-945-5811
FAX: 503-373-7823

Pennsylvania

Department of Aging
555 Walnut St., 5th Floor
Harrisburg, PA 17101-1919
717-783-1550
FAX: 717-772-3382

Rhode Island
Elderly Affairs Department
160 Pine Street
Providence, RI 02903
401-277-2858
FAX: 401-277-2130

South Carolina
Office on Aging
P.O. Box 8206
Columbia, SC 29211-8206
803-253-6177
FAX: 803-253-4173

South Dakota
Adult Services and Aging Office
Kneip Building
700 Governors Drive
Pierre, SD 57501-2291
605-773-3656
FAX: 605-773-6834

Tennessee
Aging Commission
500 Deaderic Street, 9th Floor
Nashville, TN 37243-0860
615-741-2056
FAX: 615-741-3309

Texas
Aging Department
4900 N. Lamar, 4th Floor
Austin, TX 78751
512-424-6840
FAX: 512-424-6890

Utah
Aging and Adult Services
120 North 200 West
P.O. Box 45500
Salt Lake City, UT 84145-0500
801-538-3910
FAX: 801-538-4395

Vermont
Aging and Disability Department
103 South Main Street
State Complex
Waterbury, VT 05676
802-241-2400
FAX: 802-241-2325

Virginia
Aging Department
1600 Forest Ave. #102
Richmond, VA 23219-2327
804-662-9333
FAX: 804-662-9354

Washington
Aging and Adult Services
P.O. Box 45050
Olympia, WA 98504-5050
360-586-8753
FAX: 360-902-7848

West Virginia
W. Virginia Bureau of Senior Services
Holly Grove Bldg.
1900 Kanawha Blvd.
Charleston, WV 25305-0160
304-558-3317
FAX: 304-558-0004

Wisconsin
Aging and Long Term Care Bureau
P.O. Box 7851
Madison, WI 53707
608-266-2536
FAX: 608-267-3203

Wyoming
Aging Division
117 Hathaway Building, Room 139
Cheyenne, WY 82002-0710
307-777-7986
FAX: 307-777-5340

INDEX

A

B

C

D

E

F

G

H

I

N

O

P

Q

R

S

T

		PRICE	CODE
🖫	Nolo's Will Book (Book w/Disk—PC)	$34.95	SWIL
	Plan Your Estate	$34.95	NEST
	Quick & Legal Will Book (Quick & Legal Series)	$21.95	QUIC
	FAMILY MATTERS		
	Child Custody: Building Parenting Agreements That Work	$29.95	CUST
	Child Support in California: Go to Court to Get More or Pay Less (Quick & Legal Series)	$24.95	CHLD
	The Complete IEP Guide	$24.95	IEP
	Divorce & Money: How to Make the Best Financial Decisions During Divorce	$34.95	DIMO
	Do Your Own Divorce in Oregon	$19.95	ODIV
	Get a Life: You Don't Need a Million to Retire Well	$19.95	LIFE
	The Guardianship Book for California	$34.95	GB
⊙	How to Adopt Your Stepchild in California (Book w/CD-ROM)	$34.95	ADOP
	A Legal Guide for Lesbian and Gay Couples	$25.95	LG
🖫	The Living Together Kit (Book w/Disk—PC)	$34.95	LTK
	Nolo's Pocket Guide to Family Law	$14.95	FLD
	Using Divorce Mediation: Save Your Money & Your Sanity	$21.95	UDMD
	GOING TO COURT		
	Beat Your Ticket: Go To Court and Win! (National Edition)	$19.95	BEYT
	The Criminal Law Handbook: Know Your Rights, Survive the System	$29.95	KYR
	Everybody's Guide to Small Claims Court (National Edition)	$18.95	NSCC
	Everybody's Guide to Small Claims Court in California	$24.95	CSCC
	Fight Your Ticket ... and Win! (California Edition)	$24.95	FYT
	How to Change Your Name in California	$34.95	NAME
	How to Collect When You Win a Lawsuit (California Edition)	$29.95	JUDG
	How to Mediate Your Dispute	$18.95	MEDI
	How to Seal Your Juvenile & Criminal Records (California Edition)	$29.95	CRIM
	How to Sue for Up to $25,000...and Win! (California Edition)	$29.95	MUNI
	Mad at Your Lawyer	$21.95	MAD
	Nolo's Deposition Handbook	$29.95	DEP
	Represent Yourself in Court: How to Prepare & Try a Winning Case	$29.95	RYC
	HOMEOWNERS, LANDLORDS & TENANTS		
	California Tenants' Rights	$24.95	CTEN
🖫	Contractors' and Homeowners' Guide to Mechanics' Liens (Book w/Disk—PC)	$39.95	MIEN
	The Deeds Book (California Edition)	$24.95	DEED
	Dog Law	$14.95	DOG
⊙	Every Landlord's Legal Guide (National Edition, Book w/CD-ROM)	$44.95	ELLI
	Every Tenant's Legal Guide	$26.95	EVTEN
	For Sale by Owner in California	$24.95	FSBO
	How to Buy a House in California	$24.95	BHCA
	The Landlord's Law Book, Vol. 1: Rights & Responsibilities (California Edition)	$44.95	LBRT
⊙	The California Landlord's Law Book, Vol. 2: Evictions (Book w/CD-ROM)	$44.95	LBEV
	Leases & Rental Agreements (Quick & Legal Series)	$24.95	LEAR
	Neighbor Law: Fences, Trees, Boundaries & Noise	$24.95	NEI
⊙	The New York Landlord's Law Book (Book w/CD-ROM)	$39.95	NYLL
	Renters' Rights (National Edition—Quick & Legal Series)	$19.95	RENT
	Stop Foreclosure Now in California	$34.95	CLOS
	IMMIGRATION		
	How to Get a Green Card: Legal Ways to Stay in the U.S.A.	$29.95	GRN
	U.S. Immigration Made Easy	$44.95	IMEZ

🖫 Book with disk ⊙ Book with CD-ROM

MONEY MATTERS

	PRICE	CODE
101 Law Forms for Personal Use (Quick & Legal Series, Book w/disk—PC)	$29.95	SPOT
Bankruptcy: Is It the Right Solution to Your Debt Problems? (Quick & Legal Series)	$19.95	BRS
Chapter 13 Bankruptcy: Repay Your Debts	$29.95	CH13
Credit Repair (Quick & Legal Series, Book w/disk—PC)	$18.95	CREP
The Financial Power of Attorney Workbook (Book w/disk—PC)	$29.95	FINPOA
How to File for Chapter 7 Bankruptcy	$29.95	HFB
IRAs, 401(k)s & Other Retirement Plans: Taking Your Money Out	$24.95	RET
Money Troubles: Legal Strategies to Cope With Your Debts	$24.95	MT
Nolo's Law Form Kit: Personal Bankruptcy	$16.95	KBNK
Stand Up to the IRS	$29.95	SIRS
Surviving an IRS Tax Audit (Quick & Legal Series)	$24.95	SAUD
Take Control of Your Student Loan Debt	$24.95	SLOAN

PATENTS AND COPYRIGHTS

	PRICE	CODE
The Copyright Handbook: How to Protect and Use Written Works (Book w/CD-ROM)	$34.95	COHA
Copyright Your Software	$24.95	CYS
Getting Permission: How to License and Clear Copyrighted Materials Online and Off (Book w/disk—PC)	$34.95	RIPER
How to Make Patent Drawings Yourself	$29.95	DRAW
The Inventor's Notebook	$19.95	INOT
License Your Invention (Book w/Disk—PC)	$39.95	LICE
Patent, Copyright & Trademark	$29.95	PCTM
Patent It Yourself	$46.95	PAT
Patent Searching Made Easy	$29.95	PATSE
Software Development: A Legal Guide (Book with CD-ROM)	$44.95	SFT
Trademark: Legal Care for Your Business and Product Name	$39.95	TRD
The Trademark Registration Kit (Quick & Legal Series)	$19.95	TREG

RESEARCH & REFERENCE

	PRICE	CODE
Government on the Net (Book w/CD-ROM)	$39.95	GONE
Legal Research: How to Find & Understand the Law	$29.95	LRES

SENIORS

	PRICE	CODE
Beat the Nursing Home Trap: A Consumer's Guide to Assisted Living and Long-Term Care	$21.95	ELD
The Conservatorship Book for California	$44.95	CNSV
Social Security, Medicare & Pensions	$24.95	SOA

SOFTWARE

Call or check our website at www.nolo.com for special discounts on Software!

	PRICE	CODE
LeaseWriter CD—Windows/Macintosh	$129.95	LWD1
Living Trust Maker CD—Windows/Macintosh	$89.95	LTD3
Patent It Yourself CD—Windows	$229.95	PPC12
Personal RecordKeeper 5.0 CD—Windows/Macintosh	$59.95	RKD5
Small Business Pro 4 CD—Windows/Macintosh	$89.95	SBCD4
WillMaker 7.0 CD—Windows/Macintosh	$69.95	WMD7

Special Upgrade Offer

Save 35% on the latest edition of your Nolo book

Because laws and legal procedures change often, we update our books regularly. To help keep you up-to-date, we are extending this special upgrade offer. Cut out and mail the title portion of the cover of your old Nolo book and we'll give you **35% off** the retail price of the NEW EDITION of that book when you purchase directly from Nolo.com. This offer is to individuals only.

Call us today at 1-800-992-6656

Prices subject to change without notice.

ORDER 24 HOURS A DAY

Call 800-992-6656 • www.nolo.com • Mail or fax the order form in this book

Take 2 Minutes & Give Us Your 2 cents

Your comments make a big difference in the development and revision of Nolo books and software. Please take a few minutes and register your Nolo product—and your comments—with us. Not only will your input make a difference, you'll receive special offers available only to registered owners of Nolo products on our newest books and software. Register now by:

PHONE
1-800-992-6656

FAX
1-800-645-0895

EMAIL
cs@nolo.com

or **MAIL** us
this registration card

REMEMBER:
Little publishers have big ears. We really listen to you.

fold here

nolo

REGISTRATION CARD

NAME ______________________ DATE ______________________

ADDRESS ______________________

____

CITY ______________________ STATE __________ ZIP __________

PHONE ______________________ E-MAIL ______________________

WHERE DID YOU HEAR ABOUT THIS PRODUCT? ______________________

WHERE DID YOU PURCHASE THIS PRODUCT? ______________________

DID YOU CONSULT A LAWYER? (PLEASE CIRCLE ONE) YES NO NOT APPLICABLE

DID YOU FIND THIS BOOK HELPFUL? (VERY) 5 4 3 2 1 (NOT AT ALL)

COMMENTS ______________________

____

____

WAS IT EASY TO USE? (VERY EASY) 5 4 3 2 1 (VERY DIFFICULT)

DO YOU OWN A COMPUTER? IF SO, WHICH FORMAT? (PLEASE CIRCLE ONE) WINDOWS DOS MAC

❑ If you do not wish to receive mailings from these companies, please check this box.
❑ You can quote me in future Nolo.com promotional materials. Daytime phone number ______________________.

SOA 7.2

"Nolo helps lay people perform legal tasks without the aid—or fees—of lawyers."
—USA TODAY

Nolo books are ..."written in plain language, free of legal mumbo jumbo, and spiced with witty personal observations."
—ASSOCIATED PRESS

"...Nolo publications...guide people simply through the how, when, where and why of law."
—WASHINGTON POST

"Increasingly, people who are not lawyers are performing tasks usually regarded as legal work... And consumers, using books like Nolo's, do routine legal work themselves."
—NEW YORK TIMES

"...All of [Nolo's] books are easy-to-understand, are updated regularly, provide pull-out forms...and are often quite moving in their sense of compassion for the struggles of the lay reader."
—SAN FRANCISCO CHRONICLE

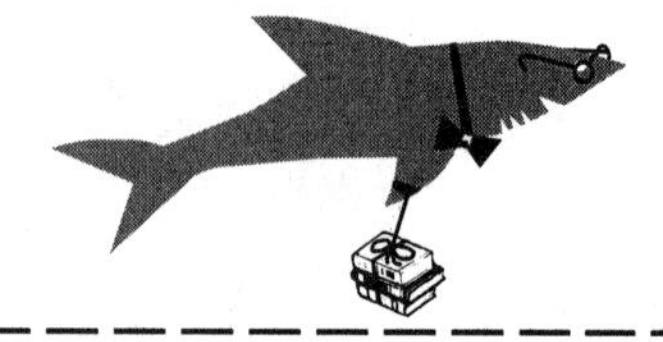

fold here

Place stamp here

Attn: SOA 7.2